KU-491-337

The sword of the revolution

Bookmarks
London, Chicago and Melbourne

Trotsky:
The sword of the revolution
1917-1923

Tony Cliff

Trotsky: The sword of the revolution 1917-1923 / *Tony Cliff*
First published July 1990.
Bookmarks, 265 Seven Sisters Road, London N4 2DE, England
Bookmarks, PO Box 16085, Chicago, IL 60616, USA
Bookmarks, GPO Box 1473N, Melbourne 3001, Australia
Copyright © Bookmarks and Tony Cliff

ISBN 0 906224 60 8

Printed by Cox and Wyman Limited, Reading, England
Cover design by Roger Huddle

Bookmarks is linked to an international grouping of socialist organisations:
Australia: *International Socialists*, GPO Box 1473N, Melbourne   3001
Belgium: *Socialisme International,* rue Lovinfosse 60, 4030 Grivegnée
Britain: *Socialist Workers Party,* PO Box 82, London E3
Canada: *International Socialists,* PO Box 339, Station E, Toronto,
Ontario M6H 4E3
Denmark: *Internationale Socialister,* Ryesgade 8, 3, 8000 Århus C
France: *Socialisme International*, BP 189, 75926 Paris Cedex 19
Greece: *Organosi Sosialistiki Epanastasi*, PO Box 8161, 10010 Omonia,
Athens.
Holland: *Groep Internationale Socialisten*, PO Box 9720, 3506 GR Utrecht.
Ireland: *Socialist Workers Movement,* PO Box 1648, Dublin 8
Norway: *Internasjonale Sosialister,* Postboks 5370, Majorstua, 0304 Oslo 3
United States: *International Socialist Organization,* PO Box 16085,
Chicago, IL 60616
West Germany: *Sozialistische Arbeiter Gruppe,* Wolfgangstrasse 81, 6000
Frankfurt 1

Contents

Acknowledgements

Several people have helped in the writing of this book. Many thanks are due to Chris Bambery, Alex Callinicos, Donny Gluckstein and Chris Harman. I owe a debt to Linda Aitken and Ahmed Shawki for help in locating material. Thanks are due in particular to John Molyneux for expert critical comment and most valuable stylistic suggestions, and to Peter Marsden for editing and advice. Chanie Rosenberg deserves a special thanks for participating in the editing of the manuscript and for typing it.

Tony Cliff, April 1990

Tony Cliff is a member of the Socialist Workers Party in Britain. and has written many previous books. The first volume of this biography, **Trotsky: Towards October 1879-1917**, was published by Bookmarks in July 1989. His other books include the classic **State Capitalism in Russia** (1974) and two previous political biographies: **Rosa Luxemburg** (1959) and **Lenin** (in three volumes 1975-79).

This book is published with the aid of the Bookmarks Publishing Co-operative. Many socialists have some savings put aside, probably in a bank or savings bank. While it is there, this money is being loaned out by the bank to some business or other to further the capitalist search for profit. We believe it is better loaned to a socialist venture to further the struggle for socialism. That's how the co-operative works: in return for a loan, repayable at a month's notice, members receive free copies of books published by Boookmarks. At the time this book was published, the co-operative had around 400 members, from as far apart as London and Malaysia, Canada and Norway.
Like to know more? Write to the Bookmarks Publishing Co-operative, 265 Seven Sisters Road, Finsbury Park, London N4 2DE, England.

Preface

THIS IS the second volume of a political biography of Leon Trotsky. It starts with the consolidation of Bolshevik power after the October revolution of 1917, follows Trotsky as commissar for foreign affairs in the peace negotiations with Germany, Austria-Hungary, Bulgaria and Turkey at Brest-Litovsk, and deals with his greatest achievement in these years: his creation and leadership of the Red Army in the civil war. The book ends with Trotsky's isolation in the politburo after Lenin's disappearance from the political scene.

Trotsky's building of the Red Army is rightly considered a gigantic achievement. By combining contradictory elements he produced a mighty army out of a void. The defence of the workers' revolution called for a correct military strategy, which meant that Trotsky had to use former Tsarist officers—yet a social abyss separated these from the mass of the soldiers on whose enthusiasm and self-sacrifice the Red Army depended. It was against these same officers that the soldiers of the Tsarist army had rebelled. The conflict between soldiers and officers was congruent with that between peasants and landlords. Nonetheless, Trotsky argued strongly that without the passionate support of the soldiers *and* the technique of the professionals the Red Army could not be victorious.

The heterogeneous nature of the soldiers of the Red Army—a minority of workers in a sea of peasants—added to the difficulties. The proletarian elements were the backbone of the Red Army, while the peasants were unstable, vacillating throughout the civil war. They favoured the Bolsheviks for giving them the land, but resented the Soviet government that requisitioned grain and introduced compulsory conscription. Hence mass desertions were common. To keep control over the former Tsarist officers, and at the same time preserve political leadership over the mass of the soldiers, the political commissar played a crucial role.

One of the most serious developments in the Red Army was the rise of a military opposition to Trotsky. This was made up largely of old Bolsheviks, who had been commanders of Red Guard units before the Red Army was created and now resented taking orders from former Tsarist officers. They thought they did not need to learn from the specialists. They spoke about 'proletarian military strategy' and 'proletarian military doctrine'. Often half-educated, crude and conceited, they criticised Trotsky's attitude to culture in general and military doctrine in particular.

When there were setbacks in the war this military opposition became more and more aggressive, and at times very strong indeed. For instance at the Eighth Congress of the Russian Communist Party, in March 1919, the official thesis on military policy, written by Trotsky and supported by Lenin, met widespread resistance: 174 delegates voted for it, 85 against and 32 abstained.

The full significance of the early formation of the military opposition in the Red Army, as the embryo of the future Stalinist faction, became apparent only in the light of much later developments. Thus Trotsky, in his creation and leadership of the Red Army, sowed the seeds of an opposition that in the end contributed to his undoing.

The war dominated every aspect of Soviet life, and the Red Army was to a large extent the foundation of the future bureaucracy. The hierarchical structure of the Red Army, rising on a socially heterogeneous base of which the atomised peasantry formed the bulk, inevitably strengthened bureaucratic trends. The strength of the bureaucracy in an organisation is in inverse proportion to the strength of the rank and file. Party organisation in the army modelled itself along military lines. The conditions of civil war, which made it imperative for military and civilian administrators to be transferred from one place to another in order to deal with states of emergency, further strengthened this bureaucracy. Trotsky himself recognised this, writing that at the end of the civil war, 'the development of the Red Army of five millions played no small role in the formation of the bureaucracy'.

Social and political changes during the civil war also encouraged the rise of the bureaucracy. The decline in the size of the proletariat and its disintegration and atomisation, the decline of the *soviets*—the directly elected workers' councils, the merger of party and state, all contributed to the process.

At the end of the civil war, the *impasse* of War Communism encouraged Trotsky (with Lenin's agreement) to move towards using Red Army units as armies of labour and towards the militarisation of labour in general. This was the background to the trade union debate in the winter of 1920-21, when Trotsky argued for the statification of the trade unions, while the newly formed Workers' Opposition argued for the unionisation of the state. Lenin shied away from both extremes.

This volume also deals with the role of Trotsky in leading the Communist International, and in teaching its sections strategy and tactics.

It deals also with Lenin's turn on his death bed towards Trotsky, to form a bloc against the bureaucracy, against Great Russian chauvinism, and against Stalin. The final chapters discuss the Twelfth Congress of the party—the first without Lenin—at which Trotsky failed to carry out his agreement with Lenin that he would fight Stalin, and try to explain this lapse.

The volume ends in April 1923. This was a short time before a number of great historical events: Lenin's complete disappearance from the active scene, the defeat of the German revolution in October-November 1923, which marked the end of the revolutionary wave that had started at the end of 1918, the first appearance of Hitler, who led an unsuccessful coup in Bavaria in November 1923, and the formation of the Left Opposition in December 1923.

The first volume of this biography, **Trotsky: Towards October 1879-1917**,[1] covered Trotsky's life from birth to the October revolution. The first two volumes of my political biography of Lenin[2] similarly covered the period of his life up to the revolution. Only now and then throughout the long political struggles of these years did the paths of the two men cross. Trotsky met Lenin first in 1902 and a year later broke with him politically. He came to Bolshevism only in May 1917. In the five months between May and October that year Lenin and Trotsky were in very close partnership, leading the Bolshevik Party and the proletariat towards the revolution. Except for these months, however, the story told in Trotsky's biography is not congruent with Lenin's.

But when it comes to the period of Trotsky's life described in the present volume—from the October revolution until Lenin's withdrawal from political life in 1923—the story dovetails completely. In these five and a half years Lenin and Trotsky worked closely: the party at the time was often called the party of Lenin and Trotsky, likewise the government and the Communist International. In parts of the present volume, therefore, I have borrowed heavily from the third volume of my biography of Lenin.

TONY CLIFF, January 1990.

The sword of the revolution

Chapter one
The consolidation of Soviet power

ON 25 OCTOBER (7 November)* 1917 the Bolsheviks took control in Petrograd. When Lenin came out of hiding after nearly four months, he said to Trotsky: 'You know, from persecution and life underground, to come so suddenly into power...'—he paused for the right word—"*Es schwindet* (it makes one giddy)", he concluded, changing suddenly to German, and circling his hand around his head.'[1]

Trotsky goes on to recount:

The government must be formed. We number among us a few members of the central committee. A quick session opens over in a corner of the room.

'What shall we call them?' asks Lenin, thinking aloud. 'Anything but ministers—that's such a vile, hackneyed word.'

'We must call them commissars', I suggest, 'but there are too many commissars just now. Perhaps "supreme commissaries"? No, "supreme" does not sound well, either. What about "people's commissars"?'

' "People's commissars"? Well, that might do, I think,' Lenin agrees. 'And the government as a whole?'

'A *soviet*, of course... the Soviet of People's Commissars, eh?'

'The Soviet of People's Commissars?' Lenin picks it up. 'That's splendid; smells terribly of revolution!'[2]

---

* Until February 1918, Russia followed the old Julian calendar, which was 13 days behind the Gregorian calendar in use in the rest of Europe. The old calendar was abolished on 1 (14) February 1918. For dates before then, the old calendar date is given, with the new in brackets. After that date, only the new is given.

Thus the Council of People's Commissars (Sovnarkom for short) was born.

Lenin suggested that Trotsky should head the government, as he had headed the body that led the insurrection, the Military Revolutionary Committee. Trotsky resisted this suggestion. He writes that Lenin

> insisted that I take over the commissariat of the interior, saying that the most important task at the moment was to fight off a counter-revolution. I objected, and brought up, among other arguments, the question of nationality. Was it worth while to put into our enemies' hands such an additional weapon as my Jewish origin.
>
> Lenin almost lost his temper. 'We are heading a great international revolution. Of what important are such trifles?' A good-humoured bickering began. 'No doubt the revolution is great', I answered, 'but there are still a good many fools left.'
>
> 'But surely we don't keep step with fools?'
>
> 'Probably we don't, but sometimes one has to make some allowance for stupidity. Why create additional complications at the outset?'
>
> Sverdlov and other members of the central committee were won over to my side. Lenin was in the minority.[3]

Sverdlov proposed the appointment of Trotsky as commissar for foreign affairs, as he was the right man 'to confront Europe' on behalf of the revolution.

The Congress of the Soviets

On 26 October (8 November) the Second All-Russian Congress of the *Soviets* opened. Its social composition was very different from that of the First Congress, held six months earlier in June. This had been made up largely of petty-bourgeois elements: intellectuals and army officers had been prominent. The October congress was both younger and much more proletarian. As John Reed describes it:

> I stood there watching the new delegates come in—burly, bearded soldiers, workmen in black blouses, a few long-haired peasants. The girl in charge—a member of

Plekhanov's Edinstvo group—smiled contemptuously. 'These are very different people from the delegates to the first *Sezd*,' she remarked. 'See how rough and ignorant they look! The Dark People...' It was true; the depths of Russia had been stirred, and it was the bottom which came uppermost now.[4]

The political composition of the second congress was also very different from that of the first. Whereas the Social Revolutionaries and Mensheviks had predominated at the June congress, now the majority of the delegates were followers of Bolshevism. The Bolsheviks held some 390 seats out of a total of 650. The strength of the Social Revolutionaries was estimated variously as between 160 and 190. But these figures are misleading, since the Social Revolutionaries had split, and most of their delegates were supporters of the Left Social Revolutionary Party, which was pro-Bolshevik at the time. The Mensheviks, who in June had accounted for more then 200 delegates, were now reduced to a mere 60 or 70, and these were split into a number of groups. The Right Social Revolutionaries and Mensheviks together could count on fewer than 100 votes.

The congress elected a new executive. This consisted of fourteen Bolsheviks, seven Social Revolutionaries, three Mensheviks and one United Internationalist (from Maxim Gorky's group). The Right Social Revolutionaries and Mensheviks at once declared that they would refuse to share executive power with the Bolsheviks.

Martov, the Menshevik leader, then mounted the rostrum and declared that the most urgent problem was to overcome the current crisis by peaceful means. The Bolsheviks, recognising the need to expose the real nature of Social Revolutionary and Menshevik policy, did not oppose Martov's statement, despite the anti-Bolshevik tenor of his speech. 'The Bolsheviks had absolutely nothing against it; let the question of a peaceable settlement of the crisis be made the first item on the agenda. Martov's motion was voted on: against it—nobody.'[5]

However the Right Mensheviks and Right Social Revolutionary leaders flatly rejected collaboration with the 'party of insurrection'. Following their statement the entire right—Mensheviks, Right Social Revolutionaries and the Jewish Bund —walked out of the congress.

Martov continued to argue as if nothing had happened, and went on to preach conciliation. Trotsky then rounded on him:

> Now we are told: renounce your victory, make concessions, compromise. With whom? I ask: with whom ought we to compromise? With those wretched groups who have left us or who are making this proposal? But after all we've had a full view of them. No one in Russia is with them any longer. A compromise is supposed to be made, as between two equal sides, by the millions of workers and peasants represented in this congress, whom they are ready, not for the first time or the last, to barter away as the bourgeoisie sees fit. No, here no compromise is possible. To those who have left and to those who tell us to do this we must say: you are miserable bankrupts, your role is played out; go where you ought to be: into the dustbin of history!
>
> 'Then we'll leave,' Martov shouted from the platform amidst stormy applause for Trotsky.[6]

Towards a coalition government?

Avilov, speaking for the Mensheviks who had not left the congress, then argued the need to establish a socialist coalition—a coalition of all socialist parties. It should be stressed that from the outset no one among the Bolsheviks wanted an exclusively Bolshevik government, although Lenin and Trotsky did want a Bolshevik-dominated one, one that excluded any 'defencists' who had supported Russia's part in the First World War. Trotsky decisively rejected Avilov's suggestion:

> A few days ago, when the question of the uprising was raised, we were told that we were isolating ourselves, that we were drifting on the rocks... Nevertheless the revolution... gained an almost bloodless victory. If it had been really true that we were isolated, how did it happen that we conquered so easily? No... Not we but the [Provisional] Government and the democracy, or rather the quasi-democracy... were isolated from the masses. By their hesitations and compromises they lost contact with the real democracy. It is our great virtue as a party that we have a coalition with the [masses]... with the workers, soldiers, and poorest peasants.
>
> ...If a coalition is necessary, it must be a coalition with our

garrison, especially with the peasants and working classes. Of this kind of a coalition we can be proud. It has stood the test of fire...

Our whole hope is that our revolution will kindle a European revolution. If the rising of the people does not crush imperialism then we will surely be crushed. There is no doubt about that. The Russian revolution will either cause a revolution in the West, or the capitalists of all countries will strangle our [revolution].[7]

When the Menshevik motion calling for a coalition government was put to the vote it received about 150 of the 650 votes. Probably some of the moderate Bolsheviks must have voted for it.[8]

A few days later, on 29 October (11 November) the call for a coalition government of all socialist parties was again put forward by the All-Russian Executive Committee of the Railway Workers (Vikzhel), a majority of whom were Mensheviks and Right Social Revolutionaries. Vikzhel declared: 'The Council of People's Commissars formed in Petrograd rests on only one party and so cannot get recognition and support from the country as a whole. A new government must be formed...' Vikzhel demanded an end to the fight against the counter-revolution, threatening to bring the railways to a halt.[9]

At this critical moment a number of leading Bolsheviks ranged themselves against Lenin and Trotsky, demanding that the party should relinquish power to a coalition of all socialist parties. Before the October insurrection the leaders of the right wing of Bolshevism—Zinoviev, Kamenev, Rykov, Nogin and Lunacharsky—had argued that the uprising was premature and would meet defeat. Now, after the victorious insurrection, they argued that the Bolsheviks would not be able to retain power unless they entered a coalition with the Mensheviks and Social Revolutionaries.

On 29 October (11 November) the central committee of the Bolshevik Party—with both Lenin and Trotsky absent—unanimously passed a resolution to widen the base of the government.[10] Ominously, in the original secretarial note in the minutes there followed this text crossed out: 'and we agree to renounce the candidature of Trotsky and Lenin if they demand this.' After the crossed-out words is written: '(Approved)'.[11] Kamenev, chairman of the All-Russian Central Executive Committee of the Soviets (VTsIK), was authorised to organise a conference to discuss the issue of a coalition government.

The Mensheviks and Social Revolutionaries put the following conditions for their entry into the coalition: the new government was to be responsible not to the *soviets*, but to 'the broad circles of revolutionary democracy'; it was to disarm the Bolshevik detachments; and Lenin and Trotsky were to be debarred from it.[12] These conditions amounted to the demand that the Bolsheviks should declare the October Revolution null and void, that they should disarm themselves, and that they should ostracise the leaders and organisers of the insurrection.

The Bolshevik negotiators, especially Kamenev and Riazanov, stood on the right of the party, and were so anxious to come to an agreement with the Mensheviks and Right Social Revolutionaries that they were ready to accept their demands. So anxious were they for a compromise that while the battle of Pulkovo Heights was still undecided, where the Red Guards were fighting Kerensky's troops at the last line of defence on the outskirts of Petrograd, they signed a joint appeal for a ceasefire —an appeal implicitly directed against their own party and government.

On 1 (14) November Kamenev reported the demands of the Mensheviks to an enlarged meeting of the central committee. The committee split. Trotsky declared:

> One thing is clear from the report, and that is that the parties which took no part in the insurrection want to grab power from the people who overthrew them. There was no point in organising the insurrection if we do not get the majority; if the others do not want that it is obvious they do not want our programme. We must have 75 per cent. It is clear that we cannot give a right of objection, just as we cannot yield on Lenin's chairmanship; such a concession is completely unacceptable.

Dzerzhinsky asserted that 'the delegates did not observe the central committee's instruction. The central committee definitely decided that the government must be responsible to the VTsIK... We always stated definitely that we would not allow objections to Lenin and Trotsky. None of this was implemented, and I propose an expression of no confidence in the delegation and that they be recalled and others sent.' The same hard line was taken by Uritsky: '...there is no doubt that we must not yield on either Lenin or Trotsky, for in a certain sense this would be renunciation of our programme; there is no need to insist on the others.'

Lenin then stated:

It is time to make an end of vacillation. It is clear that Vikzhel is on the side of the Kaledins and the Kornilovs [Tsarist generals]. There can be no wavering. The majority of the workers, peasants and army are for us. No one here has proved that the rank and file are against us; choose between Kaledin's agents and the rank and file. We must rely on the masses, and send agitators into the villages.

The right-wingers on the central committee, however, were unyielding in their fight for a coalition. Rykov declared: 'If we break off [the negotiations] we will lose the groups which are supporting us... and we will be in no position to keep power. Kamenev conducted the talks absolutely correctly.' Miliutin raised 'the question of whether we are going to insist on keeping power exclusively in our hands... if we do not get carried away... it will become clear to us that we cannot sustain a long civil war'.

After heated discussion the question, whether to break off the talks or not, was put to the vote. The result was: for breaking off—four; against—10. The intransigent Lenin and Trotsky found themselves in a minority,[13] and the Bolshevik delegates continued their effort to form a coalition government.

On the same day, a debate on the same subject took place in the Petrograd committee of the party. Lenin did not mince his words:

...now, at such a moment, when we are in power, we are faced with a split. Zinoviev and Kamenev say that we will not seize power [in the country as a whole]. I am in no mood to listen to this calmly. I view this as treason... Zinoviev says that we are not the Soviet power. We are, if you please, only the Bolsheviks, left alone since the departure of the Social Revolutionaries and the Mensheviks, and so forth and so on. But we are not responsible for that. We have been elected by the Congress of the Soviets...

As for conciliation, I cannot even speak about that seriously. Trotsky long ago said that unification is impossible. Trotsky understood this, and from that time on there has been no better Bolshevik.

They [Zinoviev, Kamenev and company] say that we will be unable to maintain our power alone, and so on. But we are not alone. The whole of Europe is before us. We must make the beginning.

Lenin went on: 'Our present slogan is: No compromise... for a homogeneous Bolshevik government'. He did not hesitate to use the threat, which he meant seriously, to 'appeal to the sailors': 'If you get the majority, take power in the central executive committee and carry on, but we will go to the sailors.'

Opposing Lenin's views, Lunacharsky argued that the coalition government was a necessity. He pointed to the sabotage carried out by technical personnel as proof of the need of the Bolsheviks to join a coalition. 'We cannot manage with our forces. Famine will break out.'

Trotsky came out strongly in support of Lenin's point of view: against conciliation and against a coalition government with the Mensheviks and Social Revolutionaries.

We are told that we are incapable of building up. In that case we should simply surrender power to those who were correct in struggling against us... We are told that we cannot sit on bayonets. But neither can we manage without bayonets. We need bayonets *there* in order to be able to sit *here*... Conciliation with Vikzhel will not do away with the conflict with the Junker detachments of the bourgeoisie. No. A cruel class struggle will continue to be waged against us in the future as well...

We are confronted with armed violence which can be overcome only by means of violence on our part. Lunacharsky says that blood is flowing. What to do? Evidently we should never have begun. Then why don't you openly admit that the biggest mistake was committed not so much in October but towards the end of February when we entered the arena of future civil war.

We already have a coalition. Our coalition is with the

peasants—the soldiers who are now fighting for the Bolshevik power. The All-Russian Congress of Soviets transmitted power to a certain party. You simply forget this. If after taking power we are incapable of realising our own programme, then we ought to go to the soldiers and workers and declare ourselves bankrupt. But nothing whatever can come of merely leaving a few Bolsheviks in a coalition government. We have taken power; we must also bear the responsibilities.

Following this speech by Trotsky, Nogin again argued the case for the conciliators:

The Social Revolutionists left the *soviets* after the revolution; the Mensheviks did likewise... this means that the *soviets* will fall apart. Such a state of affairs in the face of complete chaos in the country will end with the shipwreck of our party in a very brief interval.

Then a number of speakers came on Lenin's and Trotsky's side: Globov, Slutsky and Boki. And Trotsky spoke again:

We have had rather profound differences in our party prior to the insurrection, within the central committee as well as in the broad party circles. The same things were said; the same expressions were used then as now in arguing against the insurrection as hopeless. The old arguments are now being repeated after the victorious insurrection, this time in favour of a coalition. There will be no technical apparatus, mind you. You lay the colours on thick in order to frighten, in order to hinder the proletariat from utilising its victory... I repeat that we shall be able to draw the petty bourgeoisie behind us only by showing that we have in our hands a material fighting force. We can conquer the bourgeoisie only by overthrowing it. This is the law of the class struggle. This is the guarantee of our victory. Then and only then will the Vikzhel follow us. The same might be said about other technical branches. The apparatus will place itself at our service only when it sees that we are a force.
...You keep repeating that we cannot sit on bayonets. But in order for us to carry on these discussions here it is indispensible to have bayonets at Tsarskoe Selo [where Red

Guards were fighting Kerensky's troops].

All government is based on force and not conciliation. Our government is the force exercised by the majority of the people against the minority. This is beyond dispute. This is the ABC of Marxism.[14]*

The right-wing Bolsheviks did not limit the expression of their opinion to a discussion within the party. At a meeting of the central executive committee of the *soviets* Larin, a recent convert to Bolshevism from Menshevism, moved a resolution criticising the Soviet government for violating freedom of the press:

At the present moment, on the eve of the elections to the Constituent Assembly, the situation in regard to the press needs to be improved. The measures taken against press [freedom] could be justified during the actual course of the struggle [for power], but not now... Censorship of every kind must be completely eliminated.[17]

Kamkov, the Left Social Revolutionary, supported Larin's argument. Trotsky defended the Soviet government's policy limiting press freedom:

To demand that all repressive measures should be abandoned during a civil war is equivalent to demanding that the war itself should cease. Such a demand could come only from adversaries of the proletariat. Our opponents are not offering us peace. I assert that no one can provide a guarantee against a [victory of] the Kornilovites. In the circumstances of civil war it is legitimate to suppress newspapers that support the other side...

But when we are finally victorious our attitude toward the press will be analogous to that on freedom of trade. Then we

---

* The minutes of this meeting were omitted when the collected protocols of the Petrograd committee for 1917 were published in 1927. The proof sheet immediately reached Trotsky from one of his supporters, and he immediately published it in facsimile in the bulletin of the opposition,[15] and later reprinted it in his book **The Stalin School of Falsification**.[16] A comparison of the type with that of the published edition leaves little doubt that it is genuine. The facsimile bears a large fat question mark against a passage in Lenin's speech which refers with praise to Trotsky's attitude on coalition. In the same pencil is noted in the corner of the proof sheet, 'Scrap'.

shall naturally move on to a [regular] regime in press matters.[18]

Two resolutions were tabled: Larin's, which failed by 31 votes to 22, and Trotsky's, which passed by 34 votes to 24 with one abstention.[19] Two Bolsheviks, Riazanov and Lozovsky, voted against Trotsky's resolution.

The same day four people's commissars—Nogin, Rykov, Miliutin and Teodorovich—resigned from the government, and Shliapnikov, people's commissar for labour, declared his political solidarity with them but did not resign.

The open revolt of the right-wing Bolsheviks against Lenin and Trotsky seemed to be just what the Mensheviks had hoped for when they banked on the peaceful liquidation of the new regime. Answering the members of the Menshevik central committee who had opposed the decision to negotiate with the Bolsheviks, the Menshevik leader Dan argued that the agreement was impossible 'without a split in Bolshevism', that the Leninists' rejection of the agreement was costing the Bolsheviks 'enormous masses of workers', and that 'thanks to our tactics, the Bolsheviks are already splitting.'[20]

But Dan miscalculated. Lenin, Trotsky and the majority of the Bolshevik central committee were not going to be intimidated by the Bolshevik leaders who resigned their offices. On 3 (16) November these were charged with violating party discipline, and threatened with expulsion from the party:

> The CC is forced to repeat its ultimatum and to suggest that you either give an immediate undertaking in writing to submit to CC decisions and to promote its policy in all your speeches, or withdraw from all public party activity and resign all responsible posts in the workers' movement until the party congress.
>
> If you refuse to make one of these two pledges, the CC will be obliged to raise the question of your immediate expulsion from the party.[21]

Kamenev was replaced as chairman of the VTsIK by Sverdlov. No concession was made to the viewpoint of those who had resigned. On the contrary, the negotiations with the Mensheviks and Social Revolutionaries were allowed to collapse.

The right-wing opposition in the central committee then also collapsed. On 7 (20) November, Zinoviev surrendered and asked to be taken back on the committee. In words foreshadowing his future, more tragic capitulations, Zinoviev appealed to his friends:

> ...we remain attached to the party, we prefer to make mistakes together with millions of workers and soldiers and to die together with them than to step to one side at this decisive, historic moment.[22]

Three weeks later, on 30 November (12 December), similar statements were issued by Rykov, Kamenev, Miliutin and Nogin. Thus a very threatening split in the party at a critical moment of history was averted.

The logic of the class struggle was far too strong to be blocked by the right-wing Bolsheviks. Not only did Lenin and Trotsky oppose them, but the Menshevik and Social Revolutionary leaders pulled the rug from under their feet by putting forward demands more appropriate for victors than vanquished:

> (1) that the Red or Workers' Guard be disarmed.
> (2) that the garrison be placed under orders of the city council, and
> (3) that an armistice be declared, offering for their part to secure a pledge that the troops of Kerensky on entering the city would not fire a shot or engage in search and seizure. A socialist government would then be constituted, but without Bolshevik participation.[23]

At the Vikzhel conference on 1 (14) November

> the Mensheviks said that one should talk to the Bolsheviks with guns... and the central committee of the Social Revolutionaries was against an agreement with the Bolsheviks.[24]

One positive outcome of the negotiations was that the Left Social Revolutionaries, resentful of the attitude of the Mensheviks and Right Social Revolutionaries, decided to join the Bolsheviks in the government.

The intransigence of Lenin, Trotsky, Sverdlov and others overcame the vacillations of Zinoviev, Kamenev, Rykov and company. But why did they face so much opposition? Was it only a question of vacillation among a few top leaders of the party?

No. Revolutions, by their nature, generate uncertainty, for in a revolution the balance of class forces shifts continually and rapidly. There are equations with numerous unknowns. Under such conditions vacillation is extremely dangerous but also unavoidable. These vacillations of necessity affect the mass of the workers as well as the rank and file of the revolutionary party. It is the task of party leaders to reject these vacillations and overcome them, but they may also come to reflect them. Zinoviev, Kamenev, Rykov and company openly defied the central committee majority because they felt that many Bolshevik party workers throughout the country were behind them.

Some workers and their organisations *were* unsure on the question of a coalition government of all socialist parties. For example, the Petrograd Council of Trade Unions had been under Bolshevik influence for months. It had welcomed the insurrection, and on 27 October (9 November) had appealed to all Petrograd workers to support the new regime. Nevertheless, four days later, after heated debate, the council passed a resolution demanding 'immediate agreement among all socialist parties' and the formation of a coalition government.

The central committee of the Trade Union of Sailors and River Transport Workers on 29 October (11 November) also issued an appeal to support the new government, but next day it demanded a cabinet 'of all socialist parties and factions of revolutionary democracy'. Similar demands appear in resolutions of other trade unions and individual Petrograd factories.

The *soviet* of workers' and soldiers' deputies of the Vyborg district of Petrograd, the citadel of Bolshevism, on 29 October (11 November) condemned the 'traitorous path' taken by Menshevik defencists and Social Revolutionaries. But on 1 (14) November the same *soviet* issued an appeal signed by the Bolshevik, Menshevik and Social Revolutionary factions to 'end party squabbles and discord' and consolidate 'all socialist forces'.

The great Obukhov metal works provides another good illustration of the political wavering of Petrograd workers at this time. At a meeting on 19 October (1 November) the Menshevik internationalist David Dallin could not finish his speech, and other Mensheviks could not even begin theirs, because the workers objected to the least criticism of the Bolsheviks. The audience shouted for Dallin's arrest as a counter-revolutionary Kornilovite and traitor to the people. Yet the next day the workers passed a resolution in the spirit of the Vikzhel demands, and during the following night an excited delegation from the plant burst in on a meeting of the Vikzhel commission demanding peace among all socialist parties.

Even the Bolshevik sailors of the destroyer *Oleg*, which had been called out from Kronstadt, broadcast from their ship on 30 October the 'glad tidings' of negotiations among 'all socialist parties, who are trying to form a bloc'.[25]

It was the clarity of vision of Lenin and Trotsky and their intransigence that overcame the vacillations of the central committee and in the rest of the party—and that in the first few days after the victory of the October insurrection.

The beginning of the Red Terror

At the beginning the new government treated its opponents very mildly; but it quickly learned the cost of such behaviour.The military cadets that the Bolsheviks had released on parole from the Winter Palace on 26 October (8 November) betrayed their trust two days later and staged an uprising. Similarly mild treatment was shown to General Krasnov, which he also repaid with treason.

Victor Serge, in his book **Year One of the Russian Revolution**, wrote on the events in Moscow:

> The Whites surrendered at 4pm on 2 (15) November. 'The Committee of Public Safety is dissolved. The White Guard surrenders its arms and is disbanded. The officers may keep the side arms that distinguish their rank. Only such weapons as are necessary for practice may be kept in the military academies... The MRC [Military Revolutionary Committee] guarantees the liberty and inviolability of all.' Such were the principal clauses of the armistice signed between Reds and Whites. The fighters of the counter-revolution, butchers of the Kremlin, who in victory would have shown no quarter whatever to the Reds... *went free*.

Serge comments:

> Foolish clemency. These very Junkers, these officers, these

students, these socialists of counter-revolution, dispersed themselves throughout the length and breadth of Russia and there organised the civil war. The revolution was to meet them again, at Iaroslav, on the Don, at Kazan, in the Crimea, in Siberia and in every conspiracy nearer home.[26]

These were the early days of revolutionary innocence. The morning after the October insurrection, on Kamenev's initiative and in Lenin's and Trotsky's absence, the death penalty was abolished. When Lenin learned about this first piece of legislation he was very angry. 'How can one make a revolution without firing squads? Do you think you will be able to deal with all your enemies by laying down your arms. What other means of repression do you have? Imprisonment? No one attaches any importance to this during a civil war when each side hopes to win.'

'It is a mistake,' he went on, 'an inadmissible weakness, a pacifist illusion', and much more. 'Do you really think that we shall come out victorious without any revolutionary terror?'[27]

Trotsky too had no doubt that the revolution would have to use terror to fight the counter-revolution. 'We shall not enter the kingdom of socialism in white gloves on a polished floor', he told the All-Russian Congress of Peasant Deputies on 3 (16) December.[28]

On 28 October (10 November), after the suppression of the revolt of the military cadets, Sovnarkom issued a decree written by Trotsky banning the Kadet Party—the main counter-revolutionary party of the bourgeoisie:

Fully conscious of the enormous responsibility for the destiny of the people and the revolution now being placed on the soldiers of *soviet* power, the Council of People's Commissars decided that the Kadet Party, being an organisation for counter- revolutionary rebellion, is a party of *enemies of the people*.[29]

Trotsky declared:

We have made a modest beginning with the arrest of the Kadet leaders... In the French Revolution the Jacobins guillotined better men... for opposing the people's will. We have executed nobody and are not about to do so.[30]

Alas, this promise did not hold. To organise a struggle against counter-revolution, on 7 (20) December 1917, Sovnarkom established the Cheka, the All-Russian Extraordinary Commission to Fight Counter-Revolution and Sabotage. At first its staff was small, its resources limited, and the few death sentences it passed were on common criminals. M I Latsis, a member of the Cheka in 1918, states that during the first six months of its existence the Cheka had 22 people shot.[31]

The revolutionary terror in Russia, like its predecessor during the great French revolution of 1789, was a reaction to foreign invasion and the immensity of the threat to the revolution. The Paris terror of 2 September 1793 followed the Duke of Brunswick's proclamation threatening foreign invasion and ruthless repression of the revolution. In Russia too it was foreign invasion, starting with the victories of the Czechoslovak troops over the Red Army in 1918, that threatened the greatest danger to the Soviet Republic. On 20 June the popular Bolshevik orator, Volodarsky, was assassinated by counter-revolutionaries. On 30 August an attempt was made on Lenin's life. He was badly wounded and for a few days was in a critical condition. Another Bolshevik leader, Uritsky, the president of the Petrograd Cheka, was murdered. The Red Terror was unleashed in retaliation. On 2 September 500 hostages were shot in Petrograd.

Whereas between September 1917 and June 1918 the Cheka had executed 22 people, in the second half of 1918 more than 6000 executions took place.[32] In the three years of civil war, 1918-20, 12,737 people were shot.[33]

Compared with the White Terror, however, the Red Terror was mild. Thus in Finland alone, in April 1918, between 10,000 and 20,000 people were slaughtered by the counter-revolutionaries.[34] With complete justification Lenin told the Seventh Congress of Soviets on 5 December 1919:

> The terror was forced on us by the terror of the Entente, the terror of mighty world capitalism, which has been throttling the workers and peasants, and is condemning them to death by starvation because they are fighting for their country's freedom.[35]

Trotsky expressed the same idea in a speech on 11 September 1918:

Now that the workers are being charged with committing cruelties in the civil war we must reply, instructed by our experience: the only unpardonable sin which the Russian working class can commit at this moment is that of indulgence towards its class enemies. We are fighting for the sake of the greatest good of mankind, for the sake of the regeneration of mankind, to drag it out of darkness, out of slavery...[36]

Marx himself provided his followers with the clearest guide on the subject of terror. In the autumn of 1848, denouncing 'the cannibalism of the counter-revolution', he proclaimed that there was 'only one means to curtail, simplify and localise the bloody agony of the old society and the bloody birthpangs of the new, only one means—the revolutionary terror'.[37]

Trotsky, following the same line of argument, wrote in 1920:

The problem of revolution, as of war, consists in breaking the will of the foe, forcing him to capitulate and to accept the conditions of the conqueror...

The degree of ferocity of the struggle depends on a series of internal and international circumstances. The more ferocious and dangerous is the resistance of the class enemy who have been overthrown, the more inevitably does the system of repression take the form of a system of terror.[38]

Chapter two
The Peace of Brest-Litovsk

ON BECOMING commissar for foreign affairs Trotsky hastened to publish the secret treaties of the Tsarist government. He hoped this would not only embarrass the Allied governments, which were partners to these treaties, but would also encourage the German working class to fight against its own government, which had similarly made secret agreements.

On 27 October (9 November) 1917 Trotsky issued the following note on 'Secret Diplomacy and Secret Treaties':

> In undertaking the publication of the secret diplomatic documents relating to the foreign diplomacy of the Tsarist and the bourgeois coalition governments... we fulfil an obligation which our party assumed when it was the party of opposition.
>
> Secret diplomacy is a necessary weapon in the hands of the propertied minority, which is compelled to deceive the majority in order to make the latter serve its interests. Imperialism, with its worldwide plans of annexation, its rapacious alliances and machinations, has developed the system of secret diplomacy to the highest degree.
>
> The struggle against imperialism, which had bled the peoples of Europe white and destroyed them, means also a struggle against capitalist diplomacy which has reasons enough to fear the light of day. The Russian people and, with it, the peoples of Europe and the whole world, ought to know the precise truth about the plans forged in secret by the financiers and diplomatic agents... The abolition of secret diplomacy is the primary condition of an honourable, popular, really

democratic foreign policy.

The note ends:

> Our programme formulates the burning aspirations of millions of workers, soldiers and peasants. We desire the speediest peace on principles of honourable co-existence and co-operation of peoples. We wish the speediest overthrow of the rule of capital. Exposing to the whole world the work of the ruling classes as expressed in the secret documents of diplomacy, we turn to the toilers with the appeal which constitutes the firm foundation of our foreign policy: 'Proletarians of all countries unite!'[1]

In a speech to the Petrograd Soviet on 4 (17) November Trotsky explained how he saw the work of Soviet representatives in the peace negotiations:

> Sitting at one table with [the representatives of our adversaries] we shall ask them explicit questions which do not allow of any evasion, and the entire course of negotiations, every word that they or we utter, will be taken down and reported by radio telegraph to all peoples who will be the judges of our discussions. Under the influence of the masses, the German and Austrian governments have already agreed to put themselves in the dock. You may be sure, comrades, that the prosecutor, in the person of the Russian revolutionary delegation, will be in its place and will in due time make a thundering speech for the prosecution about the diplomacy of all imperialists.[2]

A couple of weeks later, on 23 November (6 December), Trotsky issued an appeal 'To the Toiling People of Europe, Oppressed and Bled White':

> We conceal from nobody that we do not consider the present capitalist governments capable of a democratic peace. Only the revolutionary struggle of the working masses against present governments can bring Europe towards such a peace. Its full realisation will be guaranteed only by a victorious proletarian revolution in all capitalist countries.
> ...in entering negotiations with present governments... the Council of People's Commissars does not deviate from the

path of social revolution.

...In the peace negotiations the Soviet power sets itself a dual task: first, to secure the quickest possible cessation of the shameful and cruel slaughter which destroys Europe, and secondly, to aid, with all means available to us, the working class of all countries to overthrow the rule of capital and to seize state power in the interests of democratic peace and socialist transformation of Europe and of all mankind.[3]

Thus Trotsky made it clear that he was going to act as a revolutionary agitator while commissar for foreign affairs.

The formal negotiations for peace with the Quadruple Alliance of Germany, Austria-Hungary, Bulgaria and Turkey were started on 9 (22) December at Brest-Litovsk, a Polish town occupied by German troops. The real negotiations began on 14 (27) December) when Trotsky arrived.

The moment Trotsky set foot in Brest-Litovsk he acted as the prosecution attorney. From the beginning he subjected the representatives of the Quadruple Alliance to a withering barrage of revolutionary invective, attacking their peace proposals, their governments and their social system.

Trotsky's Marxism gave him a great advantage in his arguments. As he wrote later: 'We had over our opponents an infinite advantage. We understood them much better than they understand us.'[4]

On arriving in Brest-Litovsk Trotsky was greeted by delegates from the local *soviets* and trade unions, which urged him to speed the negotiations and achieve a peace treaty. Count Ottokar Czernin, the Austrian foreign minister, writes in his diary on 7 January 1918:

The German officer who accompanied the Russian delegation from Dunaburg, Captain Baron Lamezan, gave us some interesting details... In the first place, he declared that the trenches in front of Dunaburg are entirely deserted, and save for an outpost or so there were no Russians there at all; also, that at many stations delegates were waiting for the deputation to pass, in order to demand that peace should be made. Trotsky had throughout answered them with polite and careful speeches, but grew ever more and more depressed.[5]

Trotsky's actions, however, were not those of a man suing for peace at all costs. One of his first steps was to make it clear that no more socialising would be allowed between the representatives of the Soviet government and those of the Quadruple Alliance:

> I decided to put an immediate stop to the familiarity that had quite imperceptibly been established during the early stages. Through our military representatives I made it known that I had no desire to be presented to the Prince of Bavaria. This was noted. I next demanded separate dinners and suppers, under the pretext that we had to hold conferences during the intervals.[6]

Count Czernin noted in his diary: 'The wind seems to be in a very different quarter now from what it was.'[7]

Trotsky was accompanied by Karl Radek, who had recently arrived in Russia and was the editor of the German Communist paper, *Die Fackel* (The Torch) which was distributed in the German trenches. On his arrival Radek, under the eyes of the officers and diplomats assembled on the platform to greet the Soviet delegation, began to distribute revolutionary pamphlets among the German soldiers.

Facing Trotsky at the negotiating table were the German foreign minister, von Kühlmann, the Austrian foreign minister, Count Czernin, and the German Major-General Max Hoffmann, who represented the German supreme command—and more than once intervened brusquely in the discussion when he felt that the civilian negotiators were not showing sufficient firmness. Count Czernin was the most conciliatory member of this triumvirate; Austria's need for peace and bread was urgent, and Czernin was seriously afraid that a breakdown of the negotiations might lead to a collapse of the Austro-Hungarian monarchy. However his influence on the course of affairs was slight, for Austria was completely dependent on Germany for everything from military support to food.

On 14-15 (27-28) December the German representative read out the draft of a harsh peace treaty that demanded the annexation of large areas of the former Russian empire to Germany. Trotsky broke off negotiations and left for Petrograd.

Differences in the Bolshevik leadership

The Bolshevik leadership was not united on the policy to be pursued in the peace negotiations. Lenin was convinced that there was no alternative but to accept the German peace terms. On 7 (20) January 1918 he wrote 'Theses on the Question of the Immediate Conclusion of a Separate and Annexationist Peace':

> That the socialist revolution in Europe must come, and will come, is beyond doubt. All our hopes for the *final* victory of socialism are founded on this certainty and on this scientific prognosis. Our propaganda activities in general, and the organisation of fraternisation in particular, must be intensified and extended. It would be a mistake, however, to base the tactics of the Russian socialist government on attempts to determine whether or not the European, and especially the German, socialist revolution will take place in the next six months (or some such brief period). Inasmuch as it is quite impossible to determine this, all such attempts, objectively speaking, would be nothing but a blind gamble.

One cannot make war without an army, and Russia had no army to speak of. 'There can be no doubt that our army is absolutely in no condition at the present moment to beat back a German offensive successfully,' wrote Lenin.

> The socialist government of Russia is faced with the question —a question whose solution brooks no delay—of whether to accept this peace with annexations now, or to immediately wage a revolutionary war. In fact, no middle course is possible.

One should not derive the necessary tactics directly from a general principle, he wrote. Some people would argue that

> such a peace would mean a complete break with the fundamental principles of proletarian internationalism.
> This argument, however, is obviously incorrect. Workers who lose a strike and sign terms for the resumption of work which are unfavourable to them, and favourable to the capitalist, do not betray socialism.

Would a peace policy harm the German revolution? asks Lenin, and answers:

> The German revolution will by no means be made more difficult of accomplishment as far as its objective premises are concerned, if we conclude a separate peace...
> A socialist Soviet Republic in Russia will stand as a living example to the peoples of all countries and the propaganda and the revolutionising effect of this example will be immense.[8]

Lenin's arguments met tough resistance in the party ranks. Those who had supported him in the days leading up to the October insurrection were by and large surprised and shocked by his stand now. On the whole the right within the party, who had opposed him in the days of October, now came to his support. The most extreme enthusiast for an immediate peace was Zinoviev. The left, which had supported Lenin during the revolution, was practically unanimous in opposing this policy.

Trotsky did not believe that Russia could carry on a revolutionary war, but he was against signing the peace treaty. He argued that prolonged negotiations could help to arouse the workers of Germany and Austria-Hungary, as well as those of the Entente, the alliance headed by Britain and France.

> A revolutionary war was impossible. About this there was not the slightest shade of disagreement between Vladimir Ilyich and myself...
> I maintained that before we proceeded to sign the peace it was absolutely imperative that we should prove to the workers of Europe, in a most striking manner, how great, how deadly, was our hatred for the rulers of Germany...
> To arouse the masses of Germany, of Austro-Hungary, as well as of the Entente—this was what we hoped to achieve by entering into peace negotiations. Having this aim in mind, we reasoned that the negotiations should drag on as long as possible, in this way giving the European workers enough time to acquire a proper understanding of the actuality of the revolution, and more especially, of the revolution's policy of peace.[9]

Trotsky persevered in arguing for neither war nor peace, hoping to continue the armistice without signing a peace agreement.

Events in Germany in the middle of January began to support Trotsky's reasoning. As Wheeler-Bennett, historian of the Brest-Litovsk negotiations, writes:

> ...a wave of strikes and outbreaks spread through Germany and Austria. *Soviets* were formed in Berlin and Vienna. Hamburg, Bremen, Leipzig, Essen and Munich took up the cry. 'All power to the *soviets*' was heard in the streets of Greater Berlin, where half a million workers downed tools. In the forefront of the demands were the speedy conclusion of peace without annexations or indemnities, on the basis of the self-determination of peoples in accordance with the principles formulated by the Russian people's commissars at Brest-Litovsk, and the participation of workers' delegates from all countries in the peace negotiations.[10]

On 18 (31) January 1918 **Pravda** appeared with the headline: 'It has happened! The head of German imperialism is on the chopping block! The mailed fist of the proletarian revolution is raised!' Although by 3 February the whole strike movement had collapsed, it was not clear at the time how long this lull would continue.

The first formal discussion at the central committee of Lenin's 'Theses on Peace' took place on 11 (24) January at a time when the wave of strikes in Germany and Austria was in full flood. At this meeting a number of others who were not central committee members were also present.

Wide sections of the party, including the great majority of the Petersburg committee and of the Moscow regional bureau, were in favour of a revolutionary war. The views of many of the rank and file could be summed up in the phrase used by Osinsky, a member of the Moscow regional bureau: 'I stand for Lenin's old position.' Bukharin argued for 'revolutionary war' against the Hohenzollerns and Hapsburgs; to accept the Kaiser's *diktat* would be to stab the German and Austrian proletariat in the back. Dzerzhinsky reproached Lenin with timidity, with surrendering the whole programme of the revolution: 'Lenin is doing in a disguised form what Zinoviev and Kamenev did in October.' In Uritsky's view Lenin approached the problem 'from Russia's angle and not from an international point of view'. Lomov argued that 'by concluding peace we capitulate to German imperialism'. On behalf of the Petrograd organisation Kosior harshly condemned Lenin's position.

Trotsky argued:

> ...the question of a revolutionary war is an unreal one. The army has to be disbanded, but disbanding the army does not mean signing a peace... By refusing to sign a peace and demobilising the army, we force the facts into the open, because when we demobilise the Germans will attack. This will be a clear demonstration to the German Social-Democrats that this is no game with previously determined roles.[11]

The most determined advocates of peace were Zinoviev, Kamenev, Sverdlov, Stalin and Sokolnikov. Stalin said: 'There is no revolutionary movement in the West, nothing existing, only a potential, and we cannot count on a potential.' As in October, Zinoviev saw no grounds for expecting revolution in the West. No matter, he said, that the peace treaty would weaken the revolutionary movement in the West: '...of course... peace will strengthen chauvinism in Germany and for a time weaken the movement everywhere in the West.'

Lenin hastened to repudiate these two clumsy supporters: 'Can't take [the revolution in the West] into account?' Lenin exclaimed on Stalin's position. It was true the revolution in the West had not yet begun, but 'if we were to change our tactics on the strength of that... then we would be betraying international socialism'. Against Zinoviev he declared that it was wrong to say

> that concluding a peace will weaken the movement in the West for a time. If we believe that the German movement can immediately develop if the peace negotiations are broken off then we must sacrifice ourselves, for the power of the German revolution will be much greater than ours.[12]

Lenin did not for a moment forget the revolutionary potential in the West:

> Those who advocate a revolutionary war point out that this will involve us in a civil war with German imperialism and in this way we will awaken revolution in Germany. But Germany is only just pregnant with revolution and we have

already given birth to a completely healthy child, a socialist republic which we may kill if we start a war.[13]

When the three positions were put to the vote Lenin received 15 votes, Trotsky 16 and Bukharin's call for 'revolutionary war' 32. However, since non-members of the central committee had taken part in the vote, it was not binding on the central committee itself.

Lenin himself was ready to let Trotsky play for time. Against Zinoviev's solitary vote the central committee decided to 'do everything to drag out the signing of a peace.'[14]

Trotsky suggested putting the following formula to the vote: halt the war, do not conclude peace, and demobilise the army. The vote on this was: nine for, seven against. Thus the central committee formally authorised Trotsky to pursue his policy at Brest-Litovsk.

After this session of the central committee, Trotsky and Lenin came to a private agreement. Trotsky promised that in certain circumstances he would abandon his own policy in favour of Lenin's. As long as the Germans allowed them to avoid the choice between war and peace Trotsky would go on with the policy of procrastination. But if the die had to be cast, Trotsky would join Lenin in supporting the signing of a peace. However, as events were to show, they each interpreted this agreement slightly differently. Lenin was under the impression that Trotsky would sign the peace agreement as soon as he was faced with a threat that the German offensive would be renewed. Trotsky thought he had committed himself to accept the peace terms of the Germans only after they had actually launched an offensive.

Throughout, Trotsky used the negotiations at Brest-Litovsk as a platform for mass propaganda. Hence he opposed all evasions. On 29 December 1917 (11 January 1918) von Kühlmann, leader of the German delegation, stated:

> Every peace treaty has to be preceded by some kind of preamble saying that the state of war is at an end and that the two parties henceforth desire to live in peace and concord...
> Trotsky intervened: I will take myself the liberty to propose the deletion of sentence two of the draft, which by reason of its profoundly conventional and ornamental character is out

of keeping, I think, with the severely businesslike purpose of this document... Such declarations, copied from one diplomatic document into another, have never yet characterised the real relations between states.[15]

At another opportunity Trotsky tore the veil hiding real political power. On 1 (14) January General Hoffmann denounced the Bolsheviks because their government was supported by force. Trotsky replied:

The general was quite right when he said that our government rests on force. Up to the present moment there has been no government dispensing with force. It will always be so as long as society is composed of hostile classes... What in our conduct strikes and antagonises other governments is the fact that instead of arresting strikers we arrest capitalists who organise lockouts; instead of shooting the peasants who demand land, we arrest and we shoot the landlords and the officers who try to fire upon the peasants...[16]

At this point Trotsky remembers Hoffmann's face grew purple.[17] Czernin comments in his diary: 'Hoffmann made his unfortunate speech. He had been working on it for several days, and is very proud of [it].'[18]

On 28 January (10 February) Trotsky broke off negotiations with the Quadruple Alliance, declaring that while Russia refused to sign the annexationist peace it also simultaneously declared the war to be at an end. After a bitter indictment of imperialism, he went on to say:

We are removing our armies and our people from the war. Our peasant soldiers must return to the land to cultivate in peace the field which the revolution has taken from the landlord and given to the peasants. Our workmen must return to the workshops and produce, not for destruction, but for creation. They must, together with the peasants, create a socialist state.

We are going out of the war. We inform all peoples and their governments of this fact. We are giving the order for a general demobilisation of all our armies opposed at present to the troops of Germany, Austria-Hungary, Turkey and Bulgaria. We are waiting in the strong belief that other peoples will soon follow our example.

At the same time we declare that the conditions as submitted to us by the governments of Germany and Austria-Hungary are opposed in principle to the interests of all peoples. These conditions are refused by the working masses of all countries, amongst them by those of Germany and Austria-Hungary... We cannot place the signature of the Russian Revolution under these conditions which bring with them oppression, misery and hate to millions of human beings. The governments of Germany and Austria-Hungary are determined to possess lands and peoples by might. Let them do so openly. We cannot approve violence. We are going out of the war, but we feel ourselves compelled to refuse to sign the peace treaty.[19]

Trotsky stayed on at Brest-Litovsk for another day and learned of the quarrel between General Hoffmann, who insisted on the resumption of hostilities, and the civilian diplomats Kühlmann and Czernin, who preferred to accept the state of neither war nor peace. It seemed as if the civilians carried the day. Trotsky therefore returned to Petrograd confident that his policy had worked. Wheeler-Bennett described Trotsky's achievements at Brest-Litovsk:

Single-handed, with nothing behind him save a country in chaos and a regime scarce established, this amazing individual, who a year before had been an inconspicuous journalist exiled in New York, was combatting successfully the united diplomatic talent of half Europe.[20]

Pravda excitedly proclaimed:

The Central Powers are placed in a quandary. They cannot continue their aggression without revealing their cannibal teeth dripping with human blood. For the sake of the interests of socialism, and of their own interests, the Austro-German working masses will not permit the violation of the revolution.[21]

On 1 (14) February Trotsky gave a lengthy report on the peace negotiations to the central executive committee of the *soviets*, in the conclusion of which he said:

Comrades, I do not want to say that a further advance of the Germans against us is out of the question. Such a statement would be too risky, considering the power of the German Imperialist Party. But I think that by the position we have taken up on the question we have made any advance a very embarrassing affair for the German militarists.[22]

But on 3 (16) February, less than 24 hours after the central executive committee had unanimously endorsed Trotsky's policy, the Germans informed the Soviet government that 'on 18 February, at 12 o'clock, the armistice concluded with the Russian Republic will end, and a state of war will again be resumed.'

Lenin wanted to ask the Germans if it was still possible to sign the peace treaty, but Trotsky continued to oppose this.

The German offensive encountered no resistance. On 18 February a force of fewer than sixty German soldiers captured Dvinsk. German troops advanced without firing a shot, using the railways. In a few days (from 18 to 24 February) they occupied Reval, Rezhitsa, Dvinsk and Minsk, and invaded the Ukraine. General Hoffmann wrote:

> It is the most comical war I have ever known. We put a handful of infantrymen with machine guns and one gun onto a train and push them off to the next station; they take it, make prisoners of the Bolsheviks, pick up a few more troops, and go on. This proceeding has, at any rate, the charm of novelty.[23]

On the morning of 18 February the central committee met. Trotsky reported on the military offensive of the Germans. Lenin moved that a telegram offering peace should be sent to Germany. Trotsky opposed this. In his autobiography Trotsky later recalled:

> When the German high command gave notice of the expiration of the truce Lenin reminded me of our agreement. I answered that by an ultimatum I had not meant simply a verbal statement, but an actual German offensive that would leave no doubt as to the real relations between the countries...
> As before, I insisted that Hoffmann be allowed actually to start an offensive so that the workers of Germany, as well as of the countries of the Allies, would learn of the offensive as

a fact rather than as a threat.

'No', rejoined Lenin. 'We can't afford to lose a single hour now. The test has been made. Hoffmann wants to and can fight. Delay is impossible. This beast jumps fast.'

In March, at the party congress, Lenin said: 'It was agreed between us [that is, Lenin and me] tht we hold out until a German ultimatum, but that after the ultimatum we were to surrender.' I described the agreement above. Lenin consented not to attack my point of view before the party only because I promised him not to support the advocates of a revolutionary war.[24]

Let us return to the central committee meeting of the morning of 18 February. The minutes of this meeting report:

Comrade Trotsky (against sending a telegram offering peace) emphasises that the masses are only just beginning now to digest what is happening; to sign peace now will only produce confusion in our ranks; the same applies to the Germans, who believe that we are only waiting for an ultimatum... we have to wait to see what impression all this makes on the German people. The end to the war was greeted with joy in Germany and it is not out of the question that the German offensive will produce a serious outburst in Germany. We have to wait to see the effect and then—we can still offer peace if it doesn't happen.

Comrade Lenin (in favour of offering peace). There is the suspicion that the Germans want an offensive to oust the Soviet government. We face a situation where we have to act.[25]

Lenin's motion was put. Six voted for, seven against.

However, when the central committee met again on the evening of the same day, 18 February, Trotsky this time voted with Lenin. The result was that when the question 'should we send the German government an offer straight away to conclude peace immediately?' was tabled, seven voted for, five against and one abstained.[26]

On 19 February the Soviet government sued for peace. The German reply was harsh. Russia was to carry out complete demobilisation; to cede Latvia and Estonia, to evacuate the

Ukraine and Finland. When on 23 February the central committee met, it was again on Trotsky's single vote that the outcome depended. Lenin made it clear that he would resign from the government if the German terms were not accepted. The minutes of the central committee report:

> Comrade Lenin considers that this is where the policy of revolutionary phrase-making ends. If this policy continues now he is leaving both the government and the CC. You need an army for a revolutionary war, and there isn't one. That means that the terms must be accepted.

Trotsky did not agree with Lenin's suggestion:

> The arguments of V I [Lenin] are far from convincing; if we had all been of the same mind, we could have tackled the task of organising defence and we could have managed it. Our role would not have been a bad one even if we had been forced to surrender Peter [Petrograd] and Moscow. We would have held the whole world in tension. If we sign the German ultimatum today, we may have a new ultimatum tomorrow. Everything is formulated in such a way as to leave an opportunity for further ultimatums. We may sign a peace; and lose support among the advanced elements of the proletariat, in any case demoralise them.[27]

But he was not ready to split the party in this dangerous situation for the revolution. Trotsky

> does not think we are threatened by destruction... There is a lot of subjectivity in Lenin's position. I am not convinced that this position is right but I do not want to do anything to interfere with party unity...[28]

Lenin then moved that 'the German proposals should be accepted immediately'.The vote was: seven for, four against and four abstentions. The abstentions were Trotsky, Krestinsky, Dzerzhinsky and Ioffe.[29]

The three leaders of the war faction who abstained —Krestinsky, Dzerzhinsky and Ioffe—explained in a statement that their abstention was a reaction to the danger of splitting the party.[30]

On 24 February Trotsky tendered his resignation from the

commissariat of foreign affairs:

> Comrade Trotsky points out that it is just when the peace is being signed that he finds it unacceptable to stay because he is forced to defend a position he does not agree with.[31]

The central committee appealed to Trotsky to stay in office until the peace was signed. He only agreed not to make public his resignation until then, and declared that he would not appear any more in any governmental institution. Prompted by Lenin, the committee obliged Trotsky to attend at least those sessions of the government at which foreign affairs were not debated.[32]

At the Seventh Congress of the party, which eventually confirmed the peace agreement in March 1918, Trotsky explained again the reasons for his abstention on the vote for peace:

> With a weak country behind us, with a passive peasantry, with a sombre mood in the proletariat, we were further threatened by a split in our ranks... Very much was at stake on my vote... I could not assume responsibility for the split. I had thought that we ought to retreat [before the German army] rather than sign peace for the sake of an illusory respite. But I could not take upon myself the responsibility for the leadership of the party...[33]

When it came to the election at the congress for a new central committee, Trotsky and Lenin obtained the highest number of votes. Rejecting Trotsky's policy, the party still gave him its complete confidence.

The harsh terms of the peace treaty

It was estimated that by the Brest-Litovsk Treaty Russia lost territories and resources approximately as follows: 1,267,000 square miles, with over 62 million population, or a quarter of its territory and 44 per cent of its population; one-third of its crops and 27 per cent of state income; 80 per cent of its sugar factories; 73 per cent of its iron and 75 per cent of its coal. Of the total of 16,000 industrial undertakings, 9000 were situated in the lost territories.[34]

Opposition to Lenin's peace policy now spread widely among the masses. In February a referendum of the views of 200 *soviets* was held. Of these a majority—105—voted for war against

Germany. In the industrial city *soviets* the majority in favour of war was overwhelming. Only two large *soviets*—Petrograd and Sebastopol—went on record as being in favour of peace. On the other hand several of the big centres—such as Moscow, Kronstadt, Ekaterinburg, Kharkov, Ekaterinoslav and Ivanovo-Voznesensk—voted against Lenin's policy with overwhelming majorities. Of the *soviets* of 42 provincial cities that were consulted six opted for peace, 20 for war; 88 county towns and villages opted for peace, 85 for war.[35]

However, the debate in the party came to an end with the specially convened Seventh Congress on 6-8 March. The day before it opened, a new daily paper appeared that opposed Lenin's policy. *Kommunist*, 'Organ of the St Petersburg committee and the St Petersburg area committee of the RSDLP', was edited by Bukharin, Radek and Uritsky, with the collaboration of a number of prominent party leaders: Bubnov, Lomov, Pokrovsky, Preobrazhensky, Piatakov, Kollontai, Inessa Armand and others. The list of names gives some idea of the strength and quality of *Kommunist*.

After a bitter debate the Seventh Congress resolved to support Lenin's policy by 30 votes to 12, with four abstentions. Local party organisations followed this line either immediately or after a time.

The resolution of the congress ratifying the peace treaty was thoroughly internationalist and revolutionary:

> The congress considers it necessary to confirm the highly distressing, degrading peace treaty with Germany which the Soviet government signed because of our lack of an army, the extremely unhealthy condition of the demoralised front-line units, the necessity of utilising any, however small, opportunity for a breathing space before the onslaught of imperialism on the Soviet socialist republic...
> The congress finds the most reliable guarantee of the strengthening of the socialist revolution, which was victorious in Russia, only in its transformation into an international workers' revolution...
> In the belief that the workers' revolution is maturing in all belligerent countries, preparing the inevitable and complete defeat of imperialism, the congress declares that the socialist

proletariat of Russia, with all its strength and all the means at its disposal, will support the fraternal revolutionary movement of the proletarians of all countries.[36]

The final ratification of the treaty took place at the Fourth Congress of *Soviets* on 15 March, by a vote of 748 to 261, with 115 abstentions. Among the latter were 64 'Left Communists'.

From then on the Left Communists lapsed into silence regarding the war question. But the Left Social Revolutionaries voiced their basically nationalist opposition to the peace policy all the more loudly and impatiently. Immediately after the ratification of the peace they withdrew from the Council of People's Commissars.

Negotiations with France and Britain

To add to the disarray in the Bolshevik leadership's ranks a new factor intervened. On 22 February Trotsky reported to the central committee an offer by France and Britain to give military aid to Russia in a war against Germany. The majority of the Left Communists were opposed in principle to accepting aid from such imperialist quarters. Trotsky came out clearly in favour of accepting aid from whatever source. 'The Left Communists' arguments do not stand up to criticism,' he said.

> As the party of the socialist proletariat which is in power and conducting a war against Germany, we mobilise every means through state institutions to arm and supply our revolutionary army in the best way possible with all necessary resources and, for that purpose, we obtain them where we can, including therefore from capitalist governments. In doing this, the Russian Social Democratic Labour Party retains full independence in its external policy, gives no political undertakings to capitalist governments and examines their proposals in each separate case according to what is expedient.

Lenin, who had not been present at this meeting of the central committee, added the following statement to the minutes of the session: 'Please add my vote *in favour* of taking potatoes and weapons from the Anglo-French imperialist robbers.'[37]

To explain his readiness to use the conflicts between the

imperialist powers in the interests of the proletariat in power, Lenin wrote on 22 February an article entitled 'The Itch'.

> Let us suppose Kaliaev*, in order to kill a tyrant and monster, acquires a revolver from an absolute villain, a scoundrel and robber, by promising bread, money and vodka for the service rendered.
>
> Can one condemn Kaliaev for 'dealing with a robber' for the sake of obtaining a deadly weapon? Every sensible person will answer 'no'. If there is nowhere else for Kaliaev to get a revolver, and if his intention is really an honourable one (the killing of a tyrant, not killing for plunder), then he should not be reproached but commended for acquiring a revolver in this way. But if a robber, in order to commit murder for the sake of plunder, acquires a revolver from another robber in return for money, vodka or bread, can one compare (not to speak of identifying) *such* a 'deal with the robber' with the deal made with Kaliaev?[38]

In a postscript to the article Lenin added:

> The North Americans in their war of liberation against England at the end of the eighteenth century got help from Spain and France, who were her competitors and just as much colonial robbers as England. It is said that there were 'Left Bolsheviks' to be found who contemplated writing a 'learned work' on the 'dirty deal' of these Americans.[39]

In the end, however, nothing came of the offer of aid.

Could Trotsky's tactic of 'Neither war nor peace' have succeeded?

In retrospect it is clear that Lenin's suggested tactics for the peace negotiations in Brest-Litovsk were correct. At the time, however, Trotsky had good grounds for believing that his policy could succeed.

Trotsky drew out the negotiations as long as he could in order

---

* Kaliaev was a member of the combat group of the Social Revolutionary Party who took part in a number of terrorist acts. On 4 (17) February 1905 he assassinated the governor-general of Moscow, the Grand Duke S A Romanov, uncle of Tsar Nikolai II. He was executed at Schlusselburg on 10 (23) May that year.

to give the European masses the possibility of realising the meaning of the Soviet government and its policy. The January 1918 strikes in Germany and Austria showed that this effort had not been in vain. One has only to read Czernin's diary to see how panicky the authorities were in Vienna, fearing starvation and revolt among the subject nations. With the Austro-Hungarian empire on the point of collapse, Czernin threatened his German colleagues with separate negotiations with Russia (although in fact the threat was an empty one because of the increasing dependence of Austria-Hungary on German help).

Wheeler-Bennett describes Czernin's position in these words: 'Peace at any price became his motto... Austria reached the end of her military power, her political structure was doomed.'[40] On 17 November 1917 Czernin wrote to one of his friends:

> To settle with Russia as speedily as possible, then break through the determination of the Entente to exterminate us, and then to make peace—even at a loss—that is my plan and the hope for which I live.[41]

An entry in Czernin's diary of 23 December 1917 states:

> Kühlmann is personally an advocate of general peace, but fears the influence of the military party, who do not wish to make peace until definitely victorious.[42]

An entry for 27 December 1917 reads:

> Matters still getting worse...
> I told Kühlmann and Hoffmann I would go as far as possible with them; but should their endeavours fail then I would enter into separate negotiatioins with the Russians... Austria-Hungary... desires nothing but final peace. Kühlmann understands my position, and says he himself would rather go than let it fail. Asked me to give him my point of view in writing, as it 'would strengthen his position'. Have done so. He has telegraphed it to the Kaiser.[43]

> 7 January 1918:
> A wire has just come in reporting demonstrations in Budapest against Germany. The windows of the German Consulate were broken, a clear indication of the state of feeling which would arise if the peace were to be lost...[44]

15 January 1918:

I had a letter today from one of our mayors at home, calling my attention to the fact that disaster due to lack of foodstuffs is now imminent.

I immediately telegraphed the Emperor as follows:

'I have just received a letter from Statthalter N N which justified all the fears I have constantly repeated to Your Majesty, and shows that in the question of food supply we are on the very verge of a catastrophe. The situation *arising out of the carelessness and incapacity of the Ministers* is terrible, and I fear it is already too late to check the total collapse which is to be expected in the next few weeks... On learning the state of affairs, I went to the Prime Minister to speak with him about it. I told him, as is the case, that in a few weeks our war industries, our railway traffic, would be at a standstill, the provisioning of the army would be impossible, it must break down, and that would mean the collapse of Austria and therewith also of Hungary. To each of these points he answered yes, that is so... We can only hope that some *deus ex machina* may intervene to save us from the worst.[45]

17 January 1918:

Bad news from Vienna and environs. Serious strike movement due to the reduction of flour rations and the tardy progress of the Brest negotiations.[46]

On the same day Czernin got a message from the Austrian emperor which stated:

I must once more earnestly impress upon you that the whole fate of the monarchy and of the dynasty depends on peace being concluded at Brest-Litovsk as soon as possible... If peace be not made at Brest, there will be revolution.[47]

On 20 January Czernin writes in his diary:

The position now is this: without help from outside, we shall... have thousands perishing in a few weeks... if we do not make peace *soon* then the troubles at home will be repeated, and each demonstration in Vienna will render peace here most costly to obtain...[48]

The Austrians were supported in their attempts to achieve unconditional peace by the Bulgarians and Turks, and, much more important, by the German foreign minister von Kühlmann and prime minister von Hertling.

Czernin describes the reaction to Trotsky's statement of 10 February withdrawing from the negotiations:

> At a meeting on 10 February of the diplomatic and military delegates of Germany and Austria-Hungary to discuss the question of what was now to be done it was agreed unanimously, save for a single dissentient, that the situation arising out of Trotsky's declarations must be accepted. The one dissentient vote—that of General Hoffmann—was to the effect that Trotsky's statement should be answered by declaring the armistice at an end, marching on Petersburg and supporting the Ukraine openly against Russia. In the ceremonial final sitting, on 11 February, Herr von Kühlmann adopted the attitude expressed by the majority of the peace delegations and set forth the same in a most impressive speech.[49]

The Austrian delegation

> wired to Vienna that peace had been concluded, with the result that the imperial capital was even now dressing itself en fête.
>
> With the sincere hope of peace in his heart, Kühlmann brought the conference proceedings to a formal conclusion on 11 February and departed for Berlin.

However at this point the tide started to turn against von Kühlmann:

> On his arrival [in Berlin] he was summoned, with the chancellor and the vice-chancellor... to the little watering place of Homburg, where the Kaiser was taking a February cure. There, throughout the 13th, raged a battle royal on the issues of peace and war, with the Emperor flitting in and out like an unhappy ghost.[50]
>
> The civilians remained opposed to the high command. They feared the effect on the internal conditions of Germany if hostilities were resumed... Kühlmann, in addition to his

general principles, warned them that a new war in the east would strain the alliance with Austria-Hungary almost to the breaking point...[51]

The memoirs of Ludendorff[52] and Kühlmann make it clear that for days there was a balance between the war party headed by the German general staff (Hindenburg, Ludendorff and Hoffmann), and the peace party, headed by von Kühlmann and von Hertling. The latter argued repeatedly that the situation on the home front did not permit a military offensive against the Russians. But the German supreme command remained adamant. In the end, with the Kaiser's backing, it won the day in the discussions at Homburg; a few days later General Hoffman declared the armistice at an end and ordered German troops to march on Petrograd.

The German revolutionary socialist Karl Liebknecht, from his prison cell, wrote that the policy of prolonged negotiations carried by Trotsky in Brest was of great benefit to the revolution in Germany:

> The result of Brest-Litovsk is not nil, even if it comes to a peace of forced capitulation. Thanks to the Russian delegates, Brest-Litovsk has become a revolutionary tribunal whose decrees are heard far and wide. It has brought about the exposure of the Central Powers; it has exposed German avidity, its cunning lies and hypocrisy. It has passed an annihilating verdict upon the peace policy of the German [Social Democratic] majority—a policy which is not so much a pious hypocrisy as it is cynicism. It has proved powerful enough to bring forth numerous mass movements in various countries.[53]

An early signing of peace by the Soviets would have damaged the German revolution, argued Liebknecht:

> In no sense can it be said that the present solution of the problem is not as favourable for the future development as a surrender at Brest-Litovsk would have been at the beginning of February. Quite the contrary. A surrender like that would have thrown the worst light on all preceding resistance and would have made the subsequent submission to force appear as 'vis haud ingrata'. The cynicism that cries to heaven and

the brutal character of the ultimate German action have driven all suspicions into the background.[54]

Contrary to the later Stalinist mythology, Lenin was not absolutely sure that Trotsky's tactic of 'neither peace nor war' was wrong. Thus Krupskaya discloses Lenin's hesitation on the issue. In her memoirs she shows that notwithstanding Lenin's steadfast support for the call for immediate peace, he was not *absolutely* convinced that Trotsky might not be right after all. Thus she describes strolling with Lenin along the Neva embankment one day towards the end of February. As they walked, Lenin

> kept repeating over and over again the reasons why the standpoint of 'no war, no peace' was fundamentally wrong. On our way back Ilyich suddenly stops and his tired face lights up and he lets forth: 'You never know!'—meaning a revolution may have started in Germany for all we know.[55]

When events proved that Lenin was right, Trotsky was generous in acknowledging this. On 3 October 1918, at a session of the central executive committee of the *soviet*, he declared:

> I regard it as my duty to declare, in this authoritative assembly, that at the time when many of us, myself included, doubted whether it was necessary or permissible for us to sign the peace of Brest-Litovsk, whether perhaps doing this would not have a hampering effect on the development of the world proletarian movement, it was Comrade Lenin alone, in opposition to many of us, who with persistence and incomparable perspicacity maintained that we must undergo this experience in order to be able to carry on, to hold out, until the coming of the world proletarian revolution. And now, against the background of recent events, we who opposed him are obliged to recognise that it was not we who were right. [*Prolonged applause*].[56]

Trotsky well knew that had he signed the peace treaty sooner the Soviet republic might have obtained less harsh terms. In that case, however, German imperialism would not have been completely unmasked, nor would the myth of Bolshevik connivance with it have been so effectively discredited. To the end of his life, Trotsky was convinced that the Brest-Litovsk negotiations had played a crucial role in the inner collapse of the Central Powers. The German and Austro-Hungarian empire hung on for nine months after the Brest-Litovsk peace, until November 1918, but the propaganda carried on by Trotsky in the peace negotiations played a significant role in their exposure to their own people.

Above all it must be stressed that, despite their tactical differences, both Lenin and Trotsky saw the foreign policy of the Soviet republic as subordinate to the needs of the international workers' revolution. This point needs special emphasis because in later years Stalin was to depict Lenin's policy as one of peaceful coexistence with the capitalist world.

One consequence of the Brest-Litovsk controversy was its effect on the standing of the various Bolshevik leaders. Lenin emerged with enormous moral authority. Zinoviev, who, in Lenin's words, had acted as 'a strikebreaker' in October, to some extent rehabilitated himself by rallying strongly to Lenin's side. Trotsky, on the other hand, suffered a certain eclipse. But this was only temporary. His standing was second to Lenin and shortly he was to reach new heights as organiser and leader of the Red Army.

Chapter three
Building the Red Army

A MONTH after the revolution the first White Guards, under the command of Kornilov, Kaledin, Alekseev and Denikin, moved into action on the River Don and the Cossacks of Orenburg rose under the *ataman* Dutov. In June 1918 30,000 Czechoslovak soldiers, who had been mobilised under the sponsorship of the Kerensky government, rose against the Bolsheviks. The Germans crushed the revolutionary regimes in Finland and the Ukraine and occupied Lithuania and Latvia. On 2 August 1918 British troops seized Archangel, overthrew the local *soviet* and set up a Provisional Government of the North. On the following day British and Japanese troops landed in Vladivostok, to be followed by US and French troops. The wars of intervention had begun and went on until November 1920.

Besides the Russian White Guard armies, many foreign armies fought the *soviets*: the German, Austrian, British, French, Japanese, American, Serbian, Polish, Ukrainian, Rumanian, Finnish, Estonian, Lithuanian, Czechoslovak...

The Red Army fought on fronts with a circumference of more than 5000 miles. The war consisted of a series of deep thrusts by White armies, now from one part of the outer fringe into the interior, now from another, followed by Red counter-thrusts. Again and again Soviet power was restricted to the principality of Moscow—the cities of Moscow and Petrograd and a small area around them. 1919 was the decisive year of the civil war. Three major campaigns formed the climaxes of the war: Kolchak's offensive undertaken from his Siberian base towards the Volga and Moscow in the spring; Denikin's advance from the south, also aiming at Moscow in summer; and Iudenich's attempt to capture

Petrograd in the autumn. It was only in November 1920, after three long bloody years, that the civil war came to an end with the defeat of Wrangel's army in the Crimea.

Trotsky's knowledge of military doctrine

On 4 March 1918 Trotsky became commissar for war and president of the supreme war council. What knowledge had he of military methods? His experience as a reporter of the Balkan Wars[1] had developed his knowledge of military affairs considerably. One military historian, Colonel Harold Walter Nelson of the US Army College in Pennsylvania, wrote about Trotsky:

> He never witnessed a battle and he was not even allowed to visit the front... However, once he became a war correspondent he demonstrated remarkable ability in his analysis of the strategic situation.[2]

Trotsky went far beyond mere reporting of the war:

> While he devoted most of his attention to describing the daily occurrences of the war, his approach to strategic questions made his occasional analyses of these questions extremely valuable and remarkably prescient.[3]

One of the first tasks of the strategist is the determination of the decisive points in the war. Having done this, he must next determine the course of action to be followed if the desired outcome is to be achieved. Again and again Colonel Nelson points out that Trotsky surpassed the Balkan generals in his grasp of strategy. After the initial great victory of the Bulgarians over the Turks on 3 November 1912 Trotsky wrote that the victory would lead to the ultimate defeat of the Bulgarian forces by the entrenched Turks defending the lines in Chataldja:

> Working with limited resources, Trotsky had derived the strategic plan and pointed out the critical areas which required special attention if victory was to be achieved. In retrospect Trotsky appears to have been a better strategist than those found on the Bulgarian general staff. He had a more perfect understanding of the need for speed rather than tactical victories, and he sensed the importance of massing

forces in the critical theatre rather than detaching troops to take political objectives. In his discussion of strategy he certainly displayed a grasp of the fundamental principles sufficient to allow valid analysis of complex military problems.[4]

In November 1914 Trotsky received an invitation to become a war correspondent for the liberal newspaper, *Kievskaya Mysl*. This led to a further improvement in his grasp of military affairs. Trotsky's creative, realistic imagination enabled him to foresee the appearance of the tank. Realising that trench warfare made for military stalemate, and that this could be broken only when one side gained the technological advantage, Trotsky discussed the possibility of overcoming the vulnerability of the internal combustion engine to devise a 'colossal war machine which can move forward through the barbed wire.'[5]

He was also very perceptive in guessing that the conservatism of the generals would delay the widespread and effective use of the tank. He wrote that 'the technological combinations achieved at the end of one war become the technical framework for the model used in laboratory work in preparation for the next war.' As a result, he predicted, it would take 'about ten years after the initial clash before the techniques of war are understood.'[6]

Colonel Nelson's comment on Trotsky's prognosis was:

Historical hindsight gives us no real grounds to revise Trotsky's assessments. Technological innovation did provide hope for strategic advantage before the war ended, with the tank and the aeroplane heading most lists of devices which had already displayed their potential for changing the nature of warfare before World War I ended. Some military theorists (Liddell Hart, J F C Fuller, Douhet, and Mitchell) understood the new techniques of warfare before Trotsky's ten-year deadline had passed, but no military establishment had the necessary acumen to adopt wholeheartedly their theories within the decade.[7]

Trotsky went beyond foreseeing the arrival of the tank. Having grasped the basic elements of trench warfare combined with the nature of the tank, Trotsky visualised a future defensive warfare based on a new kind of fortress:

Around essential strategic points there will be several concentric lines of narrow trenches connecting them to a central web of barbed wire. The trench lines will be strengthened by using the most advanced construction techniques. They will contain easily shifted artillery batteries placed underground. Reliable shelters, storehouses, workshops, and large electrical generating plants will also be built underground. All of this will be dispersed over a wide area, so that heavy artillery will have no attractive targets. Such a fortress of the future, without medieval forts, will be able to fulfil the functions fortresses ought to fulfil.[8]

This analysis of the future of defensive warfare seems to herald the French strategy that led to the construction of the Maginot Line after the end of the First World War.

Learning from history

In building the Red Army and leading it, Trotsky could use little experience from previous revolutions. The first time the working class had taken state power was in 1871 during the Paris Commune. The defeat of the Commune owed much to its failure on the military front. Lissagaray, who fought for the Commune, described the state of the troops:

> most of the battalions had been without leaders... the National Guards without *cadres*. And the generals who assumed the responsibility of leading 40,000 men had never conducted a single battalion into the field. They neglected even the most elementary precautions, knew not how to collect artillery, ammunition wagons or ambulances, forgot to make an order of the day, and left the men for several hours without food in a penetrating fog. Every Federal [soldier] chose the leader he liked best.[9]

> The men were also abandoned to themselves, being neither cared for nor controlled. Scarcely any, if any, relieving of the troops under fire ever took place. The whole strain fell upon the same men. Certain battalions remained twenty, thirty days in the trenches, while others were continually kept in reserve.[10]

There was no central direction at all. The Communards,

without directions, without military knowledge, saw no further than just their own quarter, or even their own streets; so that instead of 200 strategical, solid barricades, easy to defend with 7000 or 8000 men, hundreds were scattered about which it was impossible to arm sufficiently.[13]

So Trotsky could learn from the experience of the Paris Commune only what not to do, but little of a positive nature.

When discussing revolutionary wars, Marxists were most frequently influenced by the wars of the French Revolution. However, as Trotsky himself clearly explained, the lessons from France could be only of limited value:

> Historical analogies are very tempting. But one has to be cautious when resorting to them... France was, at the end of the 18th century, the richest and most civilised country on the continent of Europe. In the 20th century, Russia is the poorest and most backward country in Europe. Compared with the revolutionary tasks that confront us today, the revolutionary task of the French army was much more superficial in character. At that time it was a matter of overthrowing 'tyrants', of abolishing or mitigating feudal serfdom. Today it is a matter of completely destroying exploitation and class oppression.[12]

A most crucial difference between the French bourgeois revolution and the Russian proletarian revolution was that the bourgeoisie, for generations before its revolution, had already been able to break the monopoly of the nobility over education, including military education, while the proletariat remained an oppressed, intellectually deprived class. Long before the French Revolution the bourgeoisie could turn to the nobility and say to them: 'You have the land; we have money—we are richer than you. Intellectually we are also richer than you. You have the church; we have the universities. You have priests, we have professors. You have the Bible, we have the Encyclopaedia.'

When it came to knowledge of military affairs, again the bourgeoisie had already broken the nobility's monopoly. Hence when it came to the decisive moment, half of the 15,000 French royalist officers joined the revolution. The French Revolution created its army by amalgamating its revolutionary formations with the royalist battalions. As against this, the Russian Revolution had dissolved the Tsarist army completely, leaving not a trace of it, and the Red Army had to be built from the first brick.

However there was one important lesson that Trotsky could and did learn from the French revolutionary wars: that troops who understood and believed in what they were fighting for were vastly superior to ordinary mercenaries or conscripted men.

The dominance of politics

The authority most frequently cited in Trotsky's writings on war is Clausewitz. Clausewitz's central precept was that war is a continuation of politics by other means. This applies to civil war even more than to ordinary war. Politics dominates strategy, tactics and organisation. This is precisely the principle that governed Trotsky's approach to the civil war. He saw the civil war as an integral part of the revolution, as an extension of the class struggle culminating in the consolidation of political power. Politics dictates military policy, though not in an automatic way. Trotsky had to enlist the enthusiasm of revolutionaries first, as a key to the imposition of discipline upon others. It was Trotsky's *political* genius that dominated his role as head of the Red Army.

In an article entitled 'Leon Trotsky, the Organiser of Victory', Karl Radek wrote:

> The history of the proletarian revolution has shown how one can change the pen for the sword. Trotsky is one of the best writers on world socialism, and his literary qualities did not prevent him from being the first head, the first organiser of the first army of the proletariat. The revolution changed to a sword the pen of its best publicist...
>
> The need of the hour was for a man who would incarnate the call to struggle, a man who, subordinating himself completely to the need of the struggle, would become the ringing summons to arms, the will which exacts from all unconditional submission to a great, sacrificial necessity. Only a man with Trotsky's capacity for work, only a man so unsparing of himself as Trotsky, only a man who knew how to speak to the soldiers as Trotsky did—only such a man could have become the standard-bearer of the armed toilers. He was all things rolled into one.[13]

Chapter four

The structure of the Red Army

THE BOLSHEVIKS needed to build an army from scratch. In February 1917 the Tsarist army had had nine million soldiers under arms. Mass desertions followed the February revolution, and accelerated after October. By the end of November General Posokhov, chiefofstaff of the Twelfth Army, stated that 'the army just does not exist'.[1] Looking back on 10 July 1918, Trotsky wrote:

> The old army... shared the fate of the old Russia in general. If the revolt of the peasants against the landlords, of the workers against the capitalists, of the whole people against the old reign of the bureaucracy and against the Tsar himself signified the break-up of the old Russia, then the break-up of the army was predetermined precisely by this.[2]

The Bolsheviks inherited little from the old army. An official history of the civil war estimated that only some 30,000 or 50,000 of the soldiers 'remained under the banner of the revolution'. Among them were the Latvian Rifle Regiments, the Fourth Cavalry Division, some armoured car detachments and some of the army units in the Far East.[3]

In addition there was the Red Guard—the armed workers' militia. At the time of the October revolution the number of Red Guards was estimated at 20,000 in Petrograd, many of them without arms, and fewer than 10,000 in Moscow.[4]

Any attempt to carry out conscription in the first months of the revolution would have failed. The country was sick of war, and the main appeal of Bolshevism had been its search for peace. The first step in the building of the Red Army was therefore the recruitment of volunteers.

On 18 January 1918 a decree signed by Lenin brought the Red Army into formal existence. The new army was called 'The Workers' and Peasants' Red Army':

1) The Workers' and Peasants' Army is built up from the more conscious and organised elements of the working people.

2) Access to its ranks is open to all citizens of the Russian Republic who have attained the age of 18. Everyone who is prepared to devote his forces, his life, to the defence of the gains of the October revolution, the power of the *soviets*, and socialism can join the Red Army. Joining the ranks of the Red Army requires characterists [*sic*] from army committees or democratic public organisations standing on the platform of the Soviet power, party or trade union organisation, or at least two members of these organisations.[5]

Trotsky did not make a virtue out of the voluntary principle. It was a practical necessity:

Volunteering is the only possible means of forming units with any degree of combat readiness under conditions in which the old army has broken down catastrophically along with all the organs for its formation and administration.[6]

Unfortunately an army of millions could not be built on the voluntary principle—but after the proletarian core of the army had been firmly established in this way, Trotsky could think of starting to conscript the mass of workers and peasants.

The election of officers

Hand in hand with voluntary recruitment into the Red Army went the principle of the democratic election of officers by the soldiers. As early as April 1917 Lenin had posed the question: 'Should officers be elected by the soldiers?' He answered unequivocally: 'Not only must they be elected, but every step of every officer and general must be supervised by persons especially elected for the purpose by the soldiers.' Then he asked: 'Is it desirable for the soldiers, on their own decision, to displace their superiors?' And answered: 'It is desirable and essential in every way. The soldiers will obey and respect only elected authority.'[7]

The Soviet government followed this general line. Thus on 16 (29) December 1917, Sovnarkom issued a decree stating:

All power in the units and their formations is vested in the respective soldiers' committee and *soviets*...

Election of command personnel and officials is hereby introduced. Commanders up to regimental level are elected at general meetings of their squads, platoons, companies, teams, squadrons, batteries, battalions and regiments. Commanders of higher than regimental level, up to the supreme commander-in-chief, are elected by congresses or conferences convened by the respective committees.

Commanders of armies are elected by army congresses. Front commanders are elected by congresses of fronts...

Chiefs of staff are elected by congresses from among persons with special training.[8]

The move to conscription

In its early days the Red Army of volunteers was hardly distinguishable from the detachments of the Red Guards. One historian described the Red Guards thus: 'Fundamental to the Red Guards in 1917 were several features: their volunteering, self-formed and self-directed nature; their intensely local, usually factory, orientation, their hostile attitude toward established political authority; and their volatile and crisis-orientated membership.'[9] The Red Guards were effective only against Russian anti-*soviet* forces, which were equally weak in organisation and discipline and at the time less numerous and well-armed. Against a regular army such as the Germans in the Ukraine or the Czechs in Siberia and on the Volga they were helpless.

The number of volunteers to join the Red Army was also insufficient. By April 1918 the Red Army numbered nearly 200,000 men, drawn practically only from the urban proletariat.[10]

On 22 April 1918, at the all-Russian central executive committee of the *soviets*, Trotsky moved a 'Decree on Compulsory Military Training'. This established compulsory military training for all workers and for peasants who did not employ hired labour. The training was to be for twelve hours a week for eight weeks a year.[11] A month later, on 29 May, the central executive committee decreed the first step towards compulsory service in the Red Army in the Moscow, Petrograd, and the Don and Kuban areas.[12] Then on 12 June Sovnarkom decreed the mobilisation of the workers and poor peasants in the Pri-Volga, Urals and Siberian military districts, those immediately threatened by armed anti-Bolsheviks.[13]

By July the size of the Red Army had grown to 725,383.[14] Only when the proletarian corps of the army had been established was the mass conscription of poor and middle peasants begun. Thus by the end of 1919 the Red Army was three million strong.[15]

With the mass conscription of peasants into the Red Army, an element of instability was introduced. The peasants were far less reliable than the workers, and had a far more ambivalent attitude to Soviet power. They supported the Bolsheviks who gave them the land, but opposed the Communists who requisitioned their grain—sometimes not realising they were one and the same. While welcoming the protection the Bolsheviks gave them against the threat that the landlords might return in the wake of the White armies, they resisted the food requisitions and conscription into the Red Army. This is Trotsky's graphic description of the changing mood of the peasants during the civil war:

> The mood of the peasantry vacillated unceasingly. Entire regiments composed of peasants... surrendered in the first period, sometimes without putting up a fight, and then later, when the Whites had enrolled them under their flag, crossed over to our side again. Sometimes the peasant masses tried to show their independence and abandoned both Whites and Reds, going off into the forests to form their 'Green' units. But the scattered nature and political helplessness of these units foredoomed them to defeat. Thus, at the fronts of the civil war the relation between the basic class forces of the revolution found expression more vividly than anywhere else: the peasant masses, for whose allegiance the landlord, bourgeois, intellectual, counter-revolution contended with the working class, constantly wavered from this side to that; but in the end it gave its support to the working class... In this social fact is rooted the final cause of our victories.[16]

Mass desertions

The vacillation of the peasantry led to mass desertions from the Red Army. A Soviet historian of the civil war, F Nikonov, refers to desertions from military trains reaching between 25 and 30 per cent of the total numbers, and in some exceptional instances soaring up to even 50 or 70 per cent. He states that as a rule reinforcements reached the front at about two-thirds of the strength they had when they set off.[17] In February 1919 the Red Army numbered about a million; by January 1920 this had risen to three million. In the intervening year there were no fewer than 2,846,000 deserters—90 per cent of them men who simply failed to comply with their call-up orders.[18] Of these, 1,753,000 were brought back to duty.[19]

Desertion had been widespread in other revolutionary armies made up of peasants. Thus a historian writes of the army of the French Revolution that '...battalions in the army of the Ardennes were melting away. In one of them, five out of six recruits had disappeared...'[20] Again, not all army units 'were equally affected, but those who were far from home sometimes saw one-third of their men disappear.'[21]

Trotsky took steps against desertion as early as 7 October 1918, when he issued an order declaring:

1) It is the duty of rural *soviets* and Committees of the Poor to arrest deserters and bring them under secure guard to the headquarters of divisions or regiments.

If unapprehended deserters are discovered in any village, responsibility for this will be placed upon the chairman of the *soviet* and the chairman of the Committee of the Poor, who will be subject to immediate arrest.

Any deserter who immediately presents himself at the headquarters of a division or regiment and declares: 'I am a deserter, but I swear that in future I will fight with honour' is to be pardoned and allowed to perform the high duties of a warrior of the Workers' and Peasants' Army.

A deserter who offers resistance to arrest is to be shot on the spot.[22]

As potential military material, deserters were not inferior to other soldiers. On 24 February 1919 Trotsky declared:

Give me 3000 deserters, taken from wherever you like, and call them a regiment. I will give them a good, honest regimental commissar, a fighting commissar, give them the right battalion, company and platoon commanders—and I affirm that within four weeks those 3000 deserters will provide our revolutionary country with a splendid regiment. And that is not a hope, not a programme, not an idea, it has all been tested by experience...[23]

In his autobiography Trotsky describes a meeting with deserters:

The war commissariat of Riazan succeeded in gathering in some 15,000 of such deserters. While passing through Riazan, I decided to take a look at them. Some of our men tried to dissuade me. 'Something might happen,' they warned me. But everything went off beautifully. The men were called out of their barracks. 'Comrade deserters—come to the meeting. Comrade Trotsky has come to speak to you.' They ran out excited, boisterous, as curious as schoolboys. I had imagined them much worse, and they had imagined me as more terrible. In a few minutes, I was surrounded by a huge crowd of unbridled, utterly undisciplined, but not at all hostile men. The 'comrade deserters' were looking at me with such curiosity that it seemed as if their eyes would pop out of their heads. I climbed on a table there in the yard, and spoke to them for about an hour and a half. It was a most responsive audience. I tried to raise them in their own eyes; concluding, I asked them to lift their hands in token of their loyalty to the revolution. The new ideas infected them before my very eyes. They were genuinely enthusiastic; they followed me to the automobile, devoured me with their eyes, not fearfully as before, but rapturously, and shouted at the tops of their voices. They would hardly let me go. I learned afterwards, with some pride, that one of the best ways to educate them was to remind them: 'What did you promise Comrade Trotsky?' Later on, regiments of Riazan 'deserters' fought well at the fronts.[24]

The role of workers and Communists

The stability and combat efficiency of the Red Army depended above all on its proletarian core. Trotsky wrote:

Our army is made up of workers and peasants... in our workers' and peasants' army it is the workers who hold the position of leadership, as they do throughout the Soviet land in all spheres of life and work. This is given them by their greater consciousness, their greater unity, their higher degree of revolutionary tempering.[25]

An article analysing the percentage of workers in the Red Army in 1920 stated:

In the divisions that had distinguished themselves in action, the percentage of workers ranged from 26.4 (Eighth Red Cavalry Division) to 19.6 (28th Rifle Division). In Budenny's famous First Cavalry Army the percentage of workers was 21.7. On the other hand, in the Ninth Rifle Division, regarded as one of low combat value, the workers were only 10.5 per cent of the total number. In penal detachments, workers were 9.7 per cent of the total, in the detachments from apprehended deserters, 3.8 per cent. For the Red Army as a whole the percentage of workers at the time was 14.9; in the field units at the front it amounted to 16.5, while in the rear it fell to 11-13.[26]

Communist Party members were particularly crucial in giving backbone to Red Army units, in encouraging, inspiring, and steeling the mass of the soldiers. Thus in a speech on 2 September 1918 to the all-Russian central executive committee, Trotsky said:

Every train that brought to us at the front ten, fifteen, or twenty Communists... was as precious to us as a train that brought a good regiment or a plentiful quantity of guns.[27]

The role of the Communists in the Red Army was clearly formulated by an order of 9 May 1920 to the commissar and commanding personnel of the western front:

In each platoon, section and squad, there must be a Communist (who may even be only a young one, provided he is devoted to the cause) who will keep an eye on the morale of those fellow-fighters nearest to him, explain to them the tasks and aims of the war... Without such internal, unofficial, day-by-day and hour-by-hour agitation, carried on cheek-by-jowl under all conditions of the combat situation, official agitation alone, effected through articles and speeches, will not bring the necessary results.

The conduct of Communists in the Red Army has decisive significance for the morale and the combat capacity of units. It is therefore necessary to distribute Communists correctly, to guide them attentively, and to keep careful check on their work.[28]

On 13 October 1919, Trotsky wrote about the role of Communist Party organisation in steeling the Red Army:

Every fresh danger at the front causes an influx of Communists into the active units. There has never been a failure to answer the call of the central committee. On the contrary, local party organisations have met their obligations twice and thrice over, and the places of those party members who have fallen are being filled by young proletarians who, in the atmosphere of party organisation, soon acquire the revolutionary tempering they need. Petrograd remains a model in this respect.[29]

Communists fought to the bitter end. They were fanatically devoted to the cause. They knew that if they fell into the hands of the Whites and were recognised as party members, death was inevitable, so they fought with desperate courage and instilled their spirit into the mass of the soldiers. Trotsky compared the Communists with the order of the Samurai in Japan:

We once heard with interest of the Japanese caste of Samurai, who never hesitate to die for the sake of collective, national interests, the interests of the community as a whole. I must say that in our commissars, our leading Communist fighters, we have obtained a new, Communist order of Samurai who —without benefit of caste privileges—are able to die and to teach others to die, for the cause of the working class.[30]

There is abundant evidence of the leading and heroic role of Communist soldiers in the front line of the army. One historian cites instances during the Iudenich advance on Petrograd when the front lines were held by Communists alone. He quotes one of the commanders of divisions defending the city: 'Comrade Communists go to their death in the same way as they went to the factory to fulfil an important and difficult task—without any excitement or heroics.'[31]

The military historian F Nikonov suggests that during the civil war the units of the Red Army were classified with respect to their combat efficiency in accordance with the percentage of Communists within their ranks. He estimates that those with less than 4 or 5 per cent Communists amongst their personnel were regarded as ineffective. Detachments with 6 to 8 per cent were looked upon as satisfactory, with an average combat efficacy. Units with 12 to 15 per cent of Communists were considered shock troops.[32]

The Communists had special duties but not special rights, as Trotsky explains in an order of 11 December 1918 entitled 'The Role of Communists in the Red Army':

> The Communist soldier has the same rights as any other soldier, and not a hair's-breadth more: he only has incomparably more duties. The Communist soldier must be an exemplary warrior, he must always be in the forefront of the battle, he must try to lead others to the places of greatest danger, he must be a model of discipline, conscientiousness and courage... Only such a model soldier has the right to the name of Communist: otherwise he is a wretched pretender who must be called to account with two-fold severity.[33]

Communists who offended were to be punished much more severely than non-Communists. Thus an order issued by Trotsky on 8 August 1919 states:

> Communists found guilty of offences and crimes against revolutionary military duty will be punished twice as severely as non-Communists, because what may be forgiven to an ignorant, unconscious person cannot be excused in the case of a member of the party that stands at the head of the working class of the whole world.[34]

On 1 October 1919 the total number of Communists in the Red Army was 180,000. It was estimated that during the civil war some 200,000 Communists perished at the front. By the end of the civil war the number of Communists in the army was 280,000, grouped in 7000 cells.[35] Half of all party members were serving in the Red Army at the time.

The use of former Tsarist officers

With the predominance of peasants in the Red Army, with their inherent vacillation and instability, with the combination of conscription and desertion, the early method of electing officers could not survive. As Trotsky explained:

Election of commanders by the units themselves—which were politically ill-educated, being composed of recently mobilised young peasants—would inevitably have been transformed into a game of chance... the revolutionary army, as an army for action... was incompatible with a regime of elected committees, which in fact could not but destroy all centralised control, by allowing each unit to decide for itself whether it would agree to advance, or to remain on the defensive.[36]

The election of officers was especially incompatible with the employment of former Tsarist officers, which became the rule. Speaking to the Moscow *soviet* on 19 March 1918, a few days after his appointment as commissar for war, Trotsky stated the imperative need to call up the regular Tsarist officers and entrust them with responsible posts. They were called now 'Military Specialists'.

The tasks of Soviet democracy do not in the least consist in casting aside technical resources which can be usefully applied to ensure the success of its historical work...

It would be stupid to reject the use of former Tsarist officers. Casting them aside

would be just the same as if we were to say that all the machines that hitherto served to exploit the workers were now to be scrapped. That would be madness. Enlisting the scientific specialists is for us just as essential as taking over all the means of production and transport and all the wealth of the country generally.[37]

After the end of the civil war, looking back, Trotsky explained the crucial role of former Tsarist officers:

We needed them as representatives of their craft, as men who were familiar with military routine, and without whom we should have to *start from scratch*. Our foes would, in that case, hardly permit us to pursue our self-training until it had reached the required level.[38]

Trotsky referred to the experience of the French Revolution in support for the use of former Tsarist officers:

> the army of the Great French Revolution... was formed by way of an 'amalgam', as they said in those days, of the old royal battalions of the line with the new volunteer battalions.[39]

The experience of the American Civil War was similar, he argued.[40]

The overwhelming majority of commanders in the Red Army were former Tsarist officers. During the period of civil war 48,409 former Tsarist officers were taken into the Red Army, and 10,339 into the military-administrative staff; 13,949 army doctors and 26,767 lower medical and veterinary personnel were taken over from the Tsarist army. In addition 214,717 former non-commissioned officers (NCOs) were recruited from the Tsar's army. This makes 314,181 altogether.[41]

Included among the former Tsarist officers were a considerable number who saw service in the White armies before joining the Red Army: in 1921 a total of 14,390 former White Army officers were found in the Red Army.[42]

Compared with the number of former Tsarist officers, the number of graduates of the command courses run by the Red Army itself was small. During the civil war years, only 39,914 graduated from command courses.[43] Of these, 26,585 graduated in 1920, so that during the height of the civil war in 1918-19 only about 13,000 graduates of these schools were appointed to command positions.[44]

The young Red Commanders, as they were known, often served under the old former Tsarist officers upon promotion to their respective army units. In December 1921 Trotsky stated that 'Red Commanders who had passed through Soviet Military Colleges make up about 10 per cent of the total'. In addition 'former NCOs account for 13 per cent of our commanders'.[45] Commanders who were not members of the Communist Party amounted to a full 95 per cent of all officers in the Red Army.[46]

To ensure the loyalty of the former Tsarist officers, Trotsky used an adroit mixture of cajolery and pressure. On 29 July 1918, he announced that former officers who refused to serve would be placed in concentration camps. On 30 September he issued an order to use the hostage system to prevent the officers from betraying the Red Army. He knew that even the threat of capital punishment could not act as a deterrent to officers at the front, so he ordered that a register of officers' families be kept, so that a would-be traitor would know that if he went over to the enemy his wife and children would stay behind as hostages.[47] The hostage system was a harsh measure, but Trotsky knew that without it the revolution would be defeated, and the White terror would far surpass the hostage system in cruelty.

Tensions between former Tsarist officers and the rank and file of the Red Army

Trotsky again and again refers to the antagonism displayed toward the former Tsarist officers by the soldiers, and he was not ready to pander to the 'plebeian hatred' of the military specialists. Trotsky was right that there was a need for the proletarian government to utilise the inheritance from capitalism both in the form of machines and personnel—technicians and army officers. The analogy between the two legacies should not, however, be pushed too far. The use of live human beings was bound to raise far more social and psychological strains than the use of dead machinery in the factories or railroads.

Trotsky was right that without the tens of thousands of former Tsarist officers who were persuaded or forced to serve the Red Army, victory in the civil war would have been impossible. Still, cases of treason by former Tsarist officers were frequent; and they were more frequent the worse the military situation of the Red Army looked. Commanders of regiments, divisions, and even armies went over to the Whites, sometimes followed by the troops. Each case strengthened the opposition in the army and party to the employment of the former Tsarist officers.

However Trotsky warned against drawing the wrong conclusions from the betrayal by some officers:

In recent weeks there have been a few cases of betrayal among the military specialists...

As a result of the treason of a few scoundrels, distrust of military specialists in general has been intensified. There have been some clashes between commissars and military leaders. In some cases known to me, commissars have shown a clearly unjust attitude toward military specialists, lumping honourable men together with traitors. In other cases commissars have sought to concentrate in their own hands the functions of command and operations, not confining themselves to political leadership and supervisiion. Such action is fraught with danger, for the confusing of powers and duties kills the sense of responsibility.

I urgently call upon the comrade commissars not to surrender to the impressions of the moment and not to lump together the innocent and the guilty.[48]

Haughty behaviour on the part of military specialists was common. Many former Tsarist officers behaved extremely badly towards the rank and file, and abused their rank to draw unjustified privileges. Trotsky referred to the use of physical force by officers against rank-and-file soldiers:

I have received letters to the effect that in some units the practice of striking soldiers in the face is even flourishing. Even some Communists have told me frankly: 'I hit him in the teeth with the butt of my revolver'. It is one thing to shoot a man in battle, under fire, for some offence, but if a Red Army man knows that he may be struck in the teeth, that is such loss of moral dignity, such foulness, that it must be eradicated at all costs. Respect for the personality of the Red Army man must be ensured.[49]

One other element in officers' behaviour was their frequent verbal rudeness. An example of this concerned the use of the words 'ty' and 'vy' in the Red Army. Russian, like many languages, and like English in earlier times, has two forms for the second person singular—'ty' (thou) which is familiar, and 'vy' (you) which is respectful and polite. It was common for an officer to talk to soldiers using 'ty', while expecting to be addressed in reply 'vy'. On 18 July 1922 Trotsky wrote an article in *Izvestia*:

In the Red Army a commander may not use the familiar form when addressing a subordinate if the latter is expected to respond in the polite form. Otherwise an expression of inequality between persons would result, not an expression of subordination in the line of duty.

To some this may seem a trifling matter. It is not! A Red Army man must respect both himself and others. Respect for human dignity is an extremely important factor in what holds the Red Army together morally. The Red Army soldier submits to his superiors in the line of duty. The requirements of discipline are inflexible. But, at the same time, the soldier feels and knows that he is a conscious citizen, called upon to fulfil obligations of high responsibility. Military subordination must be accompanied by civic and moral equality, which does not allow the violation of personal dignity.[50]

Some inequality is inevitable, Trotsky argues, but sometimes it is completely unjustified. A letter to the revolutionary war councils of the fronts and the armies, and to all responsible workers in the Red Army and the Red Navy on 31 October 1920, entitled 'More Equality', attacked the abuse of privileges:

When the motor car is used for merry outings, before the eyes of the tired Red Army soldiers, or when commanders dress with flashy foppishness, while their men go half-naked, such facts cannot but provoke exasperation and murmuring among the Red Army soldiers.

There was the question of privileges in army leave:

It is no secret to anyone, and least of all to the Red Army men, that commanders and commissars often get leave under the guise of official missions. For example, the deputy head of the divisional ordnance depot receives a visit from his wife, which itself is contrary to regulations, and then is sent on a seven-day official mission so that he can see her home. Yet among the Red Army soldiers of the depot guard, there are men who have not seen their families for three years.

Then there were evening parties with drink, with women present, and so on and so forth:

Phenomena of this sort are by no means exceptional. Every Red Army man knows about them. They talk a lot in the units—often of course with exaggerations—about the feasting and boozing that goes on 'at headquarters'. When setbacks occur, the mass of Red Army men frequently—with or without good grounds—see the reasons for them in the excessively gay life led by the commanders.[51]

The commissars

The various elements involved in the Red Army—workers and peasants, Communists and former Tsarist officers—were not only heterogeneous, but often antagonistic to one another. Some of the officers commanding the workers and peasants were the same hated officers who a few months earlier had imposed the will of the Tsar or the Provisional Government on the rank-and-file soldiers. These officers were the scions of landlords, against whom the peasants had rebelled and whose land they had expropriated.

Again the soldiers, above all the peasant conscripts, did not show any great readiness to accept central discipline. Their loyalties tended to be local and their preferred tactics those of guerrilla warfare. To transform all the heterogeneous elements that made up the Red Army into a coherent body, to prevent rebellions, treason and mass desertion, a new institution was needed. So Trotsky turned to the idea of commissars.

Commissars were not new. The armies of the French Revolution had had them, and the form of commissar or political officer had been introduced into other armies since then. Kerensky had appointed commissars to be his agents in the army; they had been attached only to the highest commands, and their function had been insubstantial. Trotsky attached a commissar to every officer from the level of company command to the top military post, and defined his function in substantial terms. On 6 April 1918 an order by Trotsky specified the commissar's tasks:

The military commissar is the direct political organ of the Soviet power in the army. His post is one of exceptional importance. Commissars are appointed from among irreproachable revolutionaries, capable of remaining, under the most difficult circumstances, the embodiment of revolutionary duty... The military commissar must see to it that the army does not become dissociated from the Soviet system as a whole, and that particular military institutions do not become centres of conspiracy or instruments to be used against the workers and peasants. The commissar takes part in all the work of the military leaders, receives reports and dispatches along with them, and counter-signs orders. War councils will give effect only to such orders as have been signed not only by the military leaders, but also by at least one commissar. All work is to be done with the cognisance of the commissar, but leadership in the specifically military sphere is the task not of the commissar but the military specialist working shoulder to shoulder with him.

The commissar is not responsible for the expediency of purely military, operational, combat orders. Responsibility for them rests entirely with the military leader. The commissar's signature on an operational order means that the commissar vouches for this order as having been motivated by operational and not by any other (counter-revolutionary) considerations... The only operational order that may be held up is one regarding which the commissar has held a well-grounded opinion that it was inspired by counter-revolutionary motives... Responsibility for seeing to the precise fulfilment of orders rests with the commissar, and all the authority and resources of the Soviet power are at his disposal for this purpose.[52]

The theses written by Trotsky and adopted by the Eighth Congress of the party in March 1919, titled 'Our Policy in Creating the Army' state:

The commissars in the army are not only the direct and immediate representatives of the Soviet power, but also, and above all, the bearers of the spirit of our party, its discipline, its firmness and courage in the struggle to achieve the aims laid down.[53]

The final sacrifice was expected from the commissars: 'He who assumes the title of commissar must lay his life on the line!'[54]

Chapter five
The spirit of the Red Army

THE MOST IMPORTANT factor steeling the Red Army was the ideas inspiring it. Napoleon said that in war moral factors are to physical as three to one. For Trotsky the morale of the army was the most crucial factor in its formation and struggle. In a speech on 29 July 1918, 'The Socialist Fatherland in Danger', when the regime's very life was threatened by Czech troops, he said:

> ...we need to revive the traditions of [the French] revolution to the full. Remember how the Jacobins in France spoke, even while the war was still going on, about complete victory, and how the Girondins screamed at them: 'You talk about what you are going to do after victory: have you then made a pact with victory?' One of the Jacobins replied: 'We have made a pact with death.' The working class cannot be defeated. We are sons of the working class: we have made our pact with death, and, therefore, with victory![1]

At a meeting in Moscow celebrating the first anniversary of the founding of the Red Army, on 24 February 1919, Trotsky said:

> ...we did not doubt that the army would be created, if only it were given *a new idea, a new moral foundation*. There, comrades, was the whole part of the matter.
> An army is, of course, a material organisation, put together, to a certain degree, in accordance with its own internal laws, and armed with those instruments of technique that are provided by the state of industry in general, and, in particular, of military-technical science. But to see in an army only men exercising, manoeuvring and fighting, that is, to

see only their bodies, to see only rifles, machine-guns and cannon, means not to see the army, for all that is merely the outward expression of a different, an inner force. An army is strong if it is bound together by an internal ideological bond.[2]

In the past, the fighting spirit of the Russian soldier, that is, in the main, of the Russian peasant, had been passive, patient, all-enduring. They took him from his village, put him in a regiment, and drilled him. They sent the regiment off in a certain direction, and the soldier went with his regiment, he shot, slashed, chopped, and died... with each man individually unaware of why and for what he was fighting. When the soldier began to reflect and criticise, he rebelled, and the old army disappeared. To recreate it, new ideological foundations were needed: *it was necessary that every soldier should know what he was fighting for.*[3]

The Red Army men knew what they were fighting for, and believed in it passionately.

The internationalist spirit of the Red Army

Trotsky's Red Army was from its origin not simply a national organisation. E H Carr writes:

The Red Army was not in origin and conception exclusively national. Simultaneously with its creation, an appeal signed by three Americans appeared in **Pravda** of 24 February 1918, for recruits to an 'international detachment of the Red Army' whose language was to be English. The appeal itself is said to have been distributed in five languages.[4]

John Erickson, a historian of the Red Army, writes:

The search for trained men led into the prisoner-of-war camps. In January 1918 a Prisoner-of-War Congress held in Samara petitioned that it might be allowed to form Red Army units. From this point forth the Soviet command did not neglect the possibilities for winning recruits to their army from this manpower pool. The result was the formation of the 'International Battalions' of the Red Army, as well as the Chinese Battalion, which drew its recruits from the labour reserves of Chinese in the rear areas.[5]

Estimates of the number involved vary from 50,000 to 90,000.[6]

In his first speech as people's commissar for war, at the Moscow *soviet* on 19 March 1918, Trotsky emphasised the internationalist spirit that should imbue the Red Army:

> We need an army, which would give us powerful strength for the inevitable coming struggle with international imperialism. With the aid of this army we shall not only defend ourselves, but shall be in a position to help the struggle of the international proletariat.
>
> ...we, to whom history has given victory sooner than the rest... must be ready, at the first thunderclap of the world revolution, to bring armed help to our foreign brothers in revolt.[7]

On 22 April 1918, the all-Russian executive committee of the *soviet* approved the 'Oath of the Red Warrior', written by Trotsky. It included the following:

> I, a son of the working people and a citizen of the Soviet Republic, assume the title of a soldier of the Workers' and Peasants' Red Army.
>
> Before the working class of Russia and the whole world I pledge myself to bear this title with honour.
>
> ...I pledge myself to respond to the first call from the Workers' and Peasants' Government to defend the Soviet Republic against any dangers and attacks from any enemy, and to spare neither my strength nor my life in the fight for the Russian Soviet Republic and for the cause of socialism and the brotherhood of peoples.[8]

At the time when General Iudenich, armed by Britain, was threatening the very existence of Soviet rule in Petrograd, Trotsky issued an order entitled 'The Two Britains'.

> Red warriors! ...Your hearts are often filled to overflowing with hatred for predatory, lying, hypocritical, bloody Britain, and your hatred is just and holy. It multiplies tenfold your strength in the struggle against the enemy.
>
> But even today, when we are engaged in a bitter fight against Britain's hireling, Iudenich, I demand this of you: *Never forget that there are two Britains. Besides the Britain of profits,*

violence, bribery and bloodthirstiness there is the Britain of labour, of spiritual power, of high ideals, of international solidarity... The Britain of labour... will soon rise to its full height and put a strait-jacket on the criminals... Death to the vultures of imperialism! Long live workers' Britain, the Britain of labour, of the people![9]

In the midst of the Polish-Russian war, on 30 June 1920, Trotsky suspended a military journal and punished its editors for a chauvinistic attack on the Polish nation, which spoke about the 'innate Jesuitry of the Polacks', contrasting this with the honesty and straightforwardness of the Great Russians. Trotsky commented:

There is no need to explain how greatly this sort of crude and false generalisation contradicts the spirit of fraternity which inspires the attitude of the Russian working class towards the working masses of Poland...[10]

Revolutionary discipline

It was on the basis of this revolutionary inspiration that Trotsky founded the discipline necessary for victory against overwhelming odds. In his speech to the Moscow *soviet* on 19 March 1918, he said:

We must at all costs and at any price implant discipline in the Red Army—not the previous sort, the automatic discipline of the rod, but conscious, collective discipline, based on revolutionary enthusiasm and clear understanding by the workers and peasants of their duty to their own classes.[11]

Trotsky made it clear that discipline in the Red Army was qualitatively different from that in capitalist armies. In the Red Army the discipline was to be built on the awakened personality of the workers and peasants. Thus, in 'The Red Army in the Civil War', a report to the Fifth Congress of *soviets* at its session of 10 July 1918, he stated:

We do not want the old discipline, that discipline by which every ignorant peasant and worker was slotted into his regiment, his company and his platoon, and marched off without asking why they were leading him away, why they were making him shed blood.

The revolution gave land to the peasants, the revolution gave power to the workers and the peasants: these were great achievements, but no achievement of the revolution is more important than the awakening of the human personality in every oppressed and humiliated individual.

This process of awakening of the individual personality assumes chaotic form, in the early stages. Whereas yesterday still the peasant did not think of himself as a person, and was ready, at the first order from the government, to go forth blindly to shed his blood, now he is unwilling to subordinate himself blindly. He asks: where are they telling me to go, and why? And he declares: I'm not going, I don't want to submit! He says that because awareness of his human dignity, his personality has been awakened in him for the first time, and this awareness, which is as yet too crude, which is not sufficiently digested, takes anarchical forms when expressed in deeds.

We have to reach the situation when every peasant and every worker is aware of himself as a human personality with a right to respect, but also feels that he is part of the working class of republican Russia and will be prepared unquestioningly to lay down his life for this Soviet Republican Russia...

This is the psychological cement by means of which we can create a new army, a real, conscious Soviet army, bound together by a discipline that has passed through the soldiers' brains, and not just the discipline of the rod. This is the discipline we advocate, and we do not want to know any other.[12]

The higher the rank the harsher the discipline. Without iron discipline, said Trotsky, the Red Army is doomed. But discipline is not possible without the confidence of the soldiers in the ability and decisiveness of the commanders:

The soldier, the Red Army man, will execute a command precisely and sharply if the commander's voice is clear and distinct, if the commander feels within himself that he can give orders. If he is not sure of himself, if he gets confused, and his word of command sounds more like a request or a proposal, the whole unit senses that the commander lacks self-confidence. Woe to that unit, and woe to that commander...[13]

In case of the breakdown of discipline, the commander and commissars should be punished first of all. Trotsky's report to the Sixth Congress of *soviets* on 9 November 1918 stated:

...we have introduced a rule which some find severe, but which remains fully in force: for every panicky withdrawal, for every case of desertion, the commander and the commissar are to be answerable first and foremost. If they have not taken all the necessary measures, have remained unharmed, or have deserted along with their unit, then, of course, they will be the first to fall beneath the sharp blade of our revolutionary punishment. Apparently, some comrades have considered, and have voiced their opinion, that we are acting too harshly, too mercilessly. Our time is, in general, a harsh and merciless time for the working class, which is compelled to defend its power and its existence against a swarm of external foes...[14]

The bitter and heroic struggle demanded iron discipline, and Trotsky's hand did not tremble in imposing it.

The struggle for truth

One important aspect of the revolutionary discipline Trotsky sought to instil was honest reporting. Lying is a weapon of reaction, truth is a weapon of Communism; the Red Army must fight for truth, he argued. In an order of 5 June 1919, Trotsky attacked any cover-up. Keeping things in the dark, he writes,

is the despicable psychology of old-time civil servants, and not that of revolutionary warriors who must boldly face not only the enemy, but also the most cruel truth. Commanders and commissars who see the shortcomings and weaknesses of their units and frankly admit them will unfailingly take steps to eliminate these weak sides. Commanders and commissars who conceal cases of desertion or panicky retreat like a secret disease merely drive this disease inward and completely ruin their units.

...We must teach and compel commanders and commissars

to call a battle a battle, a panic a panic, a feat of arms a feat of arms, and cowardice cowardice. They must report with as much accuracy as possible the actual number of casualties, that is, the number of dead and wounded, the number of men taken prisoner, and the number of those who fled in panic —adding whether or not they came back...

Bragging, frivolous evasiveness and plain lying must all be ruthlessly eliminated from operational reports.

It was necessary to

denounce and brand the braggarts, boasters and liars. There is no place for them in the ranks of a revolutionary army, and still less in the post of commander or commissar.[15]

What, asks Trotsky, are the roots in Russian society of the prevailing inaccuracies?

Ask any peasant on a country road how many *versts* it is to Ivashkovo village. He will answer: three *versts*. From experience we know that it could turn out that the distance to Ivashkovo is seven *versts*, or even eight. If you are exigent and persistent, and start to cross-examine him as to whether it is exactly three *versts*, not more, not perhaps five or seven, in most cases your interlocutor will answer: 'Who has measured it?'...

Undoubtedly the source of this sort of attitude towards one's own and other people's time is the nature of rural Russia. There the harsh climate and the harsh enslavement to the state and landlord serve as a school of passivity and patience, and, therefore, of indifference to time. Ability to wait for hours outside someone's door, quietly, passively, is an age-old feature of the Russian peasant. 'Don't worry, he'll wait', is a very familiar 'formulation' of the mean contempt shown by the lord for the peasant's time, and his equally mean certainty that the peasant will put up with anything, since he is not used to valuing his time.[16]

Tensions in the Red Army

Because the mass of the soldiers resented the former Tsarist commanders, the commissars tended to become intermediaries between the commanders and the soldiers. Sometimes the anger of the soldiers burst upon the heads of the commissars. Thus, for instance, Commissar Bych was killed near Lvov in July 1918 during disturbances in the Red Army units of the district, created by the agitation of Left Social Revolutionaries for an offensive against the Germans in the Ukraine.[17] Again, one of the members of the revolutionary military council of an army on the eastern front, Lindov, was killed by mutinous soldiers.[18]

Often the commissar was not only in conflict with the rank-and-file soldiers on the one hand and the commanding personnel on the other, but also with the higher military authorities. Thus Trotsky's order of 30 August 1918 refers to the execution of several commissars of the Fifth Army:

> Yesterday twenty deserters were shot, having been sentenced by the field court-martial of the Fifth Army.
> The first to go were commanders and commissars who had abandoned the positions entrusted to them. Next, cowardly liars who played sick. Finally, some deserters from among the Red Army men who refused to expiate their crime by taking part in the subsequent struggle.[19]

This was the case of Commissar Panteleev, which later gained a great deal of notoriety. Trotsky brought Panteleev and the command of the regiment before a court martial for running away at the height of the battle of Sviiazhsk. The case of Panteleev was later used by opponents of Trotsky in the party to accuse him of shooting Communists.

Despite all this friction, the Red Army still worked. The Communists led the proletarian core of the army, which led the peasant conscripts. One concentric ring influenced a wider concentric ring. The conflicting camps of soldiers and former Tsarist officers would have led to blows and disintegration of the Red Army if not for the intervention of the commissar. Under the uncontrolled leadership of former Tsarist officers the army would have collapsed socially and politically. Without the officers it would have been doomed to defeat. For the control over the former officers, the commissars were crucial.

Chapter six
The Red Army blooded

Sviiazhsk

UP TO NOW we have dealt with the Red Army largely by describing its structure. However the Red Army was built and steeled in the civil war itself. Unlike 'normal' armies, which enjoy years of peace in which to be equipped and trained, the Red Army was built under the direct pressure of the civil war.

In late summer 1918 the Soviet regime faced the abyss. In the west the Germans had occupied not only Poland, Lithuania and Latvia, but also Belorussia, and a considerable part of Great Russia. The Ukraine had become an Austro-German colony. In the north the French and British occupied Murmansk and Archangel, and threatened an advance on Vologda. In Iaroslav an insurrection of White Guards was organised by Savinkov at the instigation of the French and British, with the object of connecting the northern troops with the Czechoslovaks and White Guards on the Volga.

In the south, on the Don, an uprising was spreading under the leadership of General Krasnov, then in alliance with the Germans. The newly established Tartar-Bashkir Republic was already lost to the Bolsheviks and Baku was occupied by the British. In the east the revolt of the Czechoslovak expeditionary force rapidly gained control over a huge zone, including much of the Volga region, the Urals and Siberia. On 6 August the town of Kazan fell, laying the road to Moscow open. If the Czechs had succeeded in crossing the river at this point, they could have marched unhindered across the open plain towards Moscow.

Two days later Trotsky ordered the first compulsory call-up of commissioned and non-commissioned officers, and stern measures against any dereliction of duty in the Soviet camp. On the same day he himself left for the front in the train that was to serve as his abode and mobile headquarters during the following two and a half years. In an order of the day issued before his departure, Trotsky wrote:

I send my greetings to all those who... are honestly and valiantly defending the freedom and independence of the working class and the working peasantry.

Honour and glory to the valiant fighters.

At the same time I issue this warning: no quarter will be given to the enemies of the people, the agents of foreign imperialism, the hirelings of the bourgeoisie. In the train of the People's Commissar for Military Affairs where this order is being written, a Military Revolutionary Tribunal is in session... [which] has been given unlimited powers within the zone of the railway line, which is placed under martial law.

...I warn responsible Soviet officials in all areas where military operations are in progress, and in the zone of military movements, that we shall be doubly exacting towards them. The Soviet Republic will punish its negligent and criminal servants no less severely than its enemies...

The Soviet Republic is imperilled! Woe to those who, directly or indirectly, aggravate its peril![1]

Trotsky arrived at Sviiazhsk, a little town on the western bank of the Volga, opposite Kazan. He found the Red Army completely demoralised—there had been mass desertion from the ranks and prostration among commanders and commissars. In his autobiography Trotsky described the situation he found:

Each unit lived its own distinct life, sharing in common only a readiness to retreat... The soil itself seemed to be infected with panic. The fresh Red detachments, arriving in vigorous mood, were immediately engulfed by the inertia of retreat. A rumour began to spread among the local peasantry that the Soviets were doomed. Priests and tradesmen lifted their heads. The revolutionary elements in the villages went into hiding. Everything was crumbling; there was nothing to hold to. The situation seemed hopeless.[2]

The fate of the revolution was hanging on a thread. Its territory

was now reduced to the size of the ancient Moscow principality. It had hardly any army; it was surrounded by enemies on all sides. After Kazan would have come the turn of Nizhni-Novgorod, from which a practically unobstructed road lay open to Moscow. The fate of the revolution was being decided here, at Sviiazhsk. And here, at the most critical moment, it rested on a single battalion, on one company, on the courage of one commissary.[3]

Out of the panic-stricken undisciplined mob, Trotsky created within a few weeks a fighting force which, as the Fifth Army, was one of the best of the sixteen armies that were organised during the civil war. Despite all the demoralisation in the Red Army ranks, Trotsky writes,

the revolution was saved. What was needed for that? Very little. The front ranks of the masses had to realise the mortal danger in the situation. The first requisite of success was to hide nothing, our weakness least of all. Not to trifle with the masses, but to call everything by its right name...

The propaganda throughout the country was being fed by telegrams from Sviiazhsk. The *soviets*, the party, the trade unions, all devoted themselves to raising new detachments, and sent thousands of communists to the Kazan front. Most of the youth of the party did not know how to handle arms, but they had the will to win, and that was the most important thing. They put backbone into the soft body of the army.[4]

Gusev, who later became a supporter of Stalin, was in Sviiazhsk at the time. In 1924, when he was far from friendly to Trotsky, he described the impact Trotsky had on the Red soldiers:

The arrival of Comrade Trotsky worked a decisive change in the situation. In Comrade Trotsky's train to the obscure station of Sviiazhsk there came a firm will to victory, a new sense of initiative, and resolute pressure in all phases of the army work.

From the very first days, everyone began to feel that some abrupt change had taken place, not only at the station—the active campaign headquarters of the political section and the army supply staff, crammed with the supply trains of countless regiments—but even in army units stationed about fifteen *versts* away. It was first apparent in the matter of discipline. Comrade Trotsky's harsh methods were most expedient and necessary for that period of unbdisciplined and irregular warfare. Persuasion counted for nothing, and there was no time for it. And so, during the twenty-five days that Comrade Trotsky spent at Sviiazhsk a tremendous amount of work was done, with the result that the disorganised and demoralised units of the Fifth Army were changed into the fighting units that later recaptured Kazan.[5]

Trotsky's train remained within reach of enemy fire. The local commissars proposed that he should move to a safer place on a steam boat on the Volga, but he refused, fearing the effect this might have on the troops. However, Trotsky did go with sailors from Kronstadt on a torpedo boat, part of a tiny flotilla, on an adventurous night raid on Kazan. Most of the flotilla was destroyed, but it managed to silence the enemy batteries on the banks of the river and Trotsky returned safely to his base. His courage and inspiration worked wonders. After a bitter fight, the Red Army recaptured Kazan on 10 September 1918. Trotsky wrote:

> This was a small war; on our side, there were only about 25,000 to 30,000 men engaged. But the small war differed from a big one only in scale. It was like a living model of a war. That is why its fluctuations and surprises were felt so directly. The small war was a big school.[6]

Sviiazhsk was a turning point for the young Red Army:

> The army was taking shape magnificently. The lowest ebb of the revolution—the moment of the fall of Kazan—was now behind us. Along with this, a tremendous change was taking place in the peasantry. The Whites were teaching the *muzhiks* their political abc's. During the ensuing seven months the Red Army cleared a territory of nearly a million square kilometres with a population of 40 million. The revolution was again advancing.[7]

Sviiazhsk was the 'Valmy' of the Russian Revolution. The first victory of the French revolutionary army over the Prussians had been at Valmy on 20 September 1792. Afterwards the poet Goethe said: 'From this place and from this day forth commences a new era in the world's history, and you can all say that you were present at its birth.'

At the end of September Trotsky returned to Moscow and reorganised the Supreme War Council into the Revolutionary War Council of the Republic—a body responsible for deciding military policy. Under it were the revolutionary war councils of the fourteen armies, each made up of the commander of the army and two or three commissars. Trotsky presided over the Revolutionary War Council of the Republic. His deputy, who managed the day-to-day work while Trotsky was away at the front, was Efroim Markovich Sklyansky, then 26 years old. He was a Kiev medical student who had joined the Bolsheviks in 1913, becoming an army doctor and a member of the Bolshevik military organisation. Trotsky paid generous tribute to the talent and energy of his deputy, describing him as 'the Carnot of the Russian Revolution'. *

The other members of the Revolutionary War Council of the Republic were Vatzetis, who had just been appointed Commander-in-Chief, I N Smirnov and A Rosengolts, who had served with Vatzetis on the Volga, and Raskolnikov, who commanded the Red flotilla at Kazan, Muralov and Iurenev. Thus the victors of Kazan were placed at the head of the army.

Trotsky's armoured train

The trip to Sviiazhsk was only the first of 36 long journeys to the widely separated fronts of the civil war that Trotsky made in the special train from which he guided the war. The train was the heart of the Red Army. Trotsky writes:

> During the most strenuous years of the revolution, my own personal life was bound up inseparably with the life of that train. The train, on the other hand, was inseparably bound

---

* Lazare Carnot (1753-1823) was a key member of the great Committee of Public Safety, which played the decisive role in defending the French Revolution in 1793-94 when it was besieged on all sides by invading foreign armies as well as facing internal counter-revolution. Carnot was in charge of the revolution's military defence. His brilliant success in turning the tide against the invading armies earned him a reputation as 'the organiser of victories'.

up with the life of the Red Army. The train linked the front with the base, solved urgent problems on the spot, educated, appealed, supplied, rewarded, and punished...

For two and a half years, except for comparatively short intervals, I lived in a railway coach. There I received those who brought reports, held conferences with local military and civil authorities, studied telegraphic despatches, dictated orders and articles. From it I made long trips along the front in automobiles with my co-workers. In my spare time I dictated my book against Kautsky and various other works...

...it had... become a flying apparatus of administration. Its sections included a secretariat, a printing press, a telegraph station, a radio station, an electric power station, a library, a garage, and a bath...

I haven't even the exact figures of the total distance covered by the train during the civil war. One of the notes to my military books mentions 36 trips, with a total run of over 105,000 kilometres. One of my former fellow-travellers writes that he reckons from memory that in three years we circled the earth five and a half times—he gives, that is, a figure twice as large as the one mentioned above. This does not include thousands of kilometres done by automobile from the railway line into the heart of the front line. Since the train always went to the most critical points, the diagram of its journeys gives a fairly exact and comprehensive picture of the relative importance of the different fronts.[8]

In the train, Trotsky writes,

We always had in reserve a few zealous communists to fill in the breaches, a hundred or so of good fighting men, a small stock of boots, leather jackets, medicaments, machine-guns, field-glasses, maps, watches, and all sorts of gifts. Of course, the actual material resources of the train were slight in comparison with the needs of the army. But they were constantly being replenished.[9]

The arrival of the train put the most isolated unit in touch with the whole army, and brought it into the life not only of the country, but of the entire world. Alarmist rumours and doubts were dispelled, and the spirit of the men grew firm.

This change of morale would last for several weeks, sometimes until the next visit of the train.[10]

Without constant changes and improvisations, the war would have been utterly impossible for us. The train initiated these, and at the same time regulated them. If we gave an impulse of initiative to the front and its immediate rear, we took care to direct it into the channels of the general system. I do not want to say that we always succeeded in this. But, as the civil war has demonstrated, we did achieve the principal thing —victory.[11]

In the unstable poise of a scale, only a small weight is enough to decide. The role of that weight was played by the train and its detachments a great many times during its two and a half years of travel.[12]

In the train Trotsky demonstrated how the sword and the pen could act together in complete harmony. Trotsky's prolific output is recorded in the five volumes of his **How the Revolution Armed**. This includes his articles, speeches, reports, appeals, orders, instructions, letters, telegrams and other documents devoted to the Red Army. Unfortunately the volumes do not encompass his correspondence (mostly with Lenin) and many of his speeches during the civil war. On the last point Trotsky explains:

The most important speeches, namely those which were addressed to military workers on the spot, at the fronts and in the army units, and which had profoundly practical, concrete significance, determined by the demands of the moment—these most important and significant speeches were, as a rule, not taken down in writing by anyone.[13]

The volumes of **How the Revolution Armed** are distinguished by a rich combination of broad historical sweep, originality, innovation and attention to the details of army life.

The army and society

An army is not external to society and does not develop independently from society. In any period of history military technique reflects the level of technique in the economy as a whole and the structure of the army reflects the structure of society as a whole. In medieval times the knight had a horse and a sword because the peasant had a horse and a plough. The mass armies of the First World War, involving millions, could not exist without a mass of workers working in factories producing the guns and shells. The nuclear bomb—the ability to press a button and thereby kill tens or hundreds of millions—parallels the multinational corporations and their power to telex massive sums of capital from one country to another, close factories—so sacking thousands, or open others employing thousands.

If the dominant social relations are those between feudal lords and serfs, then the same feudal relations dominate the relations between the lord and his knights. If in the capitalist factory there is a hierarchy of manager, deputy manager, foreman and workers, then the same hierarchy is reproduced—in more extreme form—in the army: from general to major, NCOs to the rank and file.

The social conditions of the Soviet Republic affected the shape and the working of the Red Army. The Red Army throughout the civil war was constantly under pressure from the localist, fragmented nature of the peasantry, as well as the small size of the proletariat and the general cultural poverty. Throughout the civil war these circumstances again and again obstructed Trotsky's efforts to secure the cohesion of the army. These conditions nurtured a continuous opposition to his military policy, which became the embryo of the Stalinist faction of the future.

The party *cadres*, reflecting the unevenness of consciousness in the working class and the conflict between the mass peasantry and the workers, showed a strong inclination towards substitutionism—the substitution of the state and party apparatus in place of the direct action of the workers—and towards the bureaucratic manipulation of the masses. This tendency was strengthened in the army, because the workers there were submerged in the sea of peasants. The fact that the army was an organism whose needs were in the highest degree demanding and imperative, and brooked no delay, further reinforced the bureaucratic, authoritarian tendencies among party *cadres*.

Chapter seven

Opposition to Trotsky in the Red Army

The fight against guerrillaism

THROUGHOUT the civil war Trotsky had to fight again and again against opposition to centralism, and against guerrillaist tendencies in the Red Army. Only towards the middle of 1919 were these tendencies effectively beaten back.

In retrospect Trotsky explained the rise of localist, guerrillaist tendencies thus:

> Indignation against the bureaucratic centralism of Tsarist Russia formed a very important constituent feature of the revolution. Regions, provinces, *uyezds* and towns vied with one another in trying to show their independence. The idea of 'power in the localities' assumed an extremely chaotic character in the initial period... among the broad masses it was an inevitable, and so far as its sources were concerned, a healthy reaction against the old regime which had stifled initiative.
>
> From a certain moment onward, however, with the tighter unification of the counter-revolutionary forces and the growth of external threats, these primitive tendencies towards autonomy became ever more dangerous, both from the political and, in particular, from the military standpoint.[1]

In his report to the Fifth Congress of *soviets* Trotsky said:

> Speaking of the difficulties we encounter in creating the new army, I must mention that the biggest of these is constituted by this dreadful localism, local patriotism. Interception, seizure and concealment of military property... of any and

every kind is being carried on by the local organs of Soviet power.

Every *uyezd*, almost every *volost*, believes that the Soviet power can best be defended by concentrating on the territory of the given *volost* as much as possible of aircraft *materiel*, radio equipment, rifles and armoured cars, and they all try to conceal this *materiel*...

We must put an end to this situation. We must wage a most severe struggle against the intercepting, appropriating and concealing of army property by local *soviets*.[2]

He returns to this theme again and again.

The social roots of guerrillaism were deep: they lay in the fragmented, atomised peasantry; and as peasants made up the overwhelming majority of Red Army soldiers, guerrillaism had massive influence throughout the army.

The peasantry, taken by itself, is incapable of creating a centralised army. It cannot get beyond local guerrilla units, the primitive 'democracy' of which is often a screen for the personal dictatorship of the *atamans*. These guerrilla tendencies... took possession of a considerable section of the Communists, especially those who came from the peasantry, or had formerly been soldiers or NCOs.[3]

The immediate experience of the revolution and the beginning of the civil war created in the Bolshevik Party itself a tradition of guerrillaism that was difficult to overcome, especially as it was embodied in the personnel commanding guerrilla groups. Trotsky explains:

...our army was formed in haste, out of guerrilla units that were hurriedly put together under fire. It was formed from the Red Guard units of Petrograd and Moscow workers. In those units the commanders were distinguished from the rank and file only by the fact that they were, perhaps, more enterprising, politically more developed, braver than the rest, but often they were lacking in even the most basic military knowledge.[4]

The leaders of the guerrilla groups, who came by and large from the *cadres* of the old Bolsheviks, developed a whole 'theory' justifying their practice as a feather in their caps:

> A view developed according to which, in a revolutionary country in a revolutionary epoch, we do not need protracted training, drill, system, we do not need regulations—a view that all that is needed is revolutionary solidarity, willingness to fight and die, and with our small, closely-welded units we shall march all across the country and, if necessary, beyond its borders into other countries, everywhere conquering our foes.[5]

Recent immediate experience gave credence to the theory of the guerrilla leaders:

> In the first period this theory seemed to be confirmed by experience. But why? Because our first adversaries were White Guard bands, because our enemy was also weak and unorganised, his troops consisting of small units... we were victorious. This gave some comrades the impression that guerrilla units were the last word in the revolutionary art of war.
>
> But as soon as our foes were able to form stronger units, and to consolidate these into regular formations, into brigades, divisions and corps, in the south and in the east, it once became apparent that loose, shaky, unstable and amorphous guerrilla units were incapable of coping with the task before us...

The organisers of the Red Army drew the right conclusions:

> ...we waged a persistent struggle to establish a regular structure for the Red Army, to replace the scattered guerrillas by a regular, centralised system of administration and command...
>
> We had to pass through a long period in 1918 and 1919 before the ideas and slogans of guerrilla-ism were finally overcome in the minds of the revolutionary workers and peasants.[6]

Guerrillaism was rooted in the peasant milieu. The peasantry had a dual nature. On the one hand it was a revolutionary force in its opposition to the big landlords; on the other it had a reactionary tendency towards individualism, conservatism and petty-bourgeois attitudes.

Trotsky saw in the guerrillaism of the peasant soldier an important element of progressive social rebellion: the awakening of personality, of which he had many times spoken—of the grey, oppressed and ignorant peasant. In a speech at the opening of the Military Academy on 8 November 1918 he said:

> It is natural that persons unaccustomed to revolution and its psychology... may view with some sorrow, if not disgust, the anarchic wildness and violence which appeared on the surface of the revolutionary events. Yet in that riotous anarchy, even in its most negative manifestation, when the soldier, yesterday's slave, all of a sudden found himself in a first-class railway carriage and tore out the velvet facings to make himself footcloths, even in such an act of vandalism, the awakening of a personality was expressed. That downtrodden, persecuted Russian peasant, who had been struck in the face and subjected to the vilest curses, found himself, for perhaps the first time in his life, in a first-class carriage and saw the velvet cushions, while on his feet he had stinking rags, and he tore up the velvet, saying that he too had the right to a piece of good silk or velvet. After two or three days, after a month, after a year—no, after a month —he understood how disgraceful it was to plunder the people's property, but the awakened personality, the individuality—not just Number Such-and-such, but human personality, will remain alive in him forever. Our task is to adjust this personality to the community, to make it feel that it is not a number, not a slave, as it was before, and not just Ivanov or Petrov, but, one, Ivanov the personality, and, two, at the same time, a part of the community of the whole people, with neither slaves nor masters.[7]

Guerrillaism was not always reactionary. It had to be approached historically. At a certain stage of the development of the revolution and civil war it had historical justification, it was necessary and legitimate:

> One cannot ask a class which does not have state power at its disposal, but is only, as yet, fighting for that, to create a regular army. Such a class will naturally direct its efforts

towards disintegrating the regular army of the ruling class, and detaching isolated units from this enemy army, or else forming such units from scratch, in the underground, and later on, in the arena of open civil war. In other words, guerrilla-ism is the weapon of a class (or an oppressed nation) which is weaker organisationally and in the purely military sense, in its struggle against the class to which the centralised state apparatus belongs. In this period, guerrilla-ism is not only a progressive factor, it is, in general, the only possible form of open struggle by the oppressed class for its own emancipation.

But at a later stage guerrillaism turns reactionary.

The historically progressive role of guerrilla struggle ceases when the oppressed class has taken state power into its own hands...

One can only ask: what, in general, is the point of the working class taking state power into its own hands if it is not then supposed to make use of this power to introduce state centralism into that sphere, which, by its very nature, calls for the highest degree of centralisation, namely, the military sphere?[8]

Yet even after the establishment of a centralised revolutionary army, the guerrilla method of struggle could not be opposed dogmatically. Even then guerrilla bands played a useful role, but on condition that they were subordinated to the centralised army. In August 1919, Mamontov and his cavalry separated themselves by hundreds of *versts* from Denikin's forces to roam the rear of the Red Armies, destroying railway lines and other vital supply links. The guerrilla raids of Mamontov forced the Red Army to use guerrilla methods in response. On 6 September 1919 Trotsky wrote an article entitled, 'Do We Need Guerrillas?' To this question he answered, emphatically, 'Yes':

Mamontov's raid forces us... to supplement and strengthen [our] centralised army with splendid guerrilla detachments, moulded from steel, which will thrust themselves like sharp thorns into the enemy's body.

This kind of guerrilla movement we must now create.[9]

The beginning of military opposition to Trotsky in the Communist Party

The strong influence of guerrillaism among the party *cadres* led to the formation of a Military Opposition, which continued throughout the civil war and which later became the core of the Stalinist faction. Trotsky wrote this about the rise of the Military Opposition:

> Since the army is the most necessary of all the organisations of the state, and since during the first years of the Soviet regime the centre of attention was the defence of the revolution, it is no wonder that all the discussions, conflicts and groupings inside the party revolved around the question of building the army. An opposition appeared almost from the moment we made our first efforts to pass from disjointed armed detachments to a centralised army.[10]

The Military Opposition

> consisted of two groups. There were the numerous underground workers who were utterly worn out by prison and exile, and who now could not find a place for themselves in the building of the army and the state. They looked with great disfavour on all sorts of upstarts—and there was no lack of them in responsible posts. But in this opposition there were also very many advanced workers, fighting elements with a fresh reserve of energy, who trembled with political apprehension when they saw yesterday's engineers, officers, teachers, professors, once again in commanding positions.[11]

The first theoretical justification for this opposition to the employment of military specialists was provided by the 'Left Communists' in the Manifesto of 20 April 1918, in *Kommunist*:

> the old officer corps and command structure of the Tsarist generals is being reconstituted...
>
> The political line set forth... may strengthen in Russia the influence of external and internal counter-revolutionary forces, destroy the revolutionary capacity of the working class and, by cutting the Russian revolution off from the international one, have pernicious effects on the interests of both.[12]

In the Red Army, the Communist military leadership at Tsaritsin played a special role in opposing Trotsky's efforts to create a centralised army. After the victory of the Red Army at Sviiazhsk and Kazan it was in the south that the White Guards had their main stronghold. The strongest Bolshevik force facing them was Klem Voroshilov's Tenth Army. But Voroshilov was refusing to abide by orders coming from Trotsky and the Revolutionary War Council of the Republic. Voroshilov had been a Bolshevik in 1905 and a volunteer to the Tsarist army in 1914. He was conceited and semi-educated. He opposed the centralised army authorities, and more especially the employment of military specialists. Trotsky writes: 'Tsaritsin, where the military workers were grouped around Voroshilov, held a special place in the Red army and in the military opposition.'[13] 'The atmosphere of Tsaritsin [was one of] administrative anarchy, guerrilla spirit, disrespect for the Centre, absence of administrative order, and provocative boorishness towards military specialists,' he wrote.[14]

Why the special role of Tsaritsin?

Their revolutionary detachments were headed chiefly by former non-commissioned officers from among the peasants of the Northern Caucasus. The deep antagonism between the Cossacks and the peasants of the southern steppes imparted a vicious ferocity to the civil war in that region. It penetrated far into the villages, and led to the wholesale extermination of entire families. This was a peasant war with its roots deep in local soil, and, in its *muzhik* ferocity, it far surpassed the revolutionary struggle in all other parts of the country. This war brought forward a good many stalwart irregulars who excelled in local skirmishing but usually failed when they had to undertake military tasks of larger scope.

...After the October revolution [Voroshilov] became the natural centre of the opposition of non-commissioned officers and irregulars against a centralised military organisation demanding military knowledge and a wider outlook.[15]

In the summer of 1918 Stalin was dispatched to the Lower Volga to ensure the transit of food supplies northwards to central Russia. At Tsaritsin, using his authority as a member of the central committee, he took charge of the defence of the city against the encircling White armies. Trotsky writes in his autobiography:

Stalin stayed in Tsaritsin for a few months, shaping his intrigue against me, with the aid of the home-bred opposition of Voroshilov and his closest associates. Even then it was assuming a very prominent place in his activities... Every day I would receive from the high command or the front commands such complaints against Tsaritsin as: it is impossible to get executions of an order, it is impossible to find out what is going on there, it is even impossible to get an answer to an enquiry. Lenin watched the conflict develop with alarm. He knew Stalin better than I did, and obviously suspected that the stubbornness of Tsaritsin was being secretly staged by Stalin.[16]

Again and again we find Stalin intriguing against Trotsky —and not only through his *protégés* of the Tsaritsin group. To give a few examples: in a message to Lenin sent on 7 July 1918 Stalin accused the military specialists of 'being asleep' and 'loafing about', of being 'bunglers'.[17] Three days later he wrote again to Lenin:

I shall myself, without any formalities, dismiss army commanders and commissars who are ruining the work. The interests of the work dictate this, and, of course, not having a paper from Trotsky is not going to deter me.[18]

On 4 August Stalin wrote to Lenin about the 'inertia of the former commander' of Tsaritsin, the 'conspiracy on the part of persons appointed by him', and about his 'criminal orders' that Stalin himself 'rescinded'. Stalin also carried out a 'timely removal of the so-called experts (staunch supporters either of the Cossacks or of the British and the French).'[19]

As against the 'military experts', as he referred to them, Stalin praised highly the new commanders rising from the ranks. In an interview in *Izvestia* on 21 September 1918, Stalin spoke about one gratifying phenomenon:

...the appearance of a new corps of commanders consisting of officers promoted from the ranks who have had practical experience in the imperialist war, and who enjoy the full confidence of the Red Army men.[20]

After a number of clashes between the Revolutionary War

Council of the Republic and Tsaritsin, Trotsky obtained Stalin's recall. On 4 October 1918 Trotsky spoke to Lenin and Sverdlov on the direct wire from Tambov:

> I categorically insist on Stalin's recall. Things are going badly on the Tsaritsin front, despite a super-abundance of military forces. Voroshilov is able to command a regiment, but not an army of 50,000 men. Nonetheless, I will retain him as commander of the Tenth Tsaritsin Army on condition that he places himself under the order of the commander of the southern front, Sytin. Right up to this day the Tsaritsin people have failed to send even operational reports to Kozlov. I had required them to submit operational and intelligence reports twice daily. If this is not carried out tomorrow, I shall commit Voroshilov and Minin for trial and announce this in an army order...
>
> Operations in strength are impossible without co-ordination of operations with Tsaritsin. There is no time for diplomatic negotiations. Tsaritsin must either obey orders or get out of the way. We have a colossal superiority of forces, but total anarchy at the top. This can be put to rights within 24 hours given firm and resolute support your end. In any event this is the only course of action that I can envisage.[21]

Stalin's sympathy with the Military Opposition was contradictory. In the government and in the central committee he strove for central authority and discipline, yet here in Tsaritsin he defied central authority. The distrust of the half-educated towards the military specialists, together with the hatred and jealousy of the embodiment of the central authority in the army—Trotsky —pulled against his normal inclination to centralism.

Let us return to the story of Tsaritsin.

Trotsky appointed Sytin, a former general in the Tsarist army, as commander of the southern front, and Shliapnikov, an old Bolshevik, replaced Stalin as chief commissar. Trotsky accompanied these appointments with a threat: 'Commanders and commissars who dare to infringe the rules of discipline shall, regardless of past merit, be immediately committed for trial before the revolutionary military tribunal of the southern front.'[22]

Trotsky also placed a man he trusted, A I Okulov, in command of the Tenth Army in order to keep Voroshilov in check.[23] Okulov, a Bolshevik since 1903, became after the February Revolution a member of the *gubernia* executive committee of Krasnoiarsk, and was later made a member of the presidium of the all-Russian central executive committee. In 1918 he was transferred to military work, first in Siberia, and later on several other fronts, being at one time a member of the Revolutionary War Council of the Republic.

Trotsky gave wide publicity to the conflict with the Tsaritsin group when he reported on the military situation to the congress of *soviets*, and pulled no punches in depicting the conditions of the Tenth Army. His conclusion:

> Not all Soviet executives have realised that a centralised administration exists, and all orders that come from above have to be obeyed, that deviation from them is impermissible, and that we shall be pitiless towards those Soviet executives who have not yet understood them. We shall dismiss them, cast them out of our ranks, subject them to repression.[24]

Commenting on this speech many years later Trotsky wrote:

> This was aimed at Stalin to a much greater extent than Voroshilov, against whom these words were ostensibly directed at the time. Stalin was present at the congress and kept silent. He was silent at the session of the politburo. He could not openly defend his behaviour. All the more did he store up his anger.[25]

In reaction to this humiliation the Tsaritsin group started a whispering campaign against Trotsky, accusing him of being a friend of Tsarist generals and a persecutor of Bolsheviks in the army. The accusation found its way into the columns of *Pravda*, at that time edited by Bukharin.

On 29 November 1918 *Pravda* carried an article by V Sorin, a Left Communist and member of the Moscow party committee, with the seemingly inoffensive title 'Commanders and Commissars in the Field Army'. Sorin attacked the set-up in the Red Army, in which, he wrote, commanders had too much power. Commanders could use discretionary measures 'in exceptional circumstances', the only limitation being that the front command had to be informed. This raised the question: 'Won't people who have nothing in common with communism possess their own personal opinion as to what is exceptional, an opinion formed even prior to the revolution?'

Moreover, wrote Sorin, since orders required the counter-signature of a commissar, this commissar would necessarily be turned into 'a figurehead obliged to sign against his own will all the commanders' directives'. Had not the powers invested in army commanders to inflict punishment been directly copied from some 'set of regulations from Tsar Nikolai's academy'? The range of his criticism broadened still further: 'To the same order of ideas belong those methods, practised in the army, which, while designed to create "iron discipline", in fact undermine and weaken the revolutionary activity of communist soldiers.'

In particular, Sorin stated, the order making commissars 'answerable with their lives' for the performance by their men of superior orders had a demoralising effect on those responsible for political matters within the Red Army: 'An order of this kind, alongside guidelines such as: "inquiries must not take too much time and disciplinary offences must be punished immediately" can at times literally strike terror into party comrades'.

At this juncture Sorin delivered a decisive blow. He cited the case of Panteleev, the commissar who had been court-martialled with others from his regiment for desertion during the battle of Sviiazhsk, then shot. Sorin presented this case as evidence that 'the fear of being shot merely for formal reasons means that the commissars are reduced to mere tools in the hand of the commander, instruments which he uses for addressing his subordinates.' Responsibility for the execution of Panteleev was laid squarely at Trotsky's door. The article concluded with a call to battle, an exhortation to 'struggle with determination against the attempt to enfeeble the dictatorship of the Communist Party in the army, to depersonalise communist soldiers, to tire out the revolutionary endeavour.'[26]

The argument over the Panteleev case ran on for months and months. The military revolutionary council of the Fifth Army raised the matter a few days earlier than Sorin; so did the Western regional executive committee.[27] Trotsky protested about this in a telegram to Lenin and Sverdlov on 23 November 1918:

The account given by these hair-splitters makes it appear that Panteleev was shot on the basis of my order solely for the fact of his regiment having deserted and regardless of the conduct of Panteleev himself. Yet Panteleev not only did not himself remain at his post... but turned up accompanied by all the deserters on board a steamship that had been seized by the deserters for the purpose of effecting their escape from the environment of Kazan to Nizhnii... It should also be added that... the commander of the regiment, also a Communist, accepted the sentence of death as his due, while Panteleev wept and promised to behave differently in future. The agitation conducted by the Western regional executive committee, of which Panteleev had been a member, is blatantly demoralising in tenor. I insist that the most resolute party measures be taken to suppress it. I am bound to add that the conduct of the Western regional executive committee in relation to the War Department has in the past amounted to systematic malicious subversion.[28]

The affair rumbled on for months. On 11 January 1919 Trotsky had to return to the issue in a letter to both *Pravda* and *Izvestia* and refute the accusation that he had had Panteleev shot without justification.[29] Furthermore the case of Panteleev had apparently been invoked against Trotsky by the military section of the Eighth Party Congress in March 1919, though the published protocol contains no reference to it.

On 18 April 1919 the minutes of the politburo of the party recorded that Trotsky asked the central committee for a second time to appoint an investigation into the case of Panteleev in view of the fact that this question had been raised anew at the party congress. The politburo asked the party's Organisational Bureau —known as the orgburo—to set up an investigation commission, which it did two days later.[30] In its report this commission upheld Trotsky's action.[31]

On 25 December 1918 *Pravda* published a further polemical article attacking Trotsky's military policy. Entitled 'It is High Time', it was written by A Kamensky, a member of the all-Russian central executive committee of the *soviets* and a Bolshevik since 1905. It denounced the employment of former Tsarist officers on the ground that military science and military art were of no value. Kamensky used his experience in Ukraine to support his contention, where the commander had been Voroshilov and

Kamensky the commissar. Kamensky attacked the section of the regulations relating to the power of army commanders as introduced by Trotsky in March 1918. According to Kamensky:

> In our language this means that the commander is an autocrat and that the members of the military council, in this case, will be attending a purely decorative signature [to the commander's orders].
>
> They have often pointed out to us that the conduct of a war is so very complicated that without military specialists we would not be able to cope. Military specialisation certainly is complicated, but it is also an integral part of something more general and delicate, the running of the whole state machine; and we have already displayed the courage to run the state by carrying out the October revolution.
>
> There are a great many deformities, but from the start we have refrained from appealing to 'princes from across the sea'; on the contrary, we have chased them away because they were carrying out sabotage...
>
> But even if we admit that the military specialists are the air without which the existence of a socialist army would be unthinkable, what good have they done? None whatever. And what harm? A vast amount! They were on the point of giving up Tsaritsin, and they would have succeeded in doing so had we not removed them in the nick of time.

Kamensky then goes on to accuse General Sytin, commander of the southern front, of readiness to shoot Communists:

> Without our agreement, and against our protests, they 'set up' in our area a group of gentlemen whom they had removed from another front and who carried on their damaging work here... Comrade Okulov, a member of the southern front military revolutionary council, has declared that during the fighting near Orenburg twenty officers fled from his staff. Another seven fled from the eastern front, and, because of this, two of our best comrades, Zalutski and Bekoi, were nearly sent before the firing squad, as happened to Panteleev, and only the fairness of Comrade Smilga saved their lives... About commissars. Having burnt our hands on more than one occasion with undeserved accusations and even with the

shooting of our best comrades, we must be prudent, Commissars are our political representatives, and it is intolerabie that they be shot without trial.

In passing, Kamensky is lavish in praising Voroshilov:

Glorious, undaunted, dedicated to the revolution, old party militant, rich in merit.[32]

Trotsky protested vehemently against Kamensky's article in a letter to the central committee, demanding that the central committee issue a public statement on the matter:

I ask the central committee:
1) To declare publicly as to whether the policy of the War Department is my personal policy, the policy of some group or other, or the policy of our party as a whole.
2) To establish for the benefit of the public opinion of the entire party the grounds which Comrade Kamensky had for his assertion about the shooting of the best comrades without trial.
3) To point out to the editorial board of the central organ the total inadmissibility of printing articles which consist not of a criticism of the general policy of the department or even of the party, but of direct, damning charges of actions of the most damning character (the shooting of the best comrades without trial) without making preliminary inquiries of party establishments as to the grounds for these charges, since it is clear that were there any sort of grounds for these charges, the matter could not rest at party polemics, but must become a subject for judicial investigation by the party.[33]

On the same day, 25 December 1918, the central committee passed a resolution condemning Kamensky and the *Pravda* editors, clearly following the points made by Trotsky.[34]

But this did not stop the sniping against Trotsky. His opponents in the party repeated the stories published in leaflets that the political departments of the White armies tried to circulate among Red soldiers, accusing the Red command—and Trotsky in particular—of bloodthirstiness.[35]

Trotsky's intransigence did not put balm on the wounds of the many slighted old Bolsheviks active in the Red Army. In his autobiography Trotsky explains:

> It is no wonder that my military work created so many enemies for me. I did not look to the side, I elbowed away those who interfered with military success, or in the haste of the work trod on the toes of the unheeding and was too busy even to apologise. Some people remember such things. The dissatisfied and those whose feelings had been hurt found their way to Stalin or Zinoviev, for these two also nourished hurts.[36]

The opposition to Trotsky's military policy was thus carried out by a combination of Left Communists such as Bukharin and the semi-literate and conceited clique of NCOs manipulated by Stalin. Another important person joined them, although surreptitiously, Zinoviev, who could not forgive Trotsky for his glorious role in October, when he, the old Bolshevik, had funked it. Zinoviev, as president of the Petrograd *soviet*, used this position as a base to oppose Trotsky.

In a series of issues of **Petrogradskaia Pravda** there appeared a long article by S I Gusev* under the title 'How to Build the Soviet Army'.[38] Gusev argued against Trotsky's imposed iron discipline in the Red Army and against the employment of the former Tsarist officers:

> Free, comradely discipline renders unnecessary and superfluous all 'strict' orders directed against 'insubordinate persons'. Every 'insubordinate person', if such persons exist and are found, will meet with severe condemnation from his own comrades.

---

* Trotsky wrote of Gusev in **My Life**: 'He was called an "old Bolshevik" because of his share in the revolution of 1905. He had retired to bourgeois life for the next ten years, but, like many others, returned to revolution in 1917. Later Lenin and I removed him from military work because of some petty intrigues, and he was immediately picked up by Stalin. His special vocation today is chiefly that of falsifying the history of the civil war, for which his main qualification is his apathetic cynicism.'[37]

In 1923 Gusev joined the control commission that played an important role in consolidating Stalin's hold over the party. In 1925-6, during the struggle to crush the Left Opposition, Gusev headed the central committee's press department. In 1929-33, at the time of the 'Third Period', he was a member of the presidium of the executive committee of the Communist International.

Further on in the article, Gusev expressed himself in favour of a still wider extension of freedom, and 'self-activity' on the part of the Red Army men, such as would put them in the position of 'semi-officers':

> The leading initiative of the officer loses its decisive importance in a troop of qualified soldiers in which each individual soldier is capable of finding his own bearings in a military situation and right there, on the battlefield, under fire, of creating, in accordance with the changing situation, a new tactical plan for carrying out the overall operational task.
>
> What flexibility, what mobility, what inventiveness, compared with the immobile, obtuse troops, stuck fast in the fulfilment of 'orders', of the bourgeois army. *Here* we see free creativity on the field of battle, within the broad limits of the operational task. *There* we see spiritual stagnation...[39]

Then Lashevich, a leader of the military organisation of the party, member of the central committee and a close friend of Zinoviev, wrote in **Petrogradskaia Pravda**:

> If people tell us that we have become infatuated with generals, I must say, and repeat, that we want to use only whatever they have that is useful—to squeeze that out of these generals, and then *to throw them away like squeezed lemons for which we have no more use*. (Emphasis added).[40]

Zinoviev spoke in the same vein:

> We know very well that the commanders whom we have invited to serve us do not have a friendly and sympathetic attitude towards us, and it would be stupid, therefore, to employ them in posts of command during a civil war, but the state of affairs at present is such that our interests —annihilating and repelling the Germans—and the interests of these generals who are patriots for their fatherland coincide and we can boldly utilise their services in the leadership of our army. And they, knowing perfectly well how strong we are, come to us actually in the role of our *batmen*. (Emphasis added).[41]

In January 1919 Stalin shot a poisoned arrow at Trotsky. On

1 January Stalin and Dzerzhinsky were sent by the central committee and the Council of Defence to investigate the reasons for the fall of Perm and the reverses on the eastern front, where the First and Second Armies were. The report they wrote was full of grave charges gainst the highest military leaders, including the Revolutionary Military Council of the Republic, in other words against Trotsky:

> the general staff and the area military commissariats, which [were] formed and sent to the front units, were patently unreliable;
> ...the Revolutionary Military Council of the Republic [with its] so-called instructions and orders disorganised the control of the front and the armies. Unless the necessary changes are made at central headquarters, there can be no guarantee of success at the fronts.[42]

The 'counter-revolutionary spirit' allegedly displayed by Soviet troops dispatched as reinforcements to the beleaguered city of Perm was due, they said, to 'the old pre-revolutionary methods of training contingents.' The Revolutionary Military Council of the Republic had demonstrated an 'intolerably criminal way of managing the front'; it had 'paralysed' the front with its 'contradictory instructions', and had deprived the Second Army 'of any chance of coming swiftly to the aid of the Third Army'.

The report spoke of 'the absolutely indiscriminate appointment of unverified officers as commanders, many of whom lured their units over to the enemy'.[43] It denounced 'the isolation of the Revolutionary Military Council of the Republic from the front and the ill-considered instructions of the commander-in-chief.'[44] Its conclusion was the need to change 'the composition of the general staff itself '.[45]

Insults were poured on the heads of the former Tsarist officers. These obstructed Trotsky's efforts to recruit these officers to the Red Army. General V F Novitsky, who had of his own accord declared his readiness to serve in the Red Army, now wrote an open letter to Trotsky in which he refused cooperation, saying that he had no desire to be, quoting Lashevich, 'squeezed and thrown away like a lemon'. Trotsky countered with an emphatic repudiation of the attacks on the officers. 'Those former generals who work conscientiously in the difficult and unfavourable conditions of today, even if they are of a conservative turn of mind, deserve incomparably more respect from the working class than pseudo-socialists who engage in intrigue.'[46]

Trotsky was disgusted with the boorish attitude towards the military specialists. He took up the subject in 'A Letter to a Friend', written on 10 January 1919. He wrote with scorn:

> Our own bureaucrat... is real historical ballast—already conservative, sluggish, complacent, unwilling to learn and even expressing enmity to anybody who reminds him of the need to learn.
>
> This is the genuine menace to the cause of communist revolution. These are the genuine accomplices of counter-revolution, even though they are not guilty of any conspiracy...
>
> Only a wretched Soviet bureaucrat, jealous for his new job, and cherishing this job because of the personal privileges it confers and not because of the interests of the workers' revolution, can have an attitude of baseless distrust towards any expert, outstanding organiser, technician, specialist or scientist—having already decided on his own account that 'me and my mates will get by somehow.'[47]

Trotsky did not spare his opponents. He argued that the crude and conceited attitude of the upstart bureaucrat was especially harmful to the working class, which suffered from ignorance because of its oppressed position in society.

> The revolutionary development of the proletariat consists... in the fact that it arrives at an understanding of its oppressed position, its poverty, and rises against the ruling classes. This gives it the possibility of seizing political power. But the taking of political power essentially reveals to the proletariat for the first time the full picture of its poverty in respect of general and specialised education and government experience. The understanding by the revolutionary class of its own inadequacies is the guarantee that these will be overcome.

The revolution would be meaningless if it only made

> it possible for thousands, or even tens of thousands of

advanced workers to settle into jobs in the *soviets* and commissariats. Our revolution will fully justify itself only when every toiling man and woman feels that his or her life has become easier, freer, cleaner and more dignified. This has not yet been achieved. A hard road still lies between us and this, our essential and only goal.[48]

Trotsky never spared his opponents. In this conflict between the boorish Military Opposition, which rejected the opportunity of learning from bourgeois specialists, and Trotsky, whose vision was of a new world in which the workers absorbed the cultural treasures of the centuries, we find in embryo the core of the future struggle of Trotsky against Stalinism. And this occurred just a year after the October revolution!

Lenin and the military front

The opposition to Trotsky's policy was all the more formidable because Lenin for a long time reserved judgment on the employment of former Tsarist officers. Trotsky had to appeal to Lenin repeatedly to support him. In August 1918 Lenin asked Trotsky's opinion about a proposal introduced by Larin to replace all officers with communists. Trotsky replied sharply in the negative:

> Many of them [former Tsarist officers] commit acts of treachery. But on the railways too instances of sabotage are in evidence in the routing of troop trains. Yet nobody suggests replacing railway engineers by communists. I consider Larin's proposal as being utterly worthless... Those who clamour the loudest against making use of officers are either people infected with panic or those who are remote from the entire work of the military apparatus, or such party military figures as are themselves worse than any saboteur —such as are incapable of keeping an eye on anything, behave like *satraps*, spend their time doing nothing, and, when they meet with failure, shuffle off the blame on to the general staff officers.[49]

On 24 November 1918 Lenin was still unconvinced, saying in a speech to Red Army officers: 'in building our new army now, we must draw our officers solely from among the people. Only

Red officers will have any respect among the soldiers and be able to strengthen socialism in our army. Such an army will be invincible.'[50]

Not until the eve of the Eighth Party Congress in March 1919 did Lenin have a clear idea of the extent to which military specialists were being used. At the beginning of March 1919, Trotsky narrates:

> Lenin wrote me a note: What if we fire all the specialists and appoint Lashevich as commander-in-chief? Lashevich was an old Bolshevik who had earned his promotion to the rank of sergeant in the 'German' war. I replied on the same note: 'Child's play!' Lenin looked slyly at me from under his heavy brows, with a very expressive grimace that seemed to say: 'You are very harsh with me'. But, deep down, he really liked abrupt answers that left no room for doubt. We came together after the meeting. Lenin asked me various things about the front. 'You asked me,' I said, 'if it would not be better to kick out all the old officers. But do you know how many of them we have in the army now?'
> 'No'.
> 'Not even approximately?'
> 'I don't know'.
> 'Not less than thirty thousand.'
> 'What?'
> 'Not less than thirty thousand. For every traitor there are a hundred who are dependable; for every one who deserts there are two or three who get killed. How are we to replace them all?'[51]

A few days later Lenin was making a speech on the problems of constructing the socialist commonwealth. He said:

> When Comrade Trotsky informed me recently that the number of officers of the old army employed by our War Department runs into several tens of thousands, I perceived concretely where the secret of using our enemy lay, how to compel those who had opposed communism to build it, how to build communism with the bricks which the capitalists had chosen to hurl against us![52]

This episode shows clearly how out of touch Lenin was with

the real issues facing the Red Army: not knowing until March 1919 what a massive number of former Tsarist officers was in the Red Army.*

In 1940 Trotsky described the relations between himself and Lenin on military affairs during the civil war thus:

It must be said... that Lenin's support was not unconditional. Lenin wavered more than once, and in several instances was gravely mistaken. My advantage over him was in the fact that I uninterruptedly travelled along the various fronts, came in contact with a tremendous number of people, from local peasants, prisoners of war, and deserters, to the highest army and party leaders at the front. This mass of varied impressions was of inestimable value. Lenin never left Moscow... He had to pass judgment on military questions, which were new to all of us, on the basis of information which for the most part came from the higher-ups of the party. No one was able to understand individual voices coming from below better than Lenin, but these reached him only on exceptional occasions.[54]

Whatever their differences on military affairs, Lenin's admiration for Trotsky's leadership of the Red Army was undiminished. In his recollections of Lenin, Gorky says:

Striking his fist on the table, he [Lenin] exclaimed: 'Show me another man who would be able in a year to organise almost a model army; yes, and win the esteem of the military specialists. We have such a man. We have everything, and you'll see miracles!'[55]

The fact that Stalin, Voroshilov and company invoked their party seniority when they came into conflict with Trotsky tended to transform the conflict into one between the party and army organisations. Lenin played a crucial role in Trotsky's victory in this conflict. As Jan M Meijer observes in his postscript to **The Trotsky Papers**:

As soon as there was opposition, Lenin had to repeat

---

* It is quite funny to read at the time of *glasnost* what the reformer Roy Medvedev writes: 'Lenin, undoubtedly, was the chief of its [the Red Army's] organisation, and the chief strategist of the civil war.'[53]

Trotsky's arguments before they carried conviction.

...Perhaps neither Trotsky nor Lenin realised how much the former owed to Lenin in maintaining contact with the second echelon of the party. In that respect Lenin became almost part of Trotsky's personality and after his death Trotsky was at a loss in his relations with the people that made up this second echelon.[56]

The Eighth Congress

Shortly before the Eighth Party Congress assembled in March 1919, Kolchak's White troops broke through on the eastern front, creating a grave threat to Soviet power. The central committee decided that Trotsky should straight away leave for the front, and the military delegates to the congress should return to their units. This raised vehement protest that Trotsky was evading criticism of his policy. The central committee therefore reversed its previous decision, allowing the military delegates to stay—but not Trotsky.

The debate at the congress on military policy was introduced by Sokolnikov, who moved the theses written by Trotsky, 'Our Policy in Creating the Army'.[57] His report was followed by a co-report by V M Smirnov, representing the Military Opposition. Smirnov argued for a new-style army based on democratic control and partisan warfare. During the public debate at the congress there were no other speeches specifically devoted to military policy besides Sokolnikov's and Smirnov's, only scattered references in a number of speeches.

The bulk of the discussion took place in a separate military section. This was composed of 85 delegates, 57 of whom had a 'deciding vote' (the rest merely 'consultative votes'.) The discussion was stormy. Most vociferous were Voroshilov and Minin of the Tsaritsin group, who led the attack on military specialists, asserting that the Red Army had in fact been built without their help.[58] Cases of treason by military specialists were quoted in suppport of the demand that their function should be cut down, and that of party workers extended. After stormy discussion, Smirnov's theses were accepted by 37 votes to 20.[59] The minority supporting Trotsky's theses walked out.

When the debate moved to the congress itself things were radically different. Lenin came out strongly in defence of Trotsky's theses. This is what he said on the Red Army:

> If the ruling class, the proletariat, wants to hold power, it must... prove its ability to do so by its military organisation. How was a class which had hitherto served as cannon fodder for the military commanders of the ruling imperialist class to create its own commanders? ...
>
> Here we were faced with a problem which a year's experience has now summed up for us. When we included the question of bourgeois specialists in the revolutionary programme of our party, we summed up the party's practical experience in one of the most important questions. As far as I remember the earlier teachers of socialism, who foresaw a great deal of what would take place in the future socialist revolution and discussed many of its features, never expressed an opinion on this question. It did not exist for them, for it arose only when we proceeded to create a Red Army. That meant creating an army filled with enthusiasm out of an oppressed class which had been used as mere cannon fodder, and it meant compelling that army to utilise all that was most coercive and abhorrent in what we had inherited from capitalism.[60]

Lenin attacked the guerrilla methods used by Voroshilov in Tsaritsin. In response to an angry interruption from Voroshilov himself, Lenin stated that the losses suffered by the Tenth Army might have been much less had more orthodox military methods been employed, and had properly trained commanders been used.[61]

Notwithstanding Lenin's strong support for Trotsky's theses*, the opposition to these was still large. Trotsky's theses received the support of 174 delegates in the full congress, while 95 voted against and 32 abstained.

On 25 March the central committee met. Trotsky was not present. Zinoviev introduced the discussion with a summary of congress resolutions on the military question. He declared that the unpublished resolutions constituted 'the expression of the genuine wishes of the congress', and were at the same time 'a

---

* One sign of the strong support Lenin gave to Trotsky was his instruction after the congress that Smirnov be relieved of his military posts.[62]

concession of a kind to the opposition'. Zinoviev said: 'Congress had, by token of its entire line of conduct on the military question, administered a serious caution', and made it clear at whom this caution was directed: 'It is essential for Comrade Lenin to talk things over with Comrade Trotsky.'[63]

Trotsky replied to the central committee, after he had read the congress and central committee resolutions, that he found the resolutions of the congress to contain 'many things that contradict the policy of the War Department'; they 'are formulated in supremely general and vague terms, and part of them are based on a misunderstanding.' Trotsky made it clear that he was irritated by Zinoviev's speech, which tried to fudge differences with the Military Opposition. Zinoviev had sought to play down the existence of the Military Opposition by neatly dividing its members into two categories: the first group, in Trotsky's words, 'the pretentious party intelligentsia, largely consisting of offended Soviet officials and cases of nervous exhaustion'; the second group—for which Zinoviev showed support—had declared themselves 'extremely dissatisfied with my attitude'.

Trotsky was not inclined to show indulgence towards the second category, in which Zinoviev had included Voroshilov. Zinoviev was, he maintained,

> obviously mistaken in regarding the voice of the second group as the voice of truth itself and in urging that we, in fact, take our cue from it. The opposition of the workers-oversimplifiers... is equally mistaken and, in point of practice, even more dangerous than the hysterical opposition of offended Soviet officials. Zinoviev named Voroshilov. I am not going to start examining psychological case-histories to see in which group Voroshilov should be put, but I will remark that the sole thing for which I can hold myself to blame with regard to him is the overlengthy, indeed two or three months long attempts to get things going by way of negotiation, exhortation and personal rearrangements, where the interests of the case required a resolute, organisational decision.

The issue was more than purely military:

> The opposition as a whole, in both its better half and in its

worse half, reflects the fearful difficulties of the dictatorship of a hungry, internally rent working class, alongside an ill-informed, discontented and mutinous peasantry. We see these difficulties on all sides. In the military sphere they assume their most concentrated form. All the shortages, discordances and shortcomings of Soviet work, all the slovenliness of Soviet officials express themselves in their most intensified form within the organism of the army.

Zinoviev argued for 'comradely discipline'. Trotsky, not ready to make any concessions, sharply rebuked him:

The army is an artificial organism, and the unity of thought and planning which sustains this artificial organism must be maintained with a firmness all the more relentless the more savage be the objective conditions that tend to undermine the army...

...because I have all too closely observed grave, even tragic episodes affecting armies in the field, I know very well how great is the temptation to substitute so-called 'comradely'... household discipline for formal discipline, but, at the same time, I became all too well persuaded that a substitution of this sort would mean the complete disintegration of the army. I think that the party relationship of Communists with one another is, in the military sphere, in fact translated into unconditional and comprehensive formal discipline.

Trotsky's letter ended with a sharp condemnation of Zinoviev and an appeal to the central committee to make its position clear:

Comrade Zinoviev's report inspires the most serious apprehension that he is seeking a solution to the question precisely along the line of an easing-off in the system and adjusting it to conform with the weariness of certain elements in our party. Insofar as the *buro* of the central committee has approved Comrade Zinoviev's report, I wish to believe that it is *not* this aspect of the report that it has approved, for, if the contrary should be the case, I personally would not myself see any possibility of counting on the party being successful in the severe struggle ahead of it.[64]

Chapter eight
Disputes on military strategy

THE EIGHTH CONGRESS did not put an end to the opposition to Trotsky's military policy. Stalin continued with his intrigues against army specialists who Trotsky supported. In a letter to Lenin of 4 June 1919 he complained about Okulov, who had been appointed by Trotsky to the Petrograd sector of the western front. He claimed that Okulov and his ilk 'urged the military specialists on against our commissars'.[1] He also stated that the all-Russian general staff was 'working for the Whites', a fact which documents at his disposal would make 'obvious'.[2] He demanded the removal of Okulov.[3] Stalin won. The politburo, in Trotsky's absence, supported Stalin and Okulov was removed.[4]

On 16 June, at the end of a really not too significant victorious military operation on the Petrograd front, which Stalin trumpeted, he wrote to Lenin that success had been secured by not hesitating to oppose mistaken orders of the professional experts.[5] Then again, in the notes exchanged between Lenin and Skliansky on the situation in Petrograd, Zinoviev's name crops up as an advocate of those rejecting the War Commissariat and the 'specialists'.[6] On 18 June Stalin again told Lenin that high-ranking officers had been hatching a plot.[7]

Following this sniping, a real crisis faced Trotsky in his leadership of the Red Army. After the Eighth Congress, the opposition shifted its attack from the organisation of the Red Army to a discussion of the strategy used in the civil war.

It was after the Eighth Congress that Lenin for the first time took an intense and direct interest in the military strategy of the Red Army. Thus he communicated directly with the military authorities in the Ukraine on the delay in the operations against

White forces in the Donets Basin.[8] He sent orders mobilising the Ukraine against Denikin,[9] and issued directives to military commanders from the western front to the Caspian.[10]

An acute disagreement took place in the summer of 1919 about the strategy needed on the eastern front. Towards the end of April, the commander on this front, S S Kamenev, a former colonel on the Tsarist general staff, carried out a successful outflanking manoeuvre against Kolchak's southern flank. Soon the White troops began to fall back in disorder toward the Urals. At this point a controversy broke out between Kamenev and the commander-in-chief, Vatsetis. Kamenev was confident he could inflict final defeat on Kolchak if he pursued him. Vatsetis vetoed the plan. He suggested that Kolchak had strong reserves in Siberia, that once Kolchak was pushed to the east of the Urals, the Red Army should not pursue him further, but should stay in the mountains for the winter. This would have enabled the Red Army to withdraw a few divisions from the east and switch them to the south, where Denikin was becoming very dangerous.

This plan, however, met with vigorous opposition from S S Kamenev, as well as from the three commissars of the eastern front —Smilga, Lashevich and Gusev. They insisted that Kolchak was so near to being defeated that only a few men were needed to follow him, and the most important thing was that he be prevented from taking a breathing spell, because in that case he would recover during the winter, and the eastern campaign would have to start all over again in the spring.

On 15 June the central committee, including Lenin, gave its backing to the plan elaborated by S S Kamenev, Smilga, Lashevich and Gusev. Trotsky supported Vatsetis, opposing the pursuit of Kolckak beyond the Urals.[11] Trotsky's decision to dismiss Kamenev from his position as commander of the eastern front was overturned.[12] At the end of June, in a letter to the eastern front military council, Lenin strongly argued the need to conquer the Urals as soon as possible by pushing on with the attack.[13]

In fact life itself proved that Trotsky was wrong, as he did not hesitate to admit later. He wrote:

> It proved to be the command of the eastern front that was right in appraising Kolchak's army... The eastern armies released some troops for the southern front and continued,

at the same time, their advance on the heel of Kolchak into the heart of Siberia.[14]

Being in the wrong on the issue of the eastern front weakened Trotsky in the face of his opponents. On 3-4 July, at a meeting of the central committee, Stalin proposed that Vatsetis, Trotsky's chosen commander-in-chief since September 1918, be replaced by S S Kamenev. The central committee agreed.[15] Trotsky resisted the change, but as he himself wrote later, Kamenev's 'success on the eastern front bribed Lenin and broke down my resistance.'[16] The Military Revolutionary Council of the Republic was reconstituted. It was now to be made up of Trotsky, Skliansky, Gusev, Smilga, Rykov and the new commander-in-chief, S S Kamenev. Thus Trotsky's friends, Smirnov, Rozengolts and Raskolnikov, were replaced with Stalin's *protégés*, Smilga and Gusev.

This double reproof was too much for Trotsky. He resigned on the spot from the politburo, the Commissariat of War and the Military Revolutionary Council of the Republic. On 5 July the politburo met and categorically rejected Trotsky's resignation. On Lenin's proposal it adopted, unanimously, a resolution assuring Trotsky of its deep respect and confidence:

> The orgburo and politburo of the CC will do all in their power to provide for the work on the southern front—the most difficult, dangerous and important of the fronts at the present time—which Comrade Trotsky chose for himself, to be so arranged as to best suit Comrade Trotsky and to yield the greatest benefit to the republic.[17]

It was on this occasion that Lenin, obviously disturbed by the incident, handed to Trotsky as a token of his confidence a blank sheet as endorsement of any order Trotsky might issue. At the bottom of the blank sheet Lenin wrote:

> Comrades! Knowing the strict character of the instructions issued by Comrade Trotsky, I am so convinced, supremely convinced that the instruction issued by Comrade Trotsky is correct, to the point, and essential for the good of the cause, that I wholly support this instruction. *V Ulianov (Lenin).*[18]

This *carte blanche* was testimony to the exceptional

confidence Lenin had in Trotsky.

The beginning of July 1919 was the low point in Trotsky's standing as head of the Red Army. The events of these days left deep traces in the relationship between Trotsky and many of the people at the centre. It was also a point when tension between Trotsky and Lenin revealed itself clearly. Probably an important element in the relationship was the fact that Trotsky saw Lenin only seldom, being almost always at the front.

Trotsky had to go on fighting against his opponents, who maintained their surreptitious attacks on the military specialists. Thus on 9 July 1919 he issued an order that was really an answer to Stalin's slander of the military specialists on the Petrograd front:

> In connection with the treacherous conspiracy by sections of the commanding personnel on the Petrograd front articles have appeared in the press which are being interpreted as a sign of change in Soviet policy in military matters, particularly where the military specialists are concerned... I therefore consider it necessary to make clear that Soviet policy in military matters remains unchanged, for it is not the product of the fantasy of particular individuals or groups but results from the collective experience of many hundreds of thousands of workers and peasants.
>
> The honourable commanders of the Red Army—and they are the overwhelming majority—will, as before, enjoy the confidence and backing of the Soviet power, as its valued collaborators in most responsible posts.[19]

On 12 July a letter by Trotsky to the revolutionary war councils of the armies and the fronts made a sharp attack on the Military Opposition.[20]

On 17 July, in an article published in a Ukrainian newspaper, Trotsky furiously attacked the military political administration of Kharkov, where Voroshilov had his headquarters. He accused the group formed round Voroshilov of taking advantage of military difficulties in the south to pander to the unwillingness of Ukrainian Communists to take orders from Moscow and to encourage guerrillaism. Trotsky did not spare Voroshilov and company, accusing them of ignorance and crass conceit:

Here again we see a criminally demagogic distortion of the facts in the interests of a lying argument... The worst-organised part of the southern front, in all respects, was the Ukrainian corner...

It is true that in the Kharkov sector a considerable number of betrayals occurred. But we have often observed on other fronts as well, during their infancy, how the work of sham-revolutionary demagogues has been complemented by treachery on the part of commanders...

...our party programme speaks clearly and precisely of the method by which the working class can and must make use of the experience of the military specialists.

There are Communists of a poor sort; who treat military specialists as though they were accursed persons, or simply persons under arrest, imagining that this is how to safeguard the interests of the revolution.

Guerrilla-ism, with its traces, vestiges and survivals, has caused both our republic and the Ukrainian republic incomparably more disasters, collapses, catastrophes and losses of war materials than all the betrayals by military specialists.

...Our party combats and will 'carry on a merciless struggle against the seemingly radical but actually ignorant and conceited opinion that the working people can overcome capitalism and the bourgeois order without learning from bourgeois specialists, without utilising them, without undergoing *a long schooling* through work alongside them.'

...The central committee calls for 'merciless struggle' against this ignorant conceit.[21]

The southern front

After the disagreement on the strategy towards Kolchak on the eastern front a conflict arose in the central committee over strategy on the southern front.

In the south, the enemy forces were composed of two separate and antagonistic groups: the Cossacks, particularly in the province of Kuban, and the Whites' volunteer army. Trotsky believed that it was necessary to use the antagonism between the two uneasy partners. S S Kamenev, the newly appointed commander-in-chief, however, thought only in logistic terms, without taking into account the socio-political implications, and suggested that the decisive blow should be delivered at the base of the volunteer army. Lenin and all other members of the central committee, except Trotsky, supported Kamenev, so that Trotsky was completely isolated. The adoption of Kamenev's plan unanimously by the central committee seems to point to quite widespread hostility to Trotsky there, as many of those involved could not have judged the issue at stake.[22] Trotsky's offer of resignation from all his posts, already referred to, was, as he wrote a few years later, 'intimately linked up with the question of the southern strategic plan'.[23]

Trotsky did not abide by the central committee decision without continuing to argue against Kamenev's strategy vis-à-vis Denikin. He also proceeded to sound out opinion among the armies immediately after the setback he had received at the hands of the central committee. He asked leading members of the Red Army whether they supported his military policy.

On 11 July Trotsky wired Skliansky with a report for the central committee:

> Today at a conference of political workers of the Eighth Army, the following question was put to the vote after a general discussion: should the present policy of the War Department remain in force or should changes be made in it. Forty-one voted in favour of retaining the present policy and two of making changes.[24]

Three days later, on 14 July, he again wired Skliansky for the central committee:

> At a meeting of senior political workers of the Thirteenth Army a resolution was unanimously adopted with one abstention (those taking part numbering 60) on the biassed and unfounded nature of the criticism of military policy made by a section of the party, and demanding the retention and further development of the same methods.[25]

But the central committee did not budge. A telegram appointing three new members to the military revolutionary council of the southern front—Smilga, Serebriakov and Lashevich (two of them members of the central committee)—was a further reprimand for Trotsky's stand.[26]

As late as 6 September Lenin cabled Trotsky, Serebriakov and Lashevich expressing the politburo's support for Kamenev, and its 'astonishment at the attempts [by Trotsky] to revise the basic strategic plan decided upon.'[27]

In this case, however, events proved without doubt that Kamenev's strategy was completely wrong and Trotsky's right. On 25 June 1919 the volunteer army occupied Kharkov, the chief city of the Ukraine. By the end of the month the Don Cossack army had cleared the Don country of Soviet forces, and the Kuban Cossacks had captured Ekaterinoslav on the lower Dnieper. On 30 June Denikin, with the help of British planes and tanks, captured Tsaritsin. On 31 July Poltava was captured. Kherson and Nikolaev on the Black Sea coast were taken on 18 August, and five days later Odessa fell. On 31 August the volunteer army marched into Kiev. Throughout September Denikin's army continued to advance. On 20 September it occupied Kursk; on 6 October Voronezh; on 13 October Orel, less than 250 miles from Moscow. E H Carr described those weeks as 'the crucial point at which the continued existence of the regime hung by a thread.'

After Denikin had seized Kiev and nearly the whole of the Ukraine, and pursued the Red Army towards Voronezh and Kursk, along the shortest line to Moscow, Trotsky demanded a change in the plan of operation. Again and again he repeated his demand, and again and again the politburo rejected it. Only when the threat to Moscow became imminent and Denikin's forces broke through towards Tula, the last important town before Moscow, while at the same time Iudenich, armed by the British and supported by the British navy, rapidly advanced from Estonia towards Petrograd and reached the outskirts of the city, only then was the politburo as well as S S Kamenev convinced of Trotsky's strategic plan. At the meetings of the central committee on 21 and 26 September Trotsky's plan for the southern front was accepted.

Trotsky commented in September on Kamenev's strategy:

The plan drawn up in advance for operations on the southern front has proved to be absolutely incorrect. Our defeats on the southern front are due primarily to the errors in the basic plan.
Fundamental to the plan was the identification of the threat from Denikin's White Guards with the Don and Kuban

Cossack communities.

...Denikin's tasks are offensive, whereas those of the Don and Kuban Cossacks are confined to the defence of their own regions. When Denikin advanced into the Donets area and the Ukraine, elementary considerations urged the need to separate his westward-moving forces from the original base, the Cossacks. A blow struck from Kharkov towards Taganrog or towards Berdiansk represented the shortest trajectory across a territory inhabited not by Cossacks but by workers and peasants, and gave promise of maximum success with minimum expenditure of forces.

As against this:

By our direct offensive against the Kuban we are bringing about a rapprochement between the Kuban Cossacks and the Denikinites...

A direct offensive along the line of most resistance proved, as had been forecast, wholly to Denikin's advantage. The Cossacks of Veshenskaia, Migulinskaia and Kazanskaia *stanitsas* mobilised to a man, swearing never to surrender. In this way, by our very offensive we provided Denikin with a substantial number of soldiers.[28]

Once Trotsky's perceptive strategy was adopted, the situation on the southern front improved radically. On 20 October the Red Army captured Orel, and four days later Budenny defeated Denikin's cavalry forces. On 15 November Denikin was defeated at Kastornaia, near Voronezh; on 17 November at Kursk; during December the retreat of his armies continued unabated. On 3 January 1920 Denikin lost Tsaritsin, on 8 January Rostov. After a closely fought battle round Rostov, it fell into Denikin's hands again on 20 January, but was recaptured three days later. The White armies continued to retreat. On 15 March Denikin lost Ekaterinodar; on 4 April he gave up the command of the Whites and left for Britain.

The Red cavalry

In the final stage of the fight against Denikin Trotsky launched the slogan 'Proletarians, to horse!' Cavalry troops dated back to the partisan period at the beginning of the Red Army.

When the army was put on a regular footing, relatively little attention was paid to cavalry. However, the success of the White cavalry brought home the necessity to revise this attitude. After the Denikin offensive, accompanied by the raids of Mamontov, Trotsky issued in September 1919 the call for all-out mobilisation of cavalry forces:

> PROLETARIANS, TO HORSE!
>
> The Red Army's principal misfortune is its shortage of cavalry. Our war is a war of manoeuvre and calls for the maximum mobility. This assigns a big role to the cavalry...
>
> Our shortage of cavalry is not accidental. The homeland of Russia's old cavalry was the steppes, and the Cossack communities settled there. The revolution of the proletariat came to birth in the great industrial centres. We have no shortage of machine-gunners and gunners, but we are experiencing a great lack of horsemen. The steppes, remote from the centres, were the hotbeds of counter-revolution. From the Don and the Urals came the Kaledins, Krasnovs and Durovs. Denikin found his most important support on the Don and the Kuban. As for the non-Cossack cavalry units, these were, from time immemorial, the appanage of the privileged and titled officers. An ultra-reactionary spirit always prevailed in the cavalry...
>
> Now, in the conditions of our civil war, we see the cavalry becoming ever more important...
>
> The Soviet Republic needs cavalry. Red cavalrymen, forward! To horse, proletarians![29]

Trotsky's initiative and daring improvisations were crucial to the victorious advance of the Red Army.

The defence of Petrograd

Besides the dispute with Lenin over the fight against Kolchak in the east and Denikin in the south, Trotsky had a disagreement with him over policy for the defence of Petrograd.

In October 1919, while Denikin was threatening Moscow, Iudenich, backed by the British navy in the Bay of Finland, was advancing rapidly from Estonia towards Petrograd. On 12 October his troops captured Iamburg, ten miles from Petrograd. By 16 October they had reached Gatchina, and shortly afterwards they were in Tsarskoe Selo, a suburban resort near Petrograd. The White generals were so confident that their operational commander is said to have declined an offer to look at Petrograd through field glasses, saying that next day he would be walking down Nevsky Prospekt, the central thoroughfare of the city.

On 15 October the politburo met. Facing the threat to both capitals, Lenin proposed to abandon Petrograd and gather all available strength round Moscow. He even envisaged the possibility of giving up Moscow and withdrawing to the Urals. Trotsky disagreed, and after some discussion the central committee, including Zinoviev and Stalin, sided with him. On 16 October Trotsky rushed in his armoured train to Petrograd. He believed they might have to defend the city street by street.

> If they broke into this gigantic city, the White Guards would find they had fallen into a stone labyrinth in which every building would be for them either a riddle, or a threat, or a mortal danger. From which direction should they expect the shot to come? From the window? From the attic? From the basement? From round the corner? From every direction! We have machine guns, rifles, revolvers, hand grenades... We can cover some streets with barbed wire entanglments, while leaving others open and turning them into traps. For this purpose all that is needed is for a few thousand men to decide firmly that they will not surrender Petrograd...
>
> Two or three days of street fighting like this would suffice for the invading bands to be transformed into a terrified, hunted herd of cowards who would surrender in groups or as individuals...[30]

If Iudenich had entered Petrograd Trotsky's urban battle programme would have been put to the test. But Trotsky's forces succeeded in holding the Whites outside the city.

All Trotsky's driving energy, all his gifts of organisation and oratory were put into effect. 'The city which has suffered so much, which has burnt with so strong an inward flame, this beautiful Red Petrograd remains what it has been, the torch of the revolution', he proclaimed to the Petrograd *soviet*.[31] On horseback he personally stopped retreating soldiers and led them back into line.

In his autobiography Trotsky describes the event:

In this brief episode, for the one and only time during the entire war I had to play the role of a regimental commander. When the retreating lines came up against the division headquarters at Alexandrovka, I mounted the first horse I could lay my hands on and turned the lines back. For the first few minutes there was nothing but confusion. Not all of them understood what was happening, and some of them continued to retreat. But I chased one soldier after another, on horseback, and made them all turn back. Only then did I notice that my orderly, Kozlov, a Muscovite peasant, and an old soldier himself, was racing at my heels. He was beside himself with excitement. Brandishing a revolver, he ran wildly along the line, repeating my appeals, and yelling for all he was worth: 'Courage, boys, Comrade Trotsky is leading you'. The men were now advancing at the pace at which they had been retreating before. Not one of them remained behind. After two *versts* the bullets began their sweetish, nauseating whistling and the first wounded began to drop. The regimental commander changed beyond recognition. He appeared at the most dangerous points, and before the regiment had recovered the position it had previously abandoned he was wounded in both legs. I returned to the staff headquarters on a truck. On the way we picked up the wounded. The impetus had been given, and with my whole being I felt that we would save Petrograd.[32]

With determination and daring the Red soldiers routed Iudenich's army. As it happened, the turning point on the Petrograd front occurred on the same day as that on the southern front: on 20 October the Red Army captured Orel.

The march on Warsaw

Another strategic question on which Trotsky found himself in conflict with Lenin and initially in a minority in the politburo was the march on Warsaw.

On 25 April 1920 Poland started a military offensive against Soviet Russia and invaded the Ukraine. The Polish troops advanced rapidly. On 6 May they entered Kiev, capital of the Ukraine, and occupied the whole of the western part of the country. On 26 May the Soviet counter-offensive started and on

5 June Budenny's Red cavalry broke through. On 12 June the Poles evacuated Kiev, and afterwards they were quickly pushed back to the border with Poland.

Up to this point, so long as the war was defensive, there were no differences between Trotsky and the rest of the party leadership regarding its conduct. Now the question was posed: should the Red Army go on to invade and occupy Poland. Lenin said 'Yes', Trotsky 'No'. Lenin's enthusiasm was fired by the desire to encourage the revolution in Germany. The march on Warsaw was to effect a junction between the Russian and German revolutions. He wanted 'to probe Europe with the bayonets of the Red Army'.[33] This wish reflected Lenin's anguish at the isolation of the Russian revolution and his desire to break out of it. The majority of the party leadership on the whole sided with Lenin. Stalin, who showed no enthusiasm for the war on Poland so long as it was not going too well,[34] now, as a result of success, became quite euphoric.

The Polish Communist leaders were split. Dzerzhinsky, Markhlevsky and above all Radek argued against the Soviet advance into Poland. Unschlicht, Lensky and Bobinsky took the opposite standpoint. Lenin showed no hesitation. Indeed, so long as the Polish war was progressing favourably his confidence increased. On 17 July he forced on the politburo, without much difficulty, a decision that the Red Army should march on to Warsaw. He overruled Trotsky's advice, proffered on behalf of the supreme command, that the offensive be halted. Lenin carried the five other members of the politburo with him.

Lenin's policy turned out to be wrong and costly. Radek argued that the Red Army would not be welcomed by the workers and peasants of Poland. Trotsky agreed with Radek. On 15 August the Soviet troops were beaten at the gates of Warsaw and were rapidly pushed back 400 kilometres, out of Polish teritory.

There were other factors that played a part in this Soviet defeat. For instance, there was an astonishing absence of co-ordination between the Soviet western and south-western commands: despite an order to the south-western command on 13 August to join the western front it played no significant part in the battle at all. Trotsky's explanation for the behaviour of the south-western command was simple and convincing: the private ambitions of Stalin, political commissar of the south-western army. Stalin was jealous of Tukhachevsky, the former Tsarist officer who commanded the western army, and of his political commissar, Smilga. Not willing to be overshadowed by their success, he wanted at all costs to capture Lvov at the same time as Tukhachevsky and Smilga entered Warsaw.

> Stalin was waging his own war. When the danger to Tukhachevsky's army became clearly evident, and the commander-in-chief ordered the south-western front to shift its direction sharply toward Zamostye-Tomashev, in order to strike at the flanks of the Polish troops and Warsaw, the command of the south-western front, encouraged by Stalin, continued to move to the west: Was it not more important to take possession of Lvov itself than to help 'others' to take Warsaw? For three or four days our general staff could not secure the execution of this order. Only after repeated demands, reinforced by threats, did the south-western command change direction, but by then the delay of several days had already played its fatal role. On 16 August the Poles took the counter-offensive and forced our troops to roll back. If Stalin and Voroshilov and the illiterate Budenny had not 'had their own war' in Galicia and the Red cavalry had been at Lublin in time, the Red Army would not have suffered the disaster.[35]

The whole concept of the march on Warsaw was a political mistake. After its failure Lenin said: 'Our offensive, our too swift advance almost as far as Warsaw, was undoubtedly a mistake.'[36] The Poles were bound to see in this invasion an attack by their hereditary enemies. Lenin was not one to hide his mistakes. He told Klara Zetkin:

> In the Red Army the Poles saw enemies, not brothers and liberators... The revolution in Poland which we counted on did not take place. The workers and peasants, deceived by Pilsudski and Daszynski, defended their class enemy and let our brave Red soldiers starve, ambushed them, and beat them to death... Radek predicted how it would turn out. He warned us. I was very angry and accused him of 'defeatism'... But he was right in his main contention.[37]

In retrospect Trotsky compared the difference between

himself and Lenin over the march on Warsaw with those over the Brest-Litovsk treaty, and he drew a sharp lesson from the mistakes made in both cases:

> In contrast with the Brest-Litovsk period, the roles had been completely reversed. *Then* it was I who demanded that the signing of the peace be delayed: that even at the price of losing some territory, we give the German proletariat time to understand the situation and get in its word. *Now* it was Lenin who demanded that our army continue its advance and give the Polish proletariat time to appraise the situation and rise up in arms. The Polish war confirmed from the opposite side what was demonstrated by the Brest-Litovsk war: that the events of war and those of the revolutionary mass movement are measured by different yardsticks. Where the action of armies is measured by days and weeks, the movement of masses of people is usually reckoned in months and years. If this difference in tempo is not taken fully into account, the gears of war will only break the teeth of the revolutionary gears, instead of setting them in motion. At any rate, that is what happened in the short Brest-Litovsk war and in the great Polish war. We passed over and beyond our own victory to a heavy defeat.[38]

Thus we have seen that Trotsky and Lenin disagreed on four strategic issues: the first the war against Kolchak on the eastern front, the second the war against Denikin on the southern front, the third the war against Iudenich outside Petrograd, and finally the march on Warsaw. On all except the first Trotsky was proved right. In passing, let us imagine what the Stalinists would have made of it had it been Trotsky who had suggested withdrawal from Petrograd. Clear proof of defeatism, even treason, they would have claimed. Whereas if Trotsky, not Lenin, had proposed the march on Warsaw, this would have been cited as evidence of the folly of the theory of permanent revolution and Trotsky's 'mad' 'Bonapartist' plans to export revolution by arms.

Chapter nine
The debate on military doctrine

AFTER the end of the civil war and the Polish campaign there was an ardent discussion on the military doctrines that the Red Army should adopt.

The question of military doctrine had been the subject of discussion in professional military circles as early as 1918 in the journal **Voennoe delo**. The journal tried to undertake a systematic study of the issue, but the immediate problems of the civil war prevented this. In 1920 it resumed the discussion, again at first amongst professional officers. But then the debate widened: the former Military Opposition joined the fray. At the Tenth Party Congress (March 1921), what became known as the 'single military doctrine' was first formulated by Mikhail Frunze, a former Tsarist NCO who had risen rapidly in the Red Army. He had been in command in Turkestan in 1919, and as commander of the southern front against Wrangel in the autumn of 1920 had gained high prestige for his victory. The theoretician of the group was Gusev. Belonging to the group were many of the former Military Opposition, including Voroshilov and Budenny.

The 'single military doctrine' reduced itself to the assertion, which had already been repeated continually in the preceding years, that there was a specifically Marxist, proletarian, revolutionary theory of military affairs. Since 'the working class will be compelled by the very course of the historical revolutionary process to pass over to the offensive against capital', it followed that this offensive must be the basis of the tactics of the Red Army.[1]

Trotsky proceeded to demolish this idea. In general the issue of military doctrine occupies an important place in the five volumes of his **How the Revolution Armed**, and he brought to this question a combination of creative originality and a broad historical standpoint. He had to fight on two fronts: against the advocates of proletarian military doctrine on the one hand and leaders of the Moscow Military Academy—professors, lecturers and old generals—on the other. The latter were so conservative as to view the civil war contemptuously, as if its experience was of no significance in contributing to any discussion of military doctrine. Trotsky criticised them for 'pedantic disdain for the military work that history is carrying on now'.

> You say... that... the present civil or small-scale war... has nothing to do with science, for science has, in general, nothing to do with all that. But I say to you, military specialist gentlemen, that this is an utterly ignorant statement...
> With the mobility and flexibility of its fronts, the civil war offers immense scope for real initiative and real military creativity, and that is where the whole problem lies— achieving maximum results with minimum expenditure of forces.

It is precisely the 1914-18 war that

> gave comparatively little scope for creativity, as was very soon revealed on the western front, in France. After that gigantic front had been established, between the Belgian coast and Switzerland, the war at once became automatic, with the art of strategy reduced to the minimum, and everything was staked on the card of mutual exhaustion —whereas our war, which is wholly an affair of mobility and maneouvres, presents opportunities for the greatest talent to be revealed in 'small-scale' war.[2]

While the old generals refused to learn the lessons of the civil war, the supporters of the 'proletarian military doctrine' refused to learn anything else. Their ambition was to create a brand new military doctrine, in the same way as others in the party leadership later wanted to produce 'proletarian culture' and 'proletarian literature'. The 'single military doctrine', they said, should fit the revolutionary mentality of the proletariat, it should disdain defensive and static warfare and adopt mobility and the offensive; only reactionary, decaying classes favoured defensive strategy.

The adherents of the 'proletarian doctrine of the offensive' theorised from their own experience of the civil war, in which rapid manoeuvre predominated.

Trotsky pointed out that the Red Army had learned manoeuvrability—now claimed as the exclusive creation of a revolutionary class—from the Whites. On 24 July 1919 he wrote:

> Newcomers to Marxism are trying to deduce from the aggressive psychology of the proletariat, in one breath, its military organisation and its class strategy. In doing so, alas, they fail to notice the fact that to the aggressive character of a class there does not always correspond a sufficient number of... cavalry horses.

On the other hand

> ...distrust of worker and peasant manpower, an abundance of experience, White-Guard-minded commanders and a comparatively plentiful supply of cavalry impelled the military leaders of the counter-revolution to take the road of light, mobile detachments and well-calculated guerrilla 'ventures'.

Just as the Red Army learned manoeuvrability from the Whites, so the latter borrowed methods of propaganda from the Reds. While the Red Army became more mobile over time, the White armies became less so:

> Having won certain successes, the White Guard generals are proceeding to conscript the peasants and even the workers, and to form a numerically imposing army—which will, naturally, lack mobility and manoeuvrability.
> ...it can be said that, as a result of the protracted civil war, the military methods of both camps are drawing closer together. While we are now giving very close attention to the creation of cavalry, the enemy, who long since followed our example by carrying out mass conscription, has begun to form his own political departments, agitational centres and agitational trains.[3]

The similarities between the manoeuvrability of armies in the Russian civil war and those in the American civil war, said Trotsky, are a proof that manoeuvrability is not derived from the class nature of the proletariat but from the nature of the terrain.[4] The fact that the Red Army is the weapon of a new class does not denote the establishment of a new military doctrine. Military doctrines cannot be reduced to politics alone:

> I said that politics rules over military affairs. That is undoubtedly the case, but if anyone thinks that politics can 'replace' military matters, he is very much mistaken. Politics rules over literature, over art, but politics does not replace literature and art. Politics rules in the sense that it reflects class ideology—it penetrates everything and compels everything, from guns to literary verses, to serve this class ideology: but that does not mean that if I know the politics of the working class I can make a gun or write lyrics. For that, one has to have talent and training, to know the laws of prosody, and so on. In order to follow the military vocation, one has to know the laws of military affairs and to know military technique...
>
> Military affairs constitute an independent sphere which lives by creative analysis, investigation of mistakes, correction of mistakes and development of accumulated knowledge.

And Trotsky poked fun at the ignoramuses who

> think that politics 'replaces' everything else, and that with this talisman in our hand we shall be able to open all doors.[5]

The dilettante strategists, who resented being told that they were ignorant and had to learn—especially from the hated former Tsarist generals, were livid at Trotsky's words.

In building the Red Army, Trotsky argued, the Bolsheviks had to combine the new and the old, to combine working-class experience with the traditions and experiences of the old armies. In an article whose title was quite insulting to the amateur 'proletarian strategist': 'Military Doctrine or Pseudo-Military Doctrinairism', Trotsky explained that from the beginning of the Red Army there had been comrades who had argued that everything should be new, different to what existed in the old army. But there was nothing of substance in their 'originality':

> As a matter of fact, the noisy innovators were themselves wholly captives of the old military doctrine. They merely tried

to put a minus sign wherever previously there was a plus. All their independent thinking came down just to that.

Actually, in creating the Red Army, the Bolsheviks had

> proceeded along a different path. We tried, especially in the beginning, to make maximum possible use of the habits, usages, knowledge and means retained from the past, and we were quite unconcerned about the extent to which the new army would differ from the old, in the formally organisational and technical sense, or, on the contrary, would resemble it. We built the army out of the human and technical material ready to hand...[6]

One should avoid, in military doctrine as in everything else, either accepting that 'nothing is new under the sun', or that everything is completely new, that the present has no connection to the past.

The proponents of proletarian military doctrine simply turned the 'eternal truths' of 'military science' inside out, but Trotsky poked fun at all these 'eternal truths':

> If... we check the inventory of eternal truths of military science, we obtain not much more than a few logical axioms and Euclidian postulates. Flanks must be protected, means of communication must be secured, the blow must be struck at the enemy's least defended point, etc. All these truths, in this all-embracing formulation, go far beyond the limits of the art of war. The donkey that steals oats from a torn sack (the enemy's least defended point) and vigilantly turns its crupper away from the side from which danger may be expected to come, acts thus in accordance with the eternal principles of military science. Yet it is unquestionable that this donkey munching oats has never read Clausewitz...
>
> War... is a social and historical phenomenon which arises, develops, changes its forms and must eventually disappear. For this reason alone war cannot have any eternal laws. But the subject of war is man, who possesses certain fixed anatomical and mental traits from which are derived certain usages and habits. Man operates in a specific and comparatively stable geographical setting. Thus, in all wars, in all ages and among all peoples, there have obtained certain common features, relatively stable but by no means absolute.

Based on these features, an art of war has developed historically. Its methods and usages undergo change, together with the social conditions which govern it (technology, class structure, forms of state power).[7]

Military science or art?

The whole argument put forward by the protagonists of proletarian military doctrine was based on a false premise: they believed that there was or would be a military science; in fact war, said Trotsky, was not a science at all, but an art.

> There is not, and never has been, a military 'science'. There are a whole number of sciences on which the soldier's trade is based. Essentially, these include all the sciences, from geography to psychology. A great military commander must necessarily know the basic elements of many sciences... War is based on many sciences, but war itself is not a science, it is a practical art, a skill...
> War cannot be turned into a science, because of its very nature, just as one cannot turn architecture, commerce or the work of a veterinary surgeon, and so on, into sciences. What people call the theory of war, or military science, is not a totality of scientific laws, which explain objective phenomena, but a totality of practical procedures, methods of adaptation and knacks which correspond to a specific task, that of crushing the enemy.[8]

Frunze and company argued that proletarian military science was derived from Marxism. However, this gave Marxism too much honour and too much insult by transforming it into a supra-historical science:

> Attempts to proclaim Marxism the method of all sciences and arts often serve as cover for a stubborn aversion from entering new fields: it is, after all, much, much easier to possess a *passe-partout*, that is, a key which opens all doors and locks, than to study book-keeping, military affairs, and so on... This is the greatest danger when people try to endow the Marxist method with such an absolute character...
> Marxism can be applied with very great success even to the history of chess. But it is not possible to learn to play chess

in a Marxist way. With the aid of Marxism we can establish that there was once an Oblomov-like nobility who were too lazy even to play chess, and that later, with the growth of towns, intellectuals and merchants appeared who felt the need to exercise their brains by playing draughts and chess. And now, in our country, workers go to chess clubs. The workers play chess because they have thrown off those who used to ride on their backs. All this can be excellently explained by Marxism. One can show the entire course of the class struggle from the angle of the history of the development of chess. I assert that one could, using Marx's method, write an excellent book on the history of the development of chess. However, to learn to play chess 'according to Marx' is altogether impossible, just as it is impossible to learn to wage war 'according to Marx'.[9]

The sad thing was that the new self-educated and half-educated military *cadres* preaching the 'proletarian military doctrine' were trying above all to be original: they had the

urge to say 'something new'. This is like someone who, because he appreciates original people, sets himself the task of becoming an original person: nothing would come of that, of course, except the most pathetic monkey-tricks.[10]

Trotsky did not pull his punches or defer to the sensibilities of the members of the Military Opposition, but his arguments did not convince many of the former NCOs, old Bolsheviks, who now commanded large army units. He merely put their backs up. His sharpness only insulted them. The shallowness and vagueness of the 'single military doctrine' was for them a source of emotional strength rather than weakness.

As already mentioned, the specific feature of proletarian military strategy according to Frunze and company was its aggressiveness. Trotsky comments on this:

The attempt to build a doctrine on this foundation appears all the more one-sided in view of the fact that during the epoch preceding the world war the strategy of the offensive was cultivated in the by no means revolutionary general staffs and military academies of nearly all the major countries of Europe. Contrary to what Comrade Frunze writes, the offensive was (and formally still remains to this day) the official doctrine of the French Republic.[11]

In any case, the mechanical juxtaposition of offensive to defensive strategy was mistaken. What was necessary was to grasp the dialectical relation between the two:

> It is precisely in a war of manoeuvre that the distinction between offensive and defensive is wiped out to an extraordinary degree.

Thus, during the civil war,

> *while taking the offensive* on one front, considered by us at a given moment as being the most important, for political or military reasons, we weakened ourselves on the other fronts, considering it possible to remain on the defensive there and to *retreat*. But, you see, what this shows is, precisely, the fact —how strange that this is overlooked!—that into our overall operational plans retreat entered, side by side with attack, as an indispensible link.
>
> ...there are strategic retreats due to an endeavour either to preserve manpower intact, or to shorten the front, or to lure the enemy in deeper, all the more surely to crush him. And if a strategical retreat is legitimate, then it is wrong to reduce all strategy to the offensive.[12]

Frunze, Budenny and company argued that the proletarian character of the leaders of the Red Army caused them to have much more initiative than the military leaders of the capitalist armies during the First World War, and this proved the superiority of 'proletarian military strategy'. Trotsky retorted:

> Comrade Budenny explained the positional character of the imperialist war as being due to the absence of great initiative, the irresolution of the leaders. 'There was no commander of genius!'... In my opinion this explanation is wrong. The crux of the matter is this, that the imperialist war was a war not of armies but of nations, and of the richest nations, huge in numbers and with huge material resources. It was a war to the death. To every blow the opposing side found an answer. Every hole was blocked. The front was steadily consolidated on both sides: artillery, shells, men were piled up both on this

side and on that. The task thus transcended the bounds of strategy. The war was transformed into a most profound process of measuring strength, one side against the other, in every direction. Neither aircraft, nor submarines, nor tanks, nor cavalry could by themselves produce a decisive result: they serve only as means for gradually exhausting the enemy's forces and constantly checking on his condition —was he still standing firm, or was he ready to collapse? This was in the fullest sense of the word a war of attrition, in which strategy is not of decisive but only of auxiliary importance.[13]

The tendency of Frunze and company to raise the experience of the civil war into a dogma was most damaging. The Red commanders did not escape the usual trap for successful generals—that of visualising the next war in terms of the last:

> The endeavour to fix as laws and erect into dogmas those features of the Red Army's strategy and tactics which were characteristic of it in the recent period could do a great deal of harm and could even prove fatal. It is possible to say in advance that operations by the Red Army on the continent of Asia—if they are destined to take place there—would of necessity be profoundly manoeuvring in character. Cavalry would have to play the most important, and in some cases the one and only role. On the other hand, however, there can be no doubt that military operations in the western theatre would be far more constrained. Operations conducted in territory with a different national composition and more densely populated, with a higher ratio between the number of troops and the given territory, would undoubtedly make the war more positional in character and would, in any case, confine freedom to manoeuvre within incomparably narrower limits.[14]

The case of Tukhachevsky

Tukhachevsky, the most gifted of the Military Opposition, insisted more emphatically than anyone else on the specifically proletarian military doctrine permeating strategy, tactics and organisation. Being of a more modern outlook than his colleagues, Tukhachevsky saw the future of the offensive—so crucial to proletarian military strategy—as conducted by means of mass formations of tanks and armoured vehicles co-operating with air forces. His offensive doctrine was associated with the idea that the Red Army's mission was to carry the proletarian revolution to other countries. Tukhachevsky was very much influenced by the Napoleonic tradition of 'revolution from without'.

The war with Poland, although it failed, still fuelled Tukhachevsky's enthusiasm for exporting the revolution on the points of bayonets. At the height of the operation against Poland, on 18 July 1920, Tukhachevsky wrote to Zinoviev, as president of the Communist International, about his new ideas:

> Considering the inevitability of a world civil war in the very near future, we must now set up the general staff of the Comintern...
>
> To avoid those difficulties and crudities, from which we suffered at the creation of our Red Army, it is vital to work out beforehand a plan for the mobilisation of the working class, worker Red officers must be trained in advance, both senior combat chiefs and staff workers must be prepared beforehand.
>
> ...It is essential for us in Soviet Russia to open a series of military instruction centres and academies of the general staff to train command staff from workers and Communists of all nationalities in their languages.
>
> It seems to me that the situation permits of no delay in this undertaking.[15]

Trotsky retorted:

> [Tukhachevsky] writes that the time has come for the Comintern to set up an international general staff. Neither more nor less! An international general staff! What's that? The Communist International is the political organisation which unites the national Communist Parties. When did the International become a possibility? When, alongside the Russian Communist Party, there appeared the German and other Communist Parties. Well, and when would a common general staff become possible? When, alongside the government of the Russian proletariat, other proletarian governments have arisen. Then and only then will it be possible to speak seriously of a common general staff, in the

military sense of the word. But, you know, this necessary pre-condition is not present!

Moreover, Trotsky argued, the policy of the Russian, as well as the other Communist parties at present, was based not on an offensive but on a retreat:

> we are now at the stage of retreat and preparation. What about our concessions to foreign capitalists? What about our recognition of the Tsarist debts? Are these, perhaps, elements in an offensive? No, they are elements of compromise and preparation... If we were now in a position to take the offensive, we should not have recognised the Tsarist debts. Concessions, the New Economic Policy, recognition of the Tsarist debts, and, along with all that, offensive war: why, it would make a cat laugh!
>
> ...What are we doing now in the military field? We are carrying out a general demobilisation. It is astonishing how inconsistent some comrades are in their thinking...
>
> ...We are demobilising because we are not at present going to fight, and, consequently, we are not going to launch an offensive. This is what we say to the workers and peasants: we have no war at present, there are no fronts, we are not going to attack anyone, and so we are demobilising.[16]

Nor did an offensive correspond to the strategy of the Comintern:

> The idea of a revolutionary offensive war can be linked with the idea of an international proletarian offensive. But is this the current slogan of the Comintern? No: we have put forward and are upholding the idea of the workers' united front, of joint actions even with the parties of the Second International, who do not want revolution—on the basis of defending the current vital interests of the proletariat, because these are being threatened on all sides by the aggressive bourgeoisie.

Of course one should not be dogmatic in opposing the offensive:

> But surely we can't renounce the idea of the political offensive in general? Of course not! We are not in the least intending to renounce the world proletarian revolution and victory over the bourgeoisie on the international scale. We should be

traitors like the gentlemen of the Second and Two-and-a-half Internationals if we were to renounce the revolutionary offensive. We are renouncing nothing, dear comrades; but all in good time. Without an offensive victory is impossible. But only a simpleton supposes that the whole of political tactics is reducible to the slogan—'Forward!'[17]

Furthermore, Trotsky argued, the social composition of the Red Army made the doctrine of the offensive absurd: to train the Red Army composed predominantly of peasants for an offensive war to support a world proletarian revolution was fanciful in the extreme.

Moreover, it would be disastrous for the Red Army to adopt Napoleonic offensive doctrine. First of all France, at the beginning of the nineteenth century, was the most civilised and technically advanced country on the continent, while Russia was one of the most backward countries in Europe. Secondly, the role of the proletariat, as the subject of history, did not at all fit in with revolution 'from without', imposed by an invading army. The proletariat had to be active in its own revolution; the mass of the people had played a relatively passive role in Napoleon's wars of conquest.

The armed militia

The tradition of the Marxist movement, including the Bolsheviks, was one of opposition to the standing army and advocacy of its replacement by a people's militia. Thus Lenin, in his **Letters from Afar**, written in Switzerland in March 1917, had called for a workers' militia that

> must, firstly, embrace the entire people, must be a mass organisation to the degree of being *universal*, must really embrace the *entire* able-bodied population of both sexes; secondly, it must proceed to combine not only purely police, but general state functions with military functions and with the control of social production and distribution.[18]

On 20 April (3 May) 1917, Lenin wrote: 'The workers do not want an army standing apart from the people; what they want is that the workers and soldiers should *merge* into a single militia consisting of all the people.'[19]

Unfortunately, in the conditions of Russia after October 1917, the militia was not feasible. First, the working class was a tiny minority, and if the army were to be built of militias recruited on a territorial principle the majority of its units would have been purely peasant in composition. This would have denied the leadership to the proletariat and would have made the army units unstable and unreliable. Secondly, the backwardness of the transport system would have made it impossible to move the militia units to the front in time. Russia's backwardness dictated to the Red Army principles of organisation that were very similar to those of the Tsarist army. The difference between the two was in the social and political leadership and outlook, not in the main in their structures.

But Trotsky never lost the vision of moving towards the militia system. The Eighth Congress of the party (March 1919) adopted Trotsky's theses on the future transition to the militia system, and the Ninth Congress (March 1920) endorsed this decision. Trotsky's 'Theses on going over to the Militia System', written on 28 February 1920, state:

> To the present period of transition, which may last for a long time, must correspond an organisation of our armed forces such that the working people acquire the necessary military training with the least possible distraction from productive labour. This system can only be a Red Workers' and Peasants' Militia constructed on territorial principles...
> In their territorial distribution the militia units (regiments, brigades, divisions) must coincide with the territorial layout of industry in order that the industrial centres, together with the agricultural peripheries which surround them and gravitate towards them, may constitute the basis for the militia units.

The immediate task was to move gradually towards the militia system:

> As the Red Army is gradually demobilised, its best *cadres* must be allocated territorially in the most expedient fashion, that is, most closely adapted to local conditions of production and way of life, so as to ensure that there is an apparatus ready to administer the militia units.

...Going over to the militia system must inevitably be a gradual process in conformity with the military and international diplomatic situation of the Soviet Republic...[20]

The programme of moving toward the militia system aroused considerable criticism, especially from the military specialists. One of Trotsky's critics was General Svechin, the author of a standard work on strategy and professor of the Military Academy. Against Svechin's conservative critique Trotsky defended the revolutionary tradition of the militia. In an article entitled 'The Militia Programme and its Academic Critic', dated 5 August 1919, Trotsky wrote:

If Professor Svechin thinks that the Communist Party has taken power in order to replace the tricolour barracks [the tricolour was the flag of Tsarist Russia] by a red one, that means that he has not mastered very well the [Communist Party programme]...

The objection that under a militia system the command would not enjoy proper authority strikes one by its political blindness. Has the authority of the present command of the Red Army been established in barracks?... A commander's authority is based today not on the statutory hypnosis of the barracks, but on the authority of the Soviet power and the Communist Party. Professor Svechin has simply overlooked the revolution and the enormous spiritual upheaval it has brought about in the Russian working man. To him the ignorant, drunken mercenary, poxed and numbed by Catholicism, who served in Wallenstein's camp, the Parisian apprentice who, led by journalists and lawyers, destroyed the Bastille in 1789, the Saxon worker and member of the Social Democratic Party in the period of the imperialist war, and the Russian proletarian who, for the first time in world history, took power—all these are to him more or less the same cannon-fodder to be meticulously moulded in the barracks. But isn't that a mockery of the history of mankind?

The revolutionary spiritual growth of the masses would be the foundation for the militia and the Communist social order:

The development of the Communist order will run parallel with the growth in the spiritual stature of the broadest masses of the people. What the party gave in the past, mainly to an advanced section of the workers, will be given increasingly to the entire people by the actual organisation of society, with all its internal relationships. If the party has in this sense 'replaced' the barracks, so that it has given its members the necessary cohesion and made them capable of self-sacrificing collective struggle, communist society will be able to do this on an incomparably vaster scale and higher level. The corporate spirit, in the broad sense, is the spirit of collectivism. It is fostered not only in barracks but in a well-ordered school, especially one which is connected with physical labour. It is fostered by the cooperative principle of labour. It is fostered by broad, purposefully organised sport... the militia will be infinitely richer in 'corporate' spirit, and this will be a spirit of much higher quality, than is the case with barracks-bred regiments.[21]

However Trotsky's dream of moving from a standing army to a militia was not to be realised. The peasant upheavals of 1920 and 1921 made it impossible to move to a territorially based army. This was explained clearly by Trotsky himself in a speech on 17 February 1921:

> Let us take the territorial principle. This has both positive and negative aspects. But they have to be examined in relation to the given conditions. If, in our economic construction, we had attained a state of affairs in which the workers and peasants were well fed, the peasants had a sufficient quantity of nails, calico, and so on, the territorial principle would possess, for us, only its positive aspect... But if, in a given locality, there is antagonism, enmity, this cohesion may be turned against the government. In the country districts, where revolts are taking place in which a considerable section of the peasants are involved, peasants who are suffering from want and deprivation, such cohesion may be turned against the military system—and not just against a militia system but against any other. We have to take all this into account.

Trotsky's conclusion was that it was necessary to be very cautious about moving to the militia system:

> The whole problem lies in the proportion in which we are to

go over to the militia system. Shall we say that we will now disband forty or fifty divisions, leaving ten or twenty; or, on the contrary, shall we keep forty or fifty divisions while at the same time setting about the creation of five or three militia divisions? that is how the practical problem presents itself. I think that we should begin with the minimum... then, shall we begin by creating three or five divisions? I think it would be more correct to start with three: in Petrograd, in Moscow and in the Urals... We ought to take as our basis three areas, the most favourable ones, with the biggest percentage of workers.[22]

The Tenth Party Congress (March 1921) devoted three closed sessions to military matters. In its resolution the fundamental attitude to the militia was not changed, but the idea of an immediate transition to a militia was put on ice.[23]

In fact, a full militia brigade was organised only in Petrograd. Again and again the backwardness of Russia and its encirclement by hostile capitalist powers blocked the achievement of Trotsky's dreams.

Chapter ten

The Red Army and the rise of the Stalinist bureaucracy

THE WAR dominated Soviet life. The whole of the economy during the years of civil war was subordinated completely to the needs of the army. The Council of Workers' and Peasants' Defence, chaired by Lenin, was set up to organise the economy for war. It was vested with 'full plenary powers in the matter of mobilising the human and material resources of the country in the interests of defence. The decisions of the Defence Council are unconditionally obligatory upon all agencies and institutions, central and local, and all citizens.' The decree placed all workers in transport, food supply and the war industries under conditions of strict military discipline and made the unification of administration in these fields the central concern of the Defence Council. Trotsky explains:

> The War Department determined the government work of the entire country. All the other governmental activity was subsidiary to it. After it in importance came the Commissariat of Supplies. Industry worked chiefly for war. All the other departments and institutions were subjected to constant contraction or reduction and some were even completely closed.[1]

In 1919, 40.4 per cent of the published enactments of the government were devoted entirely to military matters, 13.1 per cent to food supplies, 10.1 per cent to transport, and 8.1 per cent to industry, while the remaining 28.3 per cent covered fields as diverse as posts and telegraphs, health, finance, agriculture and education.[2]

The Red Army took the dominant share of all industrial and

agricultural supplies. In summer 1920 the army was taking the following proportions of the country's centralised supplies:[3]

Flour	25 per cent	Groats	50
Feedstuffs	40	Fish	60
Meat	60	Dried fruit	90
Sugar	60	Salt	15
Fats	40	Soap	40
Tobacco	100	Matches	20
Footwear	90	Cotton material	40
Other textiles	70-100		

The hierarchical structure of the Red Army, rising on a heterogeneous social base of which the atomised peasantry made up the overwhelming majority, undoubtedly strengthened bureaucratic tendencies. The strength of a bureaucracy in any organisation is in inverse proportion to the cohesion and strength of the rank and file.

By a mixture of popular support, revolutionary ardour and firm will, the Whites were beaten. But the price paid was enormous. People make history, but in conditions not of their own choosing. In the process they change both the circumstances and themselves. The exigencies of building a disciplined army out of an often indifferent peasant mass inculcated into many of the best party members authoritarian habits. It was in the Red Army, more than in any other arm of the state, that party democracy gave way to the completely bureaucratic, non-elective principle.

On 25 October 1918 it was decided to abolish completely the elected party committees in the army above the level of the party cell.[4] The decline of party democracy in the army went so far that Gusev could write in January 1919:

> party organisation in the army remodels itself along military lines and, as with the army, democratic centralism is replaced by military centralism. Instead of elections, appointment; in the place of resolutions, orders and reports. Party organisations lose all their 'political rights'. They retain one right alone, the right to work, to carry out 'without exception' the orders and instructions of the political department.[5]

The Central Political Administration, abbreviated to PUR, subordinated to the Revolutionary War Council of the Republic, of which Trotsky was the chairman, had complete control over all political work inside the army, in particular the right to make all appointments and enforce all party decisions. PUR had the power to transfer people from one section or job to another. It had jurisdiction over the political commissars.

Generally during the civil war both military and civilian administrators were transferred from one place or job to another in order to deal with the constant state of emergency. A special bureau, the Records and Assignment Department of the Central Committee (Uchraspred) was responsible for the distribution of *cadres* according to the requirements of the state.

The Red Army spearheaded the most extreme forms of bureaucratic centralism. Accordingly, at the Eighth Party Congress, V Osinsky accused Trotsky of 'implanting bureaucracy under the flag of militarisation... within our civilian apparatus there is an organic gravitation towards military methods of operation'.[6] Because of the heterogeneous composition of the Red Army—an overwhelming majority of peasants with a minority of proletarians, a combination of former Tsarist officers with Communist commissars—an iron ring was needed to hold these contradictory elements together; this strengthened bureaucracy in the army.

As the army reflects society, in more extreme forms and in both its weaknesses and its strengths, Trotsky was perceptive when he wrote:

> nearly all, if not all, the questions of principle and the difficulties of Soviet constructive work arose before us first and foremost in the sphere of military affairs—and, in extremely hard, concise and compact form. In this sphere, as a general rule, no respite was allowed us. Illusions and errors brought with them almost immediate retribution. The most responsible decisions were taken under fire.[7]

The civil war itself, by making the speedy resolution of immediate problems essential, led to increasing centralisation of government decisions and to the decline of local *soviets*. It also led to increasing fusion of state and party, and to increasing centralisation of decision-making in the party itself. At the centre the central committee was more and more replaced by the politburo and orgburo. Thus, in the eight months beginning April

1919, the central committee met at five or six-week intervals, instead of fortnightly as the party rules required, whereas the politburo met on average every five days, and the orgburo every second day.[8] The party secretariat multiplied its tentacles, as can be seen from the number of people it employed: this rose from 15 in March 1919 to 80 in December 1919, then to 150 by March 1920.[9]

It was no accident that Stalin was attracted to the military field, as Trotsky explained: 'The front attracted him, because here for the first time he could work with the most finished of all the administrative machines, the military machine.'[10] The Red Army rose above society and dominated it. Because the proletariat was a minority in the country the Red Army during the civil war, to use Gusev's words, had to 'look at itself as a foreign invader, an occupier who has seized an enemy nation, in which a significant part of the population is decidedly hostile to the invader.'[11]

In retrospect, Trotsky emphasised the crucial role of the Red Army in the formation of the bureaucracy. Thus he wrote in 1936:

> The demobilisation of the Red Army of five million played no small role in the formation of the bureaucracy. The victorious commanders assumed leading posts in the local *soviets*, in economy, in education, and they persistently introduced everywhere that regime which ensured success in the civil war. Thus on all sides the masses were pushed away gradually from actual participation in the leadership of the country.[12]

The number of soldiers in the Red Army, 5,498,000 on 1 October 1920, had fallen to 566,517 by 1 October 1923.

It was not the intrinsic nature of Bolshevism, neither its revolutionary Marxist ideology nor its democratic centralist form of organisation, that led to the rise of bureaucracy, but the objective conditions of the civil war. To quote Trotsky's words of 1940:

> The three years of civil war laid an indelible impress on the Soviet government itself by virtue of the fact that very many of the administrators, a considerable layer of them, had become accustomed to command and demand unconditional submission to their orders. Those theoreticians who attempt

to prove that the present totalitarian regime of the USSR is due not to such historical conditions, but to the very nature of Bolshevism itself, forget that the civil war did not proceed from the nature of Bolshevism, but rather from the efforts of the Russian and the international bourgeoisie to overthrow the Soviet regime. There is no doubt that Stalin, like many others, was moulded by the environment and circumstances of the civil war, along with the entire group that led him to establish his personal dictatorship—Ordzhonikidze, Voroshilov, Kaganovich—and a whole layer of workers and peasants [who were] raised to the status of commanders and administrators.[13]

The Red Army played a crucial role in the rise of the Stalinist faction that was later to be dominant in the bureaucracy. We have seen how a number of prominent army people collected around Stalin. After the end of the civil war they assumed significant positions in the party. At the Tenth Congress of the party (March 1921) Frunze, Voroshilov, Ordzhonikidze, Iaroslavsky, Mikhailov, Komarov, Tuntul, Molotov and Petrovsky, all associated with Stalin, were elected to the central committee. Gusev, Kuibyshev, Kirov and Chubar, also associated with Stalin, became its new candidate members. At the Eleventh and Twelfth Party Congresses the strength of Stalin's supporters in the central committee increased further. During the Lenin levy in 1924 nearly 4000 Red Army officers were brought into the party, thus strengthening the power of the Stalinist faction.

The *cadres* of the Stalinist faction consisted of self-educated and half-educated people. The psychology of the Stalinist bureaucracy at the time when they adopted the theory of 'socialism in one country' had already been demonstrated during the civil war in their bragging, ignorance, bluff and bluster. 'We can do anything'—this was the theme of the 'proletarian military doctrine'. They thrived in the cultural backwardness of the country. Pseudo-Marxist rejection of bourgeois specialists and bourgeois culture were a cover for their own lack of culture. These were the foundations for the national 'messianism', in which the bureaucracy saw itself as the embodiment both of Russia and of the communist future.

The full significance of the early formative phases of the

bureaucracy in the Red Army, as well as of the proto-Stalinist faction, became apparent in the light of much later developments. It was the tragic fate of Trotsky that in the Red Army, which was one of his greatest achievements, the seeds were sown of his future isolation and defeat.

Chapter eleven

War Communism at an impasse

THE IMPACT of the civil war on the economy was drastic. With the extreme scarcity of resources the Soviet government had to impose the strictest centralised control over every aspect of the economy. Industry was transformed into a supply organisation of the Red Army.

The civil war tore apart the Russian economy. The main industrial regions of northern and central Russia remained under Soviet rule throughout the civil war, but the factories in these regions and the railway system depended on sources of raw materials and fuel that were often cut off for long periods. The engineering industry of Petrograd, Briansk, Tula and other towns needed coal from the Donets Basin and iron from the Urals and the Ukraine. The Urals region was lost from summer 1918 until summer 1919, when Kolchak was driven back into Siberia. The Donets Basin was completely cut off from the German occupation of the Ukraine in spring 1918 until the retreat of Denikin's army in the latter months of 1919 (with the exception of a brief period early in 1919 when part of it was held by the Soviets). Baku oil was lost from the time the Turks occupied Baku in summer 1918 until the Red Army entered it in spring 1920. The secondary oil source in Grozny in the North Caucasus was cut off by Denikin.

The textile mills of Moscow and the ring of factory towns around it depended on cotton from Turkestan, but Turkestan was also cut off, first as a result of the Czechoslovak troops' onslaught on the Volga in the summer of 1918, and later, until the latter part of 1919, by Kolchak's advance. By that time the peasants of Turkestan had largely given up planting cotton, substituting crops that would give them something to eat.

The foreign blockade dealt another serious blow to Soviet Russia's industry:[1]

	Imports	Exports
1913	936.6	1472.1
1917	178.0	59.6
1918	11.5	1.8
1919	0.5	0.0
1920	5.2	0.7

(in million *pud*, where one *pud* = 16.4 kg = 36 lb)

A shortage of raw materials, fuel and food combined to bring a disastrous fall in industrial productivity. Starvation or semi-starvation gravely affected workers' efficiency. According to approximate calculations, the gross product per Russian worker changed as follows:[2]

Productivity per worker (in stable *rubles*)

1913	100	-
1917	85	100
1918	44	52
1919	22	25
1920	26	30

Absenteeism reached unprecedented levels. It was sometimes as high as 60 per cent, and commonly exceeded 30 per cent.[3] The average rate of absenteeism before the war had been about 10 per cent. In 1920 absenteeism in the best 'shock' plants increased threefold. In the Sormovsky plant it reached 36 per cent in July; in August it dropped to 32 per cent. At the Briansk plant it was 40 per cent during the winter months and rose to 48.5 per cent in June and to 50 per cent in August. At the Tver plant it was 44 per cent during July and August.[4]

The physical exhaustion of workers brought about by undernourishment was a major cause of the decline of labour productivity.[5] Workers were so wretchedly fed that it was not uncommon for them to faint at the workbench. It was an act of heroism to work at all. The labour front demanded no less fortitude than the military front.

Large-scale industry had suffered a catastrophic decline. By 1917 the destruction of war had already reduced production to

77 per cent of the level in 1913. This fell in the following year to 35 per cent, then to 26 per cent in 1919 and 18 per cent in 1920.[6] After the army had taken its share of the shrinking industrial output, little remained for the peasantry. The economic connection between industry and agriculture, between town and country, was therefore broken.

The collapse of industry and the violent suppression of commercial relations between town and country meant that the exchange of grain and industrial goods that took place was not a real exchange. While the better-off peasantry supplied the majority of the grain, the poor peasantry got the industrial goods. As Kritzman said: 'The state exchange of products was... not so much an exchange between industry and agriculture, as an exchange of industrial products against the services that the poor peasants gave in the extraction of products from the farms of the well-to-do layers of the village'.[7]

Hunger, epidemics and cold

Hunger stalked the towns. One result was a massive flight of the population to the countryside. The urban population, and particularly the number of industrial workers, declined sharply between 1917 and 1920. By the autumn of 1920 the population of forty provincial capitals had declined since 1917 by 33 per cent, from 6,400,000 to 4,300,000, and the population of fifty other large towns by 16 per cent, from 1,517,000 to 1,271,000. The larger the city the greater the decline. The population of Petrograd fell from 2,400,000 in 1917 to 574,000 by August 1920.

In the footsteps of hunger came epidemics, above all typhus. The following is the number of typhus victims in European Russia each year, in thousands:

1914	83	1918	180
1915	90	1919	2105
1916	102	1920	3114
1917	88		

So in two years more than *five million* people fell ill with typhus.[8]

Deaths from typhus alone in the years 1918-20 numbered 1.6 million, while typhoid, dysentry and cholera claimed another 700,000.[9] All told, the number of premature deaths is estimated for the period 1 January 1918 to 1 July 1920 at *seven million*, that is, 7 per cent of the total population.[10]

This estimate does not cover the peripheral areas of Russia such as Siberia and the south-east. If these were included the number of premature deaths must have been more than nine million. This far surpasses the number of those who died fighting during the civil war, which is estimated at about 350,000.

Trotsky: Proponent of the New Economic Policy

From the end of 1919 Trotsky devoted only minimal attention to military affairs. Instead he became absorbed in the problems of the economy. In February 1920 it became clear to him that War Communism had exhausted itself, that agriculture, and with it everything else, had arrived at a blind alley. He spent the winter months of 1919-20 in the Urals directing economic work. In February 1920 he sent a memorandum to the central committee:

> The present policy of the requisition of food products... is lowering agricultural production, bringing about the atomisation of the industrial proletariat and threatens to disorganise completely the economic life of the country.

As a fundamental practical measure Trotsky proposed:

> To replace the requisitioning of the surpluses by a levy proportionate to the quantity of production (a sort of progressive income tax) and set up in such a manner that it is nevertheless more profitable to increase the acreage sown or to cultivate it better.[11]

Lenin came out firmly against Trotsky's proposal and it was rejected in the central committee by eleven votes to four.[12] These facts were stated by Trotsky without challenge at the Tenth Party Congress.[13]

Lenin continued to oppose any move to replace requisitioning of grain by a tax in kind. In the summer of 1920, when he read a remark by Varga, inspired by the experience of the Hungarian revolution, that 'requisitions do not lead to the goal since they bring in their train a decrease of production', he put two question marks beside it.[14] A few months later, beside a statement in Bukharin's **The Economics of the Transition Period** that coercion of the peasantry was not to be regarded as 'pure constraint', since it 'lies on the path of general economic development', Lenin wrote 'very good'.[15]

As late as December 1920 Lenin still supported compulsory requisitioning. As he said to the Eighth Congress of the *soviets* on 22 December 1920: 'In a country of small peasants our chief and basic task is to be able to resort to state compulsion in order to raise the level of peasant farming.'[16]

It was indeed very late in the day—one year after Trotsky —that Lenin came to the conclusion that War Communism had entered a *cul-de-sac*. On 8 February 1921, in a politburo discussion on the agrarian question, Lenin wrote the draft of a thesis which stated:

1) Satisfy the wish of the non-party peasants for the substitution of a tax in kind for the surplus appropriation system (the confiscation of surplus grain stocks).
2) Reduce the size of this tax as compared with last year's appropriation rate.
3) Approve the principle of making the tax commensurate with the farmer's effort, reducing the rate for those making greater effort.
4) Give the farmer more leeway in using his after-tax surpluses in local trade, provided his tax is promptly paid up in full.[17]

Thus it is clear how false was the Stalinist myth that Trotsky was the enemy of the peasants in opposition to Lenin, the father of the New Economic Policy (NEP).

Trotsky's bold foresight condemned him to political solitude. At the Ninth Congress of the party, meeting in March 1920, one month after he had written the above memorandum, he did not put forward his suggestion that grain requisitioning be replaced by a tax in kind and free trade in grain be allowed. Indeed he did not even hint at it. On the contrary, as a disciplined Bolshevik, he appeared at the congress as the government's chief policy-maker and expounded a plan for the next phase of War Communism.

Labour armies

With the end of the civil war in sight, Trotsky posed the question: what was to be done with the soldiers? General demobilisation, he thought, would add to the decay of the economy. Keeping the soldiers idle was a waste. So he adopted the idea of labour armies.

On 10 January 1920 Matiiasevich, commander-in-chief of the Third Army, and Gaevsky, a member of the military revolutionary council of the Third Army, sent a memorandum to Lenin and Trotsky suggesting that armies not needed for military activity should be transformed into labour armies.

> With the aim in mind of achieving the swiftest possible re-establishment and organisation of the economy throughout the Urals and in the Ekaterinburg, Cheliabinsk and Tobolsk *guberniias*, the military revolutionary council of the Third Army recommends that:
>
> All the effectives and resources of the Third Red Army be applied to the re-establishment of transport and the organisation of the economy in the above-named areas.
>
> The Third Red Army of the eastern front be renamed the First Revolutionary Labour Army of the RSFSR...
>
> The main task of the Revolutionary Labour Army is the restoration of the national economy in the shortest possible time by means of the wide utilisation of mass operations and by means of putting into effect a general labour mobilisation.[18]

Lenin replied to the message two days later: 'I fully support your recommendation. I welcome the initiative. I will submit the question to the Council of People's Commissars.'[19] The council set up a commission to put it into practice.

On 15 January 1920 Trotsky issued an 'Order-Memorandum about the Third Red Army—First Revolutionary Labour Army':

> Conscious of its duty... the Third [Red] Army does not want to waste its time. During the weeks and months of the breathing-spell, however long this may be, it will use its forces and means to revive the economy of the country. While retaining its military strength... it will transform itself into a revolutionary labour army...
>
> The hungry workers of Petrograd, Moscow, Ivanovo-Voznesensk, the Urals and all other industrial centres and regions need food. The main task of the First Revolutionary Army is to collect, in a planned way, all surplus supplies of

grain, meat, fats and fodder in the regions where it is stationed, to keep precise record of the foodstuffs collected, to assemble those materials energetically and rapidly, at railway yards and stations, and to load them on the wagons. Industry needs fuel. A very important task for the Revolutionary Red Army is to hew and saw timber, and to transport it to the railway yards and stations...

Spring is coming—the time for work in the fields. Our exhausted factories are as yet producing few new agricultural implements. However, the peasants have many old implements, which are in need of repair. The Revolutionary Labour Army will make available its workshops and its smithies, fitters and joiners to carry out repairs of agricultural implements and machinery.

When work begins in the fields, the Red infantrymen and cavalrymen will show that they know how to use a plough to hoe the Soviet land.

Trotsky goes on to say:

A deserter from work, like a deserter from battle, is contemptible and dishonourable. Both are to be punished severely...

Soldiers of the Third Army, now the First Labour Army! Your initiative is of general significance.[20]

On 3 February 1920 Trotsky announced that in order to restore the ruined sectors of the south-eastern railway on the Moscow-Kazan-Ekaterinburg line, the Second Army was being transformed into the Railway Labour Army.

The Fifth Army was to build the railways for the transport of oil from Grozny. The Ukrainian Labour Army began work, its main task the production of coal in the Donbas. The Seventh Army, defending the approaches to Petrograd, was assigned the task of digging peat.[21] A Caucasus Labour Army was created in April, based on Stavropol *gubernia* and the Kuban and Terek regions, its objective the creation of food bases and the speeding up of oil supplies.

The whole idea of the labour armies was to stand the militia system on its head: instead of bringing the army nearer to the workers as producers, it turned the soldiers into producers. The actual results of the labour armies were poor. This, and not the ideological arguments against the concept of labour armies, led to their early demise. But from the labour armies it was only a step to a policy of general labour militarisation.

The militarisation of all labour

This policy, which in Stalinist legend is the policy of Trotsky, and Trotsky alone, was in fact the policy of the party as a whole at the time. It is true that a number of prominent Bolshevik leaders opposed the militarisation of labour—Rykov, Miliutin, Nogin, and above all Tomsky—but both Lenin and Trotsky on 12 January 1920 urged the Bolshevik leaders of the trade unions to accept the militarisation of labour. The theses of the central committee for the Ninth Congress (March 1920), drafted by Trotsky, were entitled 'On Mobilising the Industrial Proletariat, on Labour Service, on Militarising the Economy and on the Utilisation of Army Units for Economic Needs'. They stated:

> In the transitional stage of development, in a society burdened by the heritage of a very difficult past, going over to planned and organised social labour is unthinkable without measures of compulsion directed both at the parasitic elements and the backward elements of the peasantry and of the working class itself. The instrument of state compulsion is its armed force. Hence, the element of militarising of labour, to some extent, and in some form, is unavoidably inherent in the transitional economy based on universal labour service...
>
> Militarisation of labour signifies... that economic questions... must become in the minds of working people and in the practices of state institutions identified with military questions...
>
> The realisation of labour service must be based in principle upon the fulfilment of the same organisational tasks as involved in the establishment of Soviet power and the creation of the Red Army... Insofar as the army possesses the most important experience of mass Soviet organisation of this type, its methods and mode of working must (with all necessary modifications) be transferred to the sphere of labour organisation.[22]

The trade unions were to adopt 'the same rights in relation to their members as have been previously exercised only by military organisations.'[23] They were 'to distribute, to group, to transfer separate groups and separate categories of workers and individual proletarians to the place where they are needed by the state, by socialism.'[24]

In his report for the central committee to the Ninth Congress Trotsky stated:

> Militarisation is unthinkable without the militarisation of the trade unions as such, without the establishment of a regime in which every worker feels himself a soldier of labour, who cannot dispose of himself freely; if the order is given to transfer him, he must carry it out; if he does not carry it out, he will be a deserter who is punished. Who looks after this? The trade unions. It creates the new regime. This is the militarisation of the working class.[25]

In a report on 25 February 1920 to the Yekaterinburg membership of the party, Trotsky emphasised the compulsory element in the militarisation of labour:

> The party elements in the trade unions must explain the radical differences between a 'trade union' policy, which bargains and quarrels with the state, demanding concessions from it and eventually urging workers to go on strike, and a Communist policy, which proceeds from the fact that our state is a workers' state, which knows no other interests than those of the working people. Hence the trade unions must teach the workers not to haggle and fight with their own state in difficult times, but by common effort to help it get on the broad path of economic development.[26]

The Ninth Congress fully approved Trotsky's report with its call for the general militarisation of labour. This fact, in itself, gives the lie to the Stalinist legend that Trotsky alone was responsible for the militarisation policy. Nothing could be further from the truth. It is true that Trotsky was enthusiastic about the policy. But so was Lenin. Thus, for instance, Lenin told the Third All-Russian Congress of Economic Councils on 27 January 1920:

> ...in order to utilise our apparatus with the greatest possible

despatch we must create a labour army... In launching this slogan we declare that we must strain all the live forces of the workers and peasants to the utmost and demand that they give us every help in this matter. And then, by creating a labour army, by the harnessing of all the forces of the workers and peasants, we shall accomplish our main task.[27]

In a speech on 2 February Lenin reiterated that the economy must be reconstructed

by military methods with absolute ruthlessness and by the suppression of all other interests. We must at all costs create labour armies, organise ourselves like an army, reduce, even close down a whole number of institutions... in the next few months... When the all-Russia central executive committee endorses all the measures connected with labour conscription and the labour armies, when it has succeeded in instilling these ideas in the broad mass of the population and demands that they be put into practice by local officials—we are absolutely convinced that then we shall be able to cope with [the] most difficult tasks.[28]

Thus we see that for Lenin during the civil war, and especially in the latter part of it, the militarisation of labour, and the incorporation of the trade unions, their subordination to the state, were of vital and immediate importance.

It is also worth noting that Stalin himself served as chairman of the Ukrainian Council of the Labour Army.

Pravda, edited by Bukharin, was full of articles supporting the militarisation of labour and the labour armies. Thus, on 18 December 1919, Bukharin wrote that 'the model [for running the economy] is given to us by the army'. On 20 February 1920 he argued strongly the virtues of the labour armies. Throughout March *Pravda* was full of articles advocating the militarisation of labour. On 1 and 2 April Bukharin again defended this.

There was a *difference* between Trotsky's attitude to the question of the militarisation of labour and that of Lenin: Trotsky attempted to theorise and generalise the idea, whereas Lenin merely thought it a necessity in the circumstances. In his report to the Third All-Russia Congress of Economic Councils in January 1920, Trotsky posed the question: 'Why do we speak of *militarisation?*' He answers:

> No social organisation except the army has ever considered itself justified in subjecting citizens to itself to such a degree, and controlling them by its will in every aspect, as the state of the proletarian dictatorship considers itself justified in doing, and does. Only the army—just because it used to decide, in its own way, questions of the life or death of nations, states and ruling classes—was endowed with the power to demand from each and everyone complete submission to its tasks, purposes, regulations and orders. And it achieved this the more completely the more the tasks of military organisation coincided with the requirements of social development.[29]

Trotsky goes on to depict the militarisation of labour as crucial to socialism in general:

> ...militarisation of labour... is the inevitable method of organising and disciplining labour power in the period of transition from capitalism to socialism.[30]

> Labour service is compulsory, but this does not mean at all that it is coercion of the working class. If labour service were to encounter opposition from the majority of the working people, it would be shipwrecked, and with it the whole Soviet order. Militarisation of labour when the working people are against it is Arakcheevism.* Militarisation of labour by the will of the working people themselves is socialist dictatorship.[31]

Trotsky's argument was based on his idea that there was no real difference between compulsory and voluntary labour. At the Third Congress of Trade Unions (9 April 1920) when he argued the case for the militarisation of labour, he met with criticism from the Menshevik Abramovich, who argued that the militarisation of labour would lower productivity, since higher productivity could be obtained only with free labour. Trotsky denied there was any real difference between voluntary and compulsory labour:

---

* Count Arakcheev, the war minister to Tsar Alexander II, set up military settlements of peasants, who, while carrying on agricultural work, were organised on military lines and subject to military discipline.

Let the very few representatives of the Mensheviks at this congress explain to us what they mean by free, non-compulsory labour, if not the market of labour-power.

History has known slave labour. History has known serf labour. History has known the regulated labour of the medieval craft guilds. Throughout the world there now prevails hired labour, which the yellow journalists of all countries oppose, as the highest possible form of liberty, to Soviet 'slavery'. We, on the other hand, oppose capitalist slavery by socially-regulated labour on the basis of an economic plan, obligatory for the whole people and consequently compulsory for each worker in the country. Without this we cannot even dream of a transition to socialism...

If it were true that compulsory labour is unproductive always and under every condition, as the Menshevik resolution says, all our constructive work would be doomed to failure.[32]

Trotsky was right when he stated that men must work in order not to starve. In this sense all labour is compulsory. But to draw from this the conclusion that the form of compulsion is of little significance is nonsense. Under slavery or serfdom the compulsion is direct, open, legal. Under capitalism it is indirect and purely economic; the wage-earner is legally free. Marx stressed the progressive implications of this freedom. And this freedom makes the labour of the wage-earner far more productive than that of the slave or the serf. Thus Marx wrote:

This is one of the circumstances that makes production by slave labour such a costly process. The labourer here is, to use a striking expression of the ancients, distinguishable only as *instrumentum vocale*, from an animal as *instrumentum semi vocale*, and from an implement as *instrumentum mutum*. But he himself takes care to let both beast and implement feel that he is none of them, but is a man. He convinces himself with immense satisfaction that he is a different being, by treating the one unmercifully and damaging the other *con amore*. Hence the principle, universally applied in this method of production, only to employ the rudest and heaviest implements and such as are difficult to damage owing to their sheer clumsiness. In the slave states bordering on the Gulf of

Mexico down to the date of the civil war, ploughs constructed on old Chinese models, which turned up the soil like a hog or a mole, instead of making furrows, were alone to be found.[33]

It was taken for granted by all Marxists that socialism would not increase compulsion in labour compared to capitalism, but on the contrary would lighten it.

Trotsky's error lay not only, or mainly, in the fact that forced, militarised labour is not very productive, but that it is tyrannical and incompatible with working-class self-emancipation, in other words with socialism. Socialism would not only lighten compulsion in the labour field, but would transform its nature, and lead ultimately to its complete abolition.

Tsektran

Between the spring and autumn of 1920 Trotsky had an opportunity to put his scheme of militarisation of labour into practice. The transport system faced a terrible crisis. Of 70,000 *versts* of railways in European Russia, only 15,000 *versts* had remained undamaged, and 57 per cent of all locomotives were out of order.[34] In the winter of 1919-20 the condition of the railways was so catastrophic that the economy was threatened with complete breakdown. On 30 January 1920 the Council of Labour and Defence issued a decree declaring all railway workers mobilised for labour service, and a week later a further decree conferred wide disciplinary powers on the railway administration. Neither decree made any mention of the trade unions.[35]

On 1 February 1920 Lenin wrote to Trotsky:

The situation with regard to railway transport is quite catastrophic. Grain supplies no longer get through. Genuine emergency measures are required to save the position. For a period of two months (February-March), measures of the following kind must be put into force (as well as devising other measures too of a comparable kind):
1) The individual bread ration *is to be reduced* for those not engaged on transport work; and *increased* for those engaged on it.
Even if thousands more perish the country will be saved.
2) Three-quarters of the senior party workers from all

departments, except the Commissariats of Supply and of Military Affairs, are to be drafted to railway transport and maintenance work for these two months...

3) Within a 30-50 _verst_ wide zone along each side of the railway lines military law is to be introduced for the purpose of conscripting labour for clearing the tracks...[36]

The politburo asked Trotsky to take over the People's Commissariat of Transport Communication. Trotsky, in a telegraph to Lenin, explained that he was virtually unfamiliar with the administrative machinery of this commissariat.[37] Despite this, on 23 March Trotsky was appointed by VTsIK as temporary people's commissar of transport communications. The Ninth Party Congress passed a resolution declaring that improvement of transport was one of the most crucial tasks. Immediately after the congress a transport commission was established, composed of representatives of the People's Commissariat of Communication (Narkomput) and of the Supreme Council of National Economy (VSNKh). Trotsky was appointed its president.

On 22 May this commission issued its famous 'Order Number 1042' on the repair of locomotives.[38] The order was a detailed plan for the restoration of the locomotive rolling stock to its pre-war standard by the end of 1924. Standardisation was the key to 'Order 1042': individual parts were to be reduced to a minimum assortment, guaranteeing long production runs and interchangeability.[39] Practically at once the transport system began to recover from its paralysis.

On 17 August 1920 a decision was taken by the People's Commissariat of Transport Communication to merge the railway and water transportation by fusing the central bodies of the railway and water-transport unions into a joint Central Transport Committee (Tsektran) under the chairmanship of Trotsky.[40]

A state of emergency was declared in transport, and labour was mobilised. The decision to carry out these steps was taken by the central committee on 28 August 1920, supported by Lenin, Zinoviev and Stalin (against the protest of the trade union leader Tomsky).

By 22 December Trotsky could report to the Eighth All-Russian Congress of Soviets that the original five-year plan could be fulfilled in three and a half years.[41] By this time a plan for wagons had been added to the locomotive plan: Order Number 1157.

The party leaders were euphoric about Trotsky's success in improving rail transport. Thus on 27 May 1921, one year after the publication of Order 1042, Dzerzhinsky wrote: 'Orders 1042 and 1157... were *the first and brilliant experience in planned economy...*'[42]

The trade union debate

Trotsky, carried away by his success, declared at a meeting of party delegates on the eve of the All-Russian Trade Union Conference on 2 November 1920 that a 'shake-up' in other trade unions, similar to that taken on the railways, was necessary:

> We have built and rebuilt Soviet state economic organs, smashed them, and then rebuilt them once again, carefully selecting and checking the various workers and their various posts. It is quite obvious that it is necessary now to set about the reorganisation of the unions, that is to say, first of all, to pick the directing personnel of the unions.[43]

This went too far for Lenin, who openly dissociated himself from Trotsky. It also evoked immediate protest from Tomsky, chairman of the all-Russian central council of trade unions and a member of the central committee of the party.

On 8 November Tomsky decided to raise the whole issue at a meeting of the central committee, and he attacked Tsektran. He was supported by Lenin, who blamed Tsektran for having alienated the trade union Communists. Lenin at once drafted a sharp criticism of Tsektran for adoption by the Communist fraction of the All-Russian Trade Union Conference, which was still in session.[44]

The same day, 8 November, Lenin and Trotsky presented alternative drafts on trade union policy. Next day the central committee, by a majority of ten votes to four, adopted a resolution modelled on Lenin's draft:

> It is necessary to wage a most energetic and systematic struggle in order to eradicate the degeneration of centralisation and of militarised forms of work into bureaucracy, self-conceit, and petty officialdom and

interference with the trade unions. Healthy forms of militarisation of labour will be crowned with success only if the party, the *soviets*, and the trade unions succeed in explaining the necessity of these methods, if the country is to be saved, to the widest masses of the workers...

On the substantial point it prescribed that Tsektran should participate in the Central Council of Trade Unions on the same footing as the central bodies of other major unions, and decided to appoint a committee to draw fresh general instructions for the trade unions.[45] A commission was also set up by the central committee under the chairmanship of Zinoviev, charged with the duty of working out means for the wider application of democratic practice in the unions, and for the encouragement of their participation in the control of production.

The resolutions were a rebuff to Trotsky. It was decided to disband the political departments in transport and to stop the practice of appointing officials from above, who should instead be democratically elected to their posts.

These events were followed by a split within Tsektran, and on 7 December the central committee returned to the dispute in an atmosphere of increasing bitterness. Lenin, Zinoviev, Tomsky and Stalin urged the immediate abolition of Tsektran. By a vote of eight to seven the central committee refused to adopt this drastic course and accepted instead a compromise resolution proposed by Bukharin. This advocated the immediate abolition of the political directorates, but proposed to leave Tsektran in place until February. A new Tsektran would then be elected at the Congress of Railway and Water Transport Workers.[46]

Trotsky's most vocal critic was Zinoviev. In the pages of **Petrogradskaia pravda**, which he edited, there were vitriolic attacks on Tsektran with its 'police methods of dragooning the workers from above with the help of specialists'. Zinoviev largely succeeded in describing Tsektran as the brainchild of Trotsky alone, overlooking the fact that Tsektran had been set up by the central committee. He accused Trotsky of wanting to incorporate the unions into the state. But that was no more than the resolution of the Ninth Party Congress had in fact declared:

Being a proletarian dictatorship... there can be no possibility of any opposition between the trade unions and the organs of Soviet power.

...any opposition between the trade unions, as the economic organisation of the working class, and the *soviets*, as its political organisation, is completely absurd.

...the trade unions must be gradually converted into auxiliary organs of the proletarian state, and not the other way around.[47]

Now—between December 1920 and March 1921—a bitter debate on the trade union issue took place. The central committee was so divided on the question that eight separate platforms were advanced. The discussion spread throughout the party. In the four months leading up to the Tenth Party Congress, on 8 March 1921, the debate raged in party meetings and in the party press. Throughout January 1921 *Pravda* carried almost daily articles by supporters of one platform or another. Before the congress met, the principal documents were published by order of the central committee in a volume edited by Zinoviev. The party also published two issues of a special discussion sheet in order to provide a forum for a detailed exchange of views. *Pravda* published the platform of one of the contenders, the newly formed Workers' Opposition, while a pamphlet by Alexandra Kollontai putting the case for the Workers' Opposition was printed in 250,000 copies. Since coming to power the Bolsheviks had never been divided by so sharp a controversy,

In the end three platforms were presented to the congress. On one side were Trotsky, Bukharin, Andreev, Dzerzhinsky, Krestinsky, Preobrazhensky, Rakovsky and Serebriakov—eight members of the central committee. On the other side was the Workers' Opposition, whose main leaders were Shliapnikov and Kollontai. In between was the Platform of the Ten—Lenin, Zinoviev, Tomsky, Radzutak, Kalinin, Kamenev, Lozovsky, Petrovsky, Artem and Stalin.

The views of Trotsky and Bukharin

Basically the Trotsky-Bukharin group reacted to the economic collapse by arguing that army methods should be transferred from the war front to the factories and trade union organisations in order to tighten discipline. They wanted the complete 'statification' of the trade unions.

Trotsky argued that, in practice, the statification of the trade unions had already gone quite far and should be pushed to its conclusion. Secondly, the gradual transference of economic administration to the trade unions, promised by the party programme, presupposed 'the planned transformation of the unions into apparatuses of the workers' state'. This should be implemented consistently. He argued that his policy was only a continuation of the Lenin-Trotsky policy of earlier months and years.

Defending the rights of party leadership against the Workers' Opposition's demands for democracy, Trotsky employed an argument destined to haunt him in later years:

> The Workers' Opposition has come out with dangerous slogans, making a fetish of the principles of democracy. They seem to have placed the workers' right to elect their representatives above the party, as though the party did not have the right to defend its dictatorship even if that dictatorship were to clash for a time with the passing moods of the workers' democracy... What is indispensible is the awareness, so to speak, of the revolutionary historical birthright of the party, which is obliged to maintain its dictatorship in spite of the temporary wavering in the spontaneous moods of the masses, in spite of the temporary vacillation even in the working classes. This awareness is for us the indispensible unifying element. It is not on the formal principle of workers' democracy that the dictatorship is based at any given moment, though the workers' democracy is, of course, the only method by whose health the masses are increasingly drawn into political life.[48]

The Workers' Opposition

This group included, besides Kollontai, a considerable number of workers' leaders, of whom Shliapnikov, originally an engineer and the first commissar of labour, I K Lutovinov and S Medvedev, leaders of the metalworkers' union, were the most prominent.

The Workers' Opposition demanded that the management of industry should be in the hands of the trade unions. The transition to the new system should begin from the lowest industrial unit and extend upwards. At the factory level, the factory committee should regain the dominant position it had had at the beginning of the revolution. An All-Russia Producer Congress should be convened to elect the central management for the entire national economy. National congresses of separate trade unions should similarly elect managements for the various sectors of the economy.

Finally, the Workers' Opposition proposed a radical egalitarian revision of wages policies. Money wages were to be progressively replaced by rewards in kind; the basic food ration was to be made available to workers without payment. The same was to apply to meals in factory canteens, essential travel facilities and for education and leisure, lodging, lighting, and so on.

The Platform of the Ten

Lenin's attitude to the trade unions changed much more quickly than Trotsky's. The end of the civil war meant for him the end of talk about the 'statification' of the trade unions and about 'militarisation of labour'. In a speech on 30 December 1920 he came out strongly against Trotsky's position. The speech was published in a pamphlet with the title **The trade unions, the present situation and Trotsky's mistakes**. In Lenin's view the trade unions held a unique position. On the one hand, as their members made up the bulk of industrial workers, they were organisations of the ruling class—a class using state compulsion. On the other, they were not, and should not be, state bodies, organs of compulsion:

> the trade unions, which take in all industrial workers, are an organisation of the ruling, dominant, governing class, which has now set up a dictatorship and is exercising coercion through the state. But it is not a state organisation; nor is it one designed for coercion, but for education. It is an organisation designed to draw in and to train; it is, in fact, a school: a school of administration, a school of economic management, a school of communication... we have here a complex arrangement of cogwheels which cannot be a simple one; for the dictatorship of the proletariat cannot be exercised by a mass proletarian organisation. It cannot work without a number of 'transmission belts' running from the

vanguard to the mass of the advanced class, and from the latter to the mass of the working people. In Russia, this mass is a peasant one.[49]

With the end of the civil war, trade union policy had to change radically, said Lenin. Compulsion, justified in war time, was wrong now.

Where did Glavpolitput [the main political section of the People's Commissariat for Rail Transport] and Tsektran err? Certainly not in their use of coercion. That goes to their credit. Their mistake was that they failed to switch to normal trade union work at the right time; and without conflict... they failed to adapt themselves to the trade unions and help them by meeting them on an equal footing. Heroism, zeal, etc, are the positive side of military experience; red tape and arrogance are the negative side of the experience of the worst military types. Trotsky's theses, whatever his intentions, do not tend to play up the best, but the worst in military experience.[50]

Trotsky insisted that the militarisation of labour was essential for socialist reorganisation of the economy. Against this Lenin argued that militarisation could not be regarded as a permanent feature of socialist labour policy.

In his speech to the Tenth Congress Lenin said that it would be a grave mistake to assume an identity between the state—even a workers' state—and the trade unions. The unions had to defend the workers from their own state:

Trotsky seems to say that in a workers' state it is not the business of the trade unions to stand up for the material and spiritual interests of the working class. That is a mistake. Comrade Trotsky speaks of a 'workers' state'. May I say that this is an abstraction... it is... a patent error to say: 'Since this is a workers' state without any bourgeoisie, against whom then is the working class to be protected, and for what purposes?' Ours is a workers' state *with a bureaucratic twist to it*.

We now have a state under which it is the business of the massively organised proletariat to protect itself, while we, for our part, must use these workers' organisations to protect the workers from their state, and to get them to protect our state.[51]

A balance must be struck, Lenin argued, between the role of the unions in production and their role in defending their members' rights to consumption. They should not be turned into appendages of the state. They should retain a measure of autonomy, so as to be able to speak for the workers, if need be against the state.

At the same time as Lenin was fighting Trotsky on one front, both he and Trotsky were fighting much harder against the Workers' Opposition. He accused them of syndicalism, an approach that differed radically from Communism. Throughout the trade union debate both Lenin and Trotsky made it clear that the differences between them were far smaller than what separated them from the Workers' Opposition. At the height of the trade union debate, Trotsky told a meeting of the party fraction in the Miners' Congress, on 26 January 1921:

> Comrade Shliapnikov in speaking here—perhaps I express his thought a little crudely—said: 'Don't believe in this disagreement between Trotsky and Lenin. They will unite just the same and the struggle will be waged only against us!' He says: 'Don't believe'. I don't know what this means about believing or not believing. Of course, we may unite. We may dispute in deciding any very important question but the controversy only pushes our thoughts in the direction of 'unification'.[52]

Lenin too, speaking at the Tenth Congress, said that the differences between himself and Trotsky were minimal compared with their differences with the Workers' Opposition.[53]

The chief defect of the Workers' Opposition programme was that it lacked any concrete proposals for ending the economic *impasse*. Its declaration of confidence in the proletariat, when the latter was so demoralised, was no substitute for a realistic programme of action. Its demand for the immediate satisfaction of workers' needs, for equal wages for all, for free food, clothing, and such like, was totally unrealistic in a situation of general economic collapse. With the proletariat demoralised and alienated from the party, it was absurd to suggest that the immediate objective of this heterogeneous group should be the administration of industry. To talk about an All-Russian Congress of Producers when most of the producers were individualistic peasants, estranged from the dictatorship of the proletariat, was wishful thinking. (The concept of a 'producer' is, in any case, anti-Marxist—it amalgamates proletarian with petty-bourgeois elements, thus deviating from a class analysis).

In substance, the policy the Workers' Opposition advocated could be summed up in one phrase: the unionisation of the state, while Trotsky was arguing for the statification of the unions. If the proletariat is small and weak the unionisation of the state is a utopian fancy. In terms of positive policies, the Workers' Opposition had little to offer.

The conclusion of the trade union debate

The debate on the trade unions ended with an overwhelming victory for the Platform of the Ten at the Tenth Party Congress. This congress was unique in the way its delegates were elected. On 3 January 1921 the Petrograd party organisation, led by Zinoviev, issued an appeal to all party organisations. It called for elections to the forthcoming Tenth Congress on the basis of the various platforms on the trade union question. This provoked protests from the Moscow organisation and from Trotsky. On 12 January the central committee, by eight votes to seven, approved the election of delegates to the congress by platform—for the first time in the history of Bolshevism. At the Tenth Congress itself, Lenin's motion was accepted by an overwhelming majority: 336 votes for, against 50 for Trotsky's motion and only 18 for the Workers' Opposition.

Basically the trade union debate was an expression of the profound unease in the party due to the economic paralysis that ruled the country at the end of War Communism. The economy was in a total *impasse*. The Bolshevik regime, having emerged triumphant from the civil war, was losing its support even among the workers. The Workers' Opposition reflected this popular discontent.

Three years after the trade union debate Trotsky could justifiably write:

the discussion in no wise revolved around the trade unions,

nor even workers' democracy: what was expressed in these disputes was a profound uneasiness in the party, caused by the excessive prolonging of the economic regime of war communism. The entire economic organism of the country was in a vice. The discussions on the role of the trade unions and on workers' democracy covered up the search for a new economic road.[54]

Many years later Trotsky stated: 'We wished to have a change, and the discussion began on an absolutely secondary and false point.'[55]

How can we explain Trotsky's stand on the trade unions?

Trotsky's position in the trade union debate was a demonstration of substitutionism. The decline of the working class as a result of the civil war, combined with the efforts of the Red Army to hold Russian society together in the chaos of war, counter-revolution and famine, led inevitably to the rise of substitutionism. The traditions formed during the long and demanding years of the civil war were not easy for Trotsky to throw away. He considered that the only effective administration in the country was that of the Red Army.

Because under War Communism labour policy had boiled down to recruiting workers for the war effort and sending them where they were most urgently needed, and because the trade unions had been the instrument through which this policy was carried out, Trotsky naturally looked at the role of the trade unions through the same spectacles as during the civil war. During the civil war the government had had no alternative but to use workers as if they were soldiers; the mobilisation of labour had been unavoidable. But Trotsky raised the *expediency* of the civil war into a principle, turning a bitter necessity into an ideological virtue.

The sad thing is that the Bolshevik leaders again and again made a virtue out of necessity. Lenin and Trotsky argued that the labour armies were an indispensable feature of socialism. Similarly Bukharin extolled the runaway inflation and devaluation of money as a precursor of a true communist economy without money.[56] The series of war measures—egalitarianism, a result of general destitution—as well as the suppression of the market and the strengthening of militarisation in the economy and society, were described as measures of the direct transition to real communism.

Making a virtue out of necessity is in general a by-product of the extreme contradiction between the expected and the actual, when it is too painful to look reality in the face, when one is forced to do things that are in contrast to one's own beliefs and actions hitherto.

The state was in a void. The end of the civil war saw the proletariat completely atomised and demoralised, the peasantry in rebellion against the state, the party itself exhausted and under threat of fragmentation. It looked as if the only stable force was the army, the police and the state bureaucracy. These were the conditions for the rise of Trotsky's substitutionism—by which the military superstructure would attempt to shape the proletarian economic and social base. The militarisation of labour and statification of the trade unions were the children of this tragic situation.

An added factor encouraging Trotsky's stand on the trade unions was his inclination to too high a level of abstraction. The underlying assumption was that the workers could have no interest distinguishable from that of the Soviet state as a whole, and therefore needed no protection by independent trade unions. The fact that this state was under pressure from non-proletarian social forces, above all the peasantry, and suffered from bureaucratic deformations, he overlooked.

Above all Trotsky suffered from too much concentration on the administrative side of things, as Lenin would later point out in his 'Testament', where he wrote that Trotsky 'is personally perhaps the most capable man in the present CC, but he has developed excessive self-assurance and shown excessive pre-occupation with the purely administrative side of the work'.[57] Trotsky later, in his book **The Stalin School of Falsification**, commented on Lenin's words: 'I think that these words quite correctly characterised the root of that controversy [on the trade unions]'.[58]

The bitter trade union debate, following the sharp controversy on the military front, led to the undermining of Trotsky's popularity among many of the party *cadres*. Hence we find that in the elections to the central committee at the Tenth Congress Trotsky comes in tenth place out of 25. The list of those elected, with votes cast for each, was: Lenin 479, Radek 475, Tomsky 472, Kalinin 470, Rudzutak 467, Stalin 458, Rykov 458, Kamenev 457, Molotov 453, Trotsky 452. The high vote for Tomsky and Rudzutak is to be explained by their stand in the trade union debate at the congress.[59]

The new central committee elected by the congress reflected the ascendancy of many who were to be Stalin's supporters in future faction fights. Among the newly elected members were a number whose names were already closely associated with Stalin —Komarov, Molotov, Mikhailov, Iaroslavsky, Ordzhonikidze, Petrovsky, Frunze, Voroshilov and Tuntul. Among the new candidate members were Chubar, Kirov, Kuibyshev and Gusev, all known supporters of Stalin.

Of the old members of the central committee, the three secretaries friendly with Trotsky—Krestinsky, Preobrazhensky and Serebriakov—were not re-elected; neither was Andreev, who had backed the wrong side in the trade union dispute, nor I N Smirnov. Both were close to Trotsky. No doubt Trotsky's popularity among the mass of the workers was also damaged by his stand on the trade union issue; they saw in it an effort to restrict their freedom.

The discussion on the role of the trade unions proved irrelevant in practice to the search for new economic policies. Trotsky predicted at the congress that the victorious resolution would not 'survive to the Eleventh Congress'.[60] He was proved correct. As long as the party and state continued the policy of War Communism there were no measures other than administrative ones to try to get the economy out of its *impasse*. But these measures, whether the extreme ones advocated by Trotsky or the less stringent ones suggested by Lenin, proved incapable of breaking the vicious circle of War Communism.

Even if the discussion on the trade unions proved irrelevant to further development, it nevertheless demonstrated Lenin's sensitivity to the mood of the proletariat. Trotsky admitted his own error in the trade union debate a few years later:

The working masses, who had gone through three years of civil war, were more and more disinclined to submit to the ways of military rule. With his unerring political instinct, Lenin sensed that the critical moment had arrived. Whereas I was trying to get an ever more intensive effort from the trade unions, taking my stand on purely economic considerations on the basis of War Communism, Lenin, guided by political considerations, was moving towards an easing of the military pressure.[61]

Mass disaffection

Disaffection was particularly widespread amongst the peasantry. So long as the civil war continued, the peasants on the whole tolerated the Bolshevik regime as the lesser evil compared with White restoration. However resentful they were of the grain requisitions, they were far more fearful of the return of the former landowners. Armed peasants often confronted the grain collection detachments, but the scale of the opposition was not such as to threaten the regime. Now that the civil war had ended, however, waves of peasant uprisings swept rural Russia. The most serious outbreaks occurred in Tambov province, the Middle Volga area, the Ukraine, Northern Caucasus and Western Siberia.

By early 1921 some two and a half million men, nearly half the total strength of the Red Army and the majority of them peasants, had been demobilised in a situation of social unrest that threatened the very existence of the state. In February 1921 alone the Cheka, the new state police, reported 118 separate peasant uprisings in various parts of the country.[62] The fiercest uprising occurred in Tambov province and was led by A S Antonov, a former Social Revolutionary. At its height the Antonov movement involved some 50,000 peasants. It took the capable Red commander Mikhail Tukhachevsky more than a year to overpower this rebellion.

Disaffection spread to the urban proletariat, many of whose members returned to the countryside for good, while others went foraging for food again and again in the villages. The rural disturbances became contagious and led to industrial agitation and military unrest.

In February 1921 an open breach occurred between the Bolshevik regime and its principal mainstay, the working class. Since the onset of winter, unusually severe even by Muscovite standards, cold and hunger, combined with the undiminished rigours of War Communism, had produced a highly charged atmosphere in the large towns. This was particularly true of Moscow and Petrograd, where only a spark was needed to set off an explosion.

This spark was provided on 22 January when the government announced that the already meagre bread ration for the cities was to be cut by one-third. Severe though it was, the reduction was apparently unavoidable. Heavy snows and shortages of fuel had held up food trains from Siberia and the Northern Caucasus, where surpluses had been gathered to feed the hungry towns of the centre and the north. During the first ten days of February the disruption of railway links became so great that not a single carload of grain reached the empty warehouses of Moscow.[63] In early February more than 60 of the largest Petrograd factories were forced to close for lack of fuel. Meanwhile, the food supply had all but vanished.[64]

The executive committee of the Petrograd *soviet*, chaired by Zinoviev, proclaimed martial law throughout the city. An 11pm curfew was imposed, and gatherings in the streets were forbidden at any time.[65] Strikes spread throughout the Petrograd district. As Serge remembers: '...every day in Smolny the only talk was of factory incidents, strikes, and booing at party agitators. This was in November and December of 1920'.[66]

On 28 February the strike wave reached the giant Putilov metal works with its 6000 workers, a formidable body even though only a sixth of what it had been during the First World War.[67] Menshevik agitators received a sympathetic hearing at workers' meetings, and their leaflets and manifestoes went into many eager hands.[68]

Initially the resolutions passed at factory meetings dealt overwhelmingly with familiar economic issues: regular distribution of rations, the issue of shoes and warm clothing, the removal of roadblocks, permission to make foraging trips into the countryside and to trade freely with the villagers, the elimination of privileged rations for special categories of workers, and so on. But political demands came increasingly to the front—demands for the restoration of political and civil rights.[69]

This turmoil was accompanied by a flare-up of anti-semitic feelings. The Jewish inhabitants of Petrograd were apprehensive, and some left the city, fearing a pogrom if the government collapsed and the mobs had the freedom of the streets.[70]

After a week, however, Zinoviev gained control of the situation and checked the unrest. Force and propaganda alone were not enough to restore order in Petrograd. Of equal importance was a series of concessions sufficiently large to take the edge off the opposition movement. As an immediate step, extra rations were distributed to soldiers and factory workers. On 27 February Zinoviev also announced a number of additional concessions to the workers' most pressing demands. Henceforward they would be permitted to leave the city in order to look for food. To facilitate this he even promised to schedule extra passenger trains into the surrounding countryside. But most important of all, he revealed for the first time that plans were under way to abandon the forcible seizure of grain from the peasants in favour of a tax in kind, that a New Economic Policy was to replace War Communism.

By 2 or 3 March nearly every striking factory was back at work.

Kronstadt takes up arms

These strikes in Petrograd aroused the sailors of neighbouring Kronstadt to armed insurrection.

In July 1917 the island fortress of Kronstadt had earned Trotsky's accolade as 'the pride and glory of the revolution'. However, the Kronstadters had changed considerably since then. Being out of the battle area of the civil war, Kronstadt had been emptied of its original sailors, who were mobilised to the most difficult fronts and replaced by a new intake. The bulk of the Kronstadt sailors in 1921 were not those of 1917. By 1921, according to official figures, more than three-quarters of the sailors were of peasant origin, a substantially higher proportion than in 1917, when industrial workers from the Petrograd area had made up a sizeable part of the fleet.[71] In addition, three-quarters of the garrison were natives of the Ukraine, some of who had served with the anti-Bolshevik forces in the south before joining the Soviet navy.[72] This was why they were particularly influenced by the mood of the people in the rural areas.

The widespread unrest affected even party members among the sailors. In January 1921 alone some 5000 Baltic seamen left the Communist Party. Between August 1920 and March 1921 the

Kronstadt party organisation lost half its 4000 members.[73] The main reason was War Communism. The Kronstadters charged the government alone with responsibility for all the ills afflicting the country. They neglected the effects of the chaos and destruction of the civil war itself, the inescapable ravages of contending armies, the allied intervention and blockade, the unavoidable scarcity of fuel and raw materials, or the difficulties of feeding the hungry and healing the sick in a situation of famine and epidemic. All the suffering and hardship was laid at the door of the Bolshevik regime.

A degree of anti-semitic feeling was mixed with hatred of the Communist Party. The worst venom was directed at Trotsky and Zinoviev. Prejudice against Jews was widespread among the Baltic sailors, many of who came from the Ukraine and western borderlands, regions of traditionally virulent anti-semitism in Russia. For men of this peasant and working-class background the Jews had been the customary scapegoat in times of hardship and distress. For instance when Vershinin, a member of Kronstadt's revolutionary committee, came out on the ice on 8 March to parley with a Soviet detachment, he appealed: 'Enough of your "hurrahs", and join us to beat the Jews. It is their cursed domination that we workers and peasants have had to endure.'[74]

The Communist Party almost disintegrated in Kronstadt during the fortnight of the rebellion (1-17 March 1921). Trotsky estimated that 30 per cent of the Kronstadt Communists participated actively in the revolt, while 40 per cent took a 'neutral position'.[75] As has been mentioned, party membership in Kronstadt declined from 4000 in August 1920 to 2000 in March 1921, and some 500 members and 300 candidates now resigned from the party, while the remainder were badly demoralised.[76]

The slogan of the Kronstadt rising, '*Soviets* without Communists', sounds very democratic. Actually it was immediately seized upon not only by the Social Revolutionaries but also by the bourgeois liberals. The Kadet leader, Professor Miliukov, understood that to free the *soviets* from the leadership of the Bolsheviks would have meant to demolish the *soviets* themselves in a short time. The Kronstadt uprising had objectively a counter-revolutionary character. That this was so became clear from the fact that the most severe opponents of the uprising were the adherents of the Workers' Opposition: they volunteered practically to a man and woman to participate in the assault on Kronstadt.

Trotsky himself did not participate in the suppression of Kronstadt. When the rebellion broke out he was away in the Urals. From there he went directly to Moscow for the Tenth Congress of the party. He did not go to Kronstadt because at the time he was involved in the debate on the trade union question. One of his bitterest opponents in this debate was Zinoviev, who headed the Petrograd committee—in whose hands lay the political work in Kronstadt. Thus the anarchists' story of Trotsky's role in suppressing the Kronstadt rebellion is pure myth.

'The Kronstadt events', Lenin said, 'were like a flash of lightning which threw more glare upon reality than anything else.'[77]

The peasants' Brest-Litovsk

The Tenth Party Congress met on 8 March 1921 in the shadow of the Kronstadt uprising. There was clear evidence that the party was losing its grip on the people. Some idea of the alarm this caused can be seen in the fact that, on receiving the news about Kronstadt, the congress interrupted its debates and sent most of the delegates off to participate in the storming of the fortress. At no other time during the civil war had there been comparable panic.[78]

The first lesson the Bolshevik leaders drew from the peasant uprisings, from the disaffection of a broad section of the proletariat, even in Petrograd, and above all from Kronstadt, was the need to end the compulsory requisitioning of grain. This was a retreat in face of massive petty-bourgeois pressure. War Communism ended and the New Economic Policy was launched.

Three years earlier, in March 1918, the Bolsheviks had made a similar retreat on the international front when they signed the treaty of Brest-Litovsk, in order to obtain a 'breathing space'. Now, on 15 March 1921, the Tenth Congress of the party adopted what one delegate, Riazanov, called a 'Peasant Brest'.[79]

Chapter twelve

The decline of the proletariat and the rise of the bureaucracy

The proletariat burns itself out in the struggle

THE COLLAPSE of industry led to a drastic reduction in the number of workers. The number of industrial workers fell from 3,024,000 in 1917 to 1,243,000 in 1921-2, a decrease of 58.7 per cent.[1]

The drop was particularly sharp in Petrograd. While at the time of the October revolution there were 400,000 factory workers there, this fell to 120,495 by 1 April 1918. Of these 48,910 were unemployed. So the total number of workers employed in Petrograd's industry was only 71,575.[2]

The decline of the proletariat was not only quantitative but also qualitative, as Lenin explained: 'Since the war, the industrial workers of Russia have become much less proletarian than they were before, because during the war all those who desired to evade military service went into the factories. This is common knowledge.'[3] Thus many of the workers of 1921-2 were actually former students or shopkeepers, or their children. The group that was most reduced was the metal workers, the mainstay of the Bolsheviks in 1917.

Members of the working class were forced by the scarcity of food to act like small individualist traders, rather than as a collective, or a united class. It has been calculated that in 1919-20 the state supplied only 42 per cent of the grain consumed by the towns, and an even smaller percentage of other foodstuffs, all the rest being bought on the black market.[4]

In March-April 1919, 75 per cent of the Petrograd workers bought bread on the black market.[5] It was common for workers to stay away from work in order to forage in the countryside. During the civil war factories paid part of the wages in kind. The workers used a portion themselves and sold the rest on the black market. A speaker at the First All-Russian Congress of Councils of National Economy in May 1918 drew attention to this practice, which acquired the nickname 'piece-selling':

> Bagging [foraging for food by townspeople] is a terrible evil, piece-selling is a terrible evil; but it is an even greater evil when you begin to pay the workers in kind, in their own products... and when they themselves turn piece-sellers.'[6]

But the practice persisted, and the Second All-Russian Congress of Councils of National Economy in December 1918 had little option but to turn a blind eye to it, passing yet another resolution in favour of payment of wages to factory workers in kind. Two years later the scandal had grown much worse.

At the Fourth Congress of Trade Unions in May 1921 the disorganisation of industry and the demoralisation of the proletariat were illustrated by a statement that workers in factories were stealing 50 per cent of the goods produced and that the average workers' wage covered only one-fifth of their cost of living, so that they were compelled to earn the rest by illicit trading.[7] Under these circumstances workers inevitably became middlemen, parasitic on the economy and increasingly inclined to look after their own interests.

On 24 August 1919 Lenin wrote: '...industry is at a standstill. There is no food, no fuel, no industry.'[8] He summed up the disintegration of the proletariat in these words:

> The industrial proletariat... owing to the war and to the desperate poverty and ruin, has become declassed... dislodged from its class groove, and has ceased to exist as a proletariat. The proletariat is the class which is engaged in the production of material values in large-scale capitalist industry. Since large-scale capitalist industry has been destroyed, since the factories are at a standstill, the proletariat has disappeared. It has sometimes figured in statistics, but it has not been held together economically.[9]

There was a dictatorship of the proletariat, even though the proletariat had disintegrated. As Lenin put it to the Tenth

Conference of the party on 26 May 1921: 'even though the proletariat has to go through a period when it is declassed... it can nevertheless fulfil its task of winning and holding political power.'[10]

With some cynicism Shliapnikov told the Eleventh Party Congress: 'Vladimir Ilyich [Lenin] said yesterday that the proletariat as a class, in the Marxian sense, did not exist. Permit me to congratulate you on being the vanguard of a non-existing class.'[11]

Of course, to a vulgar materialist, it sounds impossible to have a dictatorship of the proletariat without the proletariat, like the smile of the Cheshire cat without the cat itself. But one must remember that the ideological as well as the political superstructure never reflect the material base *directly and immediately*. Ideas have their own momentum. Usually in 'normal' times they are a source of conservativism: long after people's material circumstances have changed, they are still dominated by old ideas. However, this disjuncture between the ideological superstructure and the economic base became a source of strength to Bolshevism during the civil war.

Marx explained that the class in itself and the class for itself are not one and the same, in other words that the class can be powerful in its position in production and yet not be conscious of this. The other side of the same coin is that a class which loses three-quarters of its economic power can, for a short period, maintain its political dominance through its experience and its established position in society and the state.

But in the not very long run, the economic enfeeblement of the proletariat must in practice lead to a catastrophic decline in morale and consciousness of the people who are supposed to form the ruling class of the new state.

The bureaucratic Leviathan

At first the congress of *soviets* met frequently. Thus in the seven months between 7 November 1917, when power was declared to be in the hands of the *soviets*, and the adoption of the constitution of 10 July 1918, there were four congresses. As against this, between November 1918 and December 1922 the congress met only annually.

The power of the congress of *soviets* shifted to its central executive committee (VTsIK). In the constitution VTsIK was subordinate to the congress. In practice, however, the power of VTsIK was whittled away by its own presidium and by Sovnarkom, the Council of People's Commissars.

VTsIK met less and less frequently. At first it was required to meet at least once every two months. At the Seventh Congress of *soviets* (December 1919) Lenin justified the infrequency of the meetings of VTsIK by the requirements of the war against the Whites. The official requirement was reduced to 'not less than three times a year' by provision of the Ninth Congress of *soviets*.

The outstanding development of the years of the civil war was the concentration of central authority in the hands of Sovnarkom at the expense of both the congress of *soviets* and VTsIK. Sovnarkom not only enjoyed full executive authority but also unlimited power of legislation by decree. In its first year it passed 480 decrees, of which only 68 were submitted to VTsIK for confirmation. Between 1917 and 1921 Sovnarkom issued 1,615 decrees, VTsIK only 375.[12] At the same time as the congress of *soviets* was being deprived of its power by Sovnarkom, the process of concentration of authority in the centre at the expense of local *soviets* was taking place. There was a massive increase in the number of officials. By the end of 1920 there were 5,880,000 state officials—five times the number of industrial workers.[13]

This state apparatus was mostly composed of people with bourgeois origins. It is true that hundreds of thousands of workers had been mobilised by the party to strengthen the new state machine, but they were a minority, and their weight was further weakened by the dominance that technical superiority and higher cultural level gave to the old officials. As Lenin said on 12 June 1920: 'The Soviet government employs hundreds of thousands of office workers, who are either bourgeois or semi-bourgeois... they have absolutely no confidence in our Soviet government.'[14] He told the Eighth Congress of the party in March 1919:

> The Tsarist bureaucrats began to join the Soviet institutions and practise their bureaucratic methods, they began to assume the colouring of communists and, to succeed better in their careers, to procure membership cards of the Russian Communist Party... What makes itself felt here most is the lack of cultured forces.[15]

From 1921 onwards Lenin's denunciations of bureaucracy became more and more vehement. In a speech on 17 October 1921 to a conference of representatives of the political education departments, he said:

> At present bribery surrounds us on all sides. In my opinion, three chief enemies now confront one... the first is communist conceit; the second—illiteracy, and the third—bribery.[16]

With the same frankness and plainness, in his last speech to the Comintern congress on 13 November 1922, Lenin indicted the bourgeois conservative nature of the existing state machine:

> the machine functions somehow; but down below government employees have arbitrary control and they often exercise it in such a way as to counteract our measures. At the top, we have, I don't know how many, but at all events, I think, no more than a few thousand, at the outside several tens of thousands of our own people. Down below, however, there are hundreds of thousands of old officials whom we got from the Tsar and from bourgeois society and who, partly deliberately and partly unwittingly, work against us.[17]

In large part this had been a result of circumstances: the civil war had shaped all state institutions. In the words of Bukharin and Preobrazhensky:

> Today, when a fierce civil war is still raging, all our organisations have to be on a war footing. The instruments of the Soviet power have had to be constructed on militarist lines... What exists today in Russia is not simply the dictatorship of the proletariat; it is a militarist-proletarian dictatorship.[18]

The Bolsheviks' political monopoly

Prior to the revolution all revolutionaries took it for granted that during the dictatorship of the proletariat more than one workers' party would continue to exist. Thus Trotsky, on being elected president of the Petrograd *soviet* on 9 (22) September 1917, said:

> We are all party people, and we shall have to cross swords more than once. But we shall guide the work of the

Petersburg *soviet* in a spirit of justice and complete independence for all fractions; the hand of the praesidium will never oppress the minority.

Sukhanov, quoting these words a few years later, commented:

Heavens! What liberal views! What self-mockery! But the point is that about three years later, while exchanging reminiscences with me, Trotsky, thinking back to this moment, exclaimed dreamily:
'What a happy time!'
Yes, wonderful! Perhaps not one person in the world, not excluding himself, will ever recall Trotsky's rule with *such* feelings.[19]

However under the iron pressure of the civil war the Bolshevik leaders were forced to move, as the price of survival, to a *one-party system*. They could not give up power just because the class they represented had largely vanished while fighting to defend that power.

The fate of the different parties was closely bound up with the development of the civil war. That the openly capitalist parties, above all the Kadets, would be ready to fight to the end against Bolshevik power was obvious. They wanted an open capitalist class dictatorship. The petty bourgeois parties—the Social Revolutionaries and Mensheviks—were less clear in their positions. On the one hand their leaders rallied again and again to the counter-revolution. On the other they were repulsed by the extremism of the White terror, which did not spare even them. The result was vacillation in the Social Revolutionary and Menshevik camps. This was combined with serious fragmentation within the two parties. In each one section joined the Kadets, another moved cautiously and gradually towards the Bolsheviks, and yet another remained neutral. The positions of the different sections depended very much on the situation on the civil war front. A few Red Army reverses were enough to push the petty bourgeoisie, perpetually hesitant, in the direction of the right.

In suppressing the extreme right, the Bolshevik government faced a dilemma. What were they to do about the petty bourgeois who protested against the 'suppression of freedom'. This dilemma became increasingly difficult to solve by moderate measures: the Right Social Revolutionaries were practically indistinguishable from the 'Left' Kadets, and protested strongly when the latter were suppressed; the Right Mensheviks protested against the suppression of the Right Social Revolutionaries; then again there was no clear boundary between the Right Social Revolutionaries and the moderate Social Revolutionaries, and between these and the Left Social Revolutionaries, and so on. The gradation was continuous. So long as the final outcome of the civil war was not certain, which was for nearly three years, the level of tolerance of both the Bolsheviks and their opponents was very low. As E H Carr put it:

> If it was true that the Bolshevik regime was not prepared after the first few months to tolerate an organised opposition, it was equally true that no opposition was prepared to remain within legal limits. The premise of dictatorship was common to both sides of the argument.[20]

The severity of civil war conditions, the weakness of the proletariat and the sullen animosity of the peasantry forced the Bolsheviks to greater and greater restriction of the freedom of action of the Mensheviks and Social Revolutionaries, of whatever variety. Had it been possible to isolate the Whites as the sole target for attack, the situation would have been very different.

The Bolshevik Party programme adopted in March 1919 made it clear that the restriction of the rights of other parties was only temporary. Thus it stated: '...the forfeiture of political rights, and whatever limitations may be imposed upon freedom, are necessary only as temporary measures.'[21] However, the circumstances conspired to demonstrate that sometimes there is nothing more permanent than what is intended to be temporary.

The Fifth All-Russian Congress of Soviets in July 1918 was the last at which the opposition was present in strength. At the next congress, held four months later with 950 delegates, there were 933 Communists, eight Revolutionary Communists, four Social Revolutionaries, two Narodnik Communists, one Maximalist, one Anarchist and one non-party delegate.[22]

With the party monopoly of power, the separation of party and state was necessarily only formal, especially as party members were bound by discipline to act as one. In fact the party and the *soviets* became increasingly fused. This fusion permeated all levels of the administration. Data from some 60 per cent of local *soviets* in the second half of 1919 showed that party members and candidates made up 89 per cent of the membership of executive committees of *guberniia* congresses of *soviets*, 86 per cent of executive committees of *uezd* congresses of *soviets*, 93 per cent of executive committees of city *soviets* in *guberniia* administrative centres, and 71 per cent of executive committees of town *soviets* in *uezd* administrative centres.[23]

The civil war changed the Bolsheviks' attitude to the issue of single-party monopoly. They turned it from a 'temporary evil' imposed by circumstances, into a virtue. Thus in 1923 Trotsky wrote: 'We are the only party in the country and, in the period of the dictatorship it could not be otherwise.'[24] The platform of the United Opposition (1927), one of whose main leaders was Trotsky, declared: 'We will struggle with all our force against the formation of two parties, for the dictatorship of the proletariat demands as its very core a united proletarian party. It demands a single party.'[25]

The establishment of the Bolshevik Party monopoly led to a deterioration of political life in general, and a decline of the *soviets* in particular, which was summed up by Victor Serge:

> With the disappearance of political debates between parties representing different social interests through the various shades of their opinion, Soviet institutions, beginning with the local *soviets* and ending with the VTsIK and the Council of People's Commissars, manned solely by communists, now function in a vacuum: since all the decisions are taken by the party, all they can do is give them the official rubber stamp.[26]

However, it is one thing to assert that the banning of all parties, except for the Bolshevik Party, must have had deleterious consequences. To assert that the Bolsheviks could have acted differently, and could have allowed freedom of parties, is altogether another. In essence the dictatorship of the proletariat *does not* represent a combination of abstract, immutable elements such as democracy and centralism, independent of time and place. The actual level of democracy, as well as of centralism, depends on three basic factors: the strength of the proletariat, the material and cultural legacy left to it by the old regime, and the strength of capitalist resistance. The level of democracy feasible must be in direct proportion to the first two factors, and in inverse proportion to the third. The captain of an ocean liner can allow football to be played on his vessel; on a tiny raft in a stormy sea the level of tolerance is far lower.

The transformation of the party

During the civil war hundreds of thousands of workers joined the party, but the effect of the struggle radically changed its social composition. With the primary task the need to run the administration, tens of thousands of worker party members became state officials. A substantial proportion of party members went into the Red Army during the civil war; in 1920 this reached about 300,000—half the total membership.[27] More than half a million communists saw service with the Red Army during the civil war, of whom roughly half were sent into the army by civilian party organisations and half were recruited by the party while on army service. Some 200,000 communists lost their lives.

One inevitable result was a catastrophic decline in the proportion of party members working at the factory bench. Thus statistics for 1919 show that only 11 per cent of party members were then working in factories; 53 per cent were working as government officials; 8 per cent were party and trade union officials and 27 per cent were in the army.[28]

At the Tenth Congress in March 1921 Shliapnikov deplored the fact that among the metal workers of Petrograd, who before the revolution had been a mainstay of Bolshevism, no more than 2 per cent were party members. The corresponding figure for Moscow was 4 per cent.[29] At the Eleventh Congress (March-April 1922) Zinoviev complained: 'It is a fact that there are big districts, mines, etc, where there are from 10,000 to 12,000 workers, where we have a party nucleus of only six.'[30]

To add to the weakness of the party, the proportion of old Bolsheviks in it was extremely small. In October 1919 only 20 per cent of members had been members before the October revolution, and only 8 per cent had joined before February 1917.[31] Zinoviev told the Eleventh Congress that only 2 per cent of the members in 1922 had been party members before February 1917.[32]

In a letter to Molotov on 26 March 1922 Lenin wrote:

If we do not close our eyes to reality we must admit that at the present time the proletarian policy of the party is not determined by the character of its membership but by the enormous undivided prestige enjoyed by the small group which might be called the old guard of the party.

The danger inherent in the situation was very great. 'A slight conflict within this group will be enough, if not to destroy this prestige, at all events to weaken the group to such a degree as to rob it of its power to determine policy.'[33]

Increasing centralisation of power in the party

The central committee, originally a small combat body and in actuality the *decision-making body* of the party, came increasingly to ratify rather than to make decisions.

At first it was required to meet twice a month, following a resolution of the Eighth Party Congress and the 1919 Party Rules.[34] In 1921 the Tenth Congress modified this requirement to once in two months.[35]

Immediately after the October revolution, the central committee had met very frequently. We have the minutes of 17 such meetings for a period of a little over three months,[36] while the minutes of a number of other meetings in the same period have not survived. Subsequently, during the civil war, meetings became less frequent. There were only six between April and July 1918, and between July and November 1918 the central committee did not meet at all. (This was complained of at the Eighth Congress in March 1919). Later the meetings became more regular: between April and October 1919 there were six; between April 1920 and March 1921 there were 29.[37] But these were still far less frequent than those of the politburo.

The central committee met only six times between March and December 1919, while the politburo and orgburo had 29 and 110 meetings respectively. During this period there were also ten joint politburo-orgburo meetings. From December 1919 to September 1920 the central committee met only nine times, while the politburo and orgburo met 77 and 64 times respectively. Between September 1920 and March 1921—the time of the trade union debate—the central committee met more often, with 24 meetings, almost one a week, while the politburo and orgburo had 26 and

47 sessions respectively. Between May and August 1921 the central committee held nine meetings and the politburo and orgburo 39 and 48. Between September and December 1921 the central committee met five times, while the politburo and orgburo met 44 and 63 times respectively.[38]

In practice the politburo and orgburo increasingly usurped the power of the central committee.

Another party institution whose power continued to increase was the secretariat. To achieve coordination between the politburo and the orgburo, the secretary of the party was a member of both.

The secretariat greatly expanded its staff; from 15 in March 1919 it grew to 80 in November 1919 to 80, in eight departments (general administration, finance, information, orgnisation, distribution, inspection, peasantry and women's work).[39] In March 1920 its staff rose to 150 and a year later it totalled 602 —plus a military detachment of 140 as guards and messengers).[40]

One of the most important powers controlled by the secretariat was the appointment of personnel. Since 1920 one of the three party secretaries had been in charge of what was called the 'accounts and distribution section' (Uchraspred), which kept account of party manpower and supervised its distribution. In its report to the Tenth Congress it showed that in a period of less than twelve months it had been responsible for the transfer and appointment of 42,000 party members.[41] Uchraspred had become a powerful organ of control over state and party institutions.

Zinoviev explained at the Twelfth Party Congress (1923) that the presidents of the executive committees of provincial *soviets* were appointed by the central committee of the party and that this was necessarily so.[42] In fact it was the secretariat that had this power of nomination.

There were also widespread appointments in internal party bodies. During the civil war, when local party committees, including those representing large territorial units, expressed opposition to the central committee in Moscow, they were often summarily sacked. In the spring of 1919, for instance, the central committee dissolved the elected central committee of the Ukraine and appointed a new one. Between March 1922 and March 1923 the secretariat appointed 42 secretaries of provincial committees.[43]

Even delegates to party congresses were often nominated rather than elected.

The fight to defend party democracy

The undermining of inner party democracy did not take place without vigorous protests from party members. K K Iurenev, for example, spoke at the Ninth Congress of the methods used by the central committee to suppress criticism, including the virtual exile of the critics: 'One goes to Christiana, another sent to the Urals, a third—to Siberia'.[44] He said that in its attitude towards the party the central committee had become 'not accountable ministry, but unaccountable government'.

At the same congress, V N Maksimovsky counterposed 'democratic centralism' to the 'bureaucratic centralism' for which the centre was responsible. 'It is said,' he commented, 'that fish begin to putrefy from the head. The party begins to suffer at the top from the influence of bureaucratic centralism.'[45] Iakovlev stated: 'Ukraine has become a place of exile. Comrades unwanted for one reason or another in Moscow are exiled there.'[46] Sapronov declared: 'However much you talk about electoral rights, about the dictatorship of the proletariat, the striving of the central committee for party dictatorship in fact leads to the dictatorship of the party bureaucracy.'[47]

Nevertheless, throughout the civil war, the atmosphere of free discussion in party conferences and congresses was maintained. During the debate on the Brest-Litovsk peace treaty the party enjoyed, in the words of E H Carr, 'a freedom and publicity of discussion rarely practised by any party on vital issues of public policy.'[48] Bukharin's pamphlet defending 'Left Communism' against Lenin's position was published in May 1918 in one million copies.[49]

In the trade union debate the democratic traditions of Bolshevism remained clear. As Robert V Daniels, a historian not sympathetic to Bolshevism, put it: 'The fall of 1920 was the high point of open discussion in the Communist Party and of free opposition to the leaders' authority.'[50] Victor Serge wrote of the situation in the party during the civil war:

> [The party's] thinking is... very lively and free. It welcomes the anarchists and Left Social Revolutionaries of yesterday...

Nobody is afraid to contradict Lenin or to criticise him. His authority was so little imposed, the democratic manners of the revolution were still so natural, that it was a matter of course for any revolutionary, no matter how recent a recruit, to express himself frankly in the presence of the man who headed the party and the state. Lenin was more than once criticised unsparingly, in factories or conferences, by totally unknown people. He listened to his contestants coolly and replied to them in a commonsense manner.[51]

The banning of factions

At the Tenth Party Congress, meeting in the shadow of the Kronstadt uprising, Lenin moved a resolution to ban all factions, which the congress approved:

> The congress orders the immediate dissolution, without exception, of all groups that have been formed on the basis of some platform or other, and instructs all organisations to be very strict in ensuring that no manifestations of factionalism of any sort be tolerated. Failure to comply with this resolution of the congress is to entail unconditional and immediate expulsion from the party.[52]

To this was added a secret article giving the central committee unlimited disciplinary discretion:

> the congress authorises the central committee, in cases of breach of discipline or of a revival or toleration of factionalism, to apply all party penalties, including expulsion.

Members of the central committee could themselves be expelled from the party by a two-thirds vote at a combined meeting of the central committee and the party control commission.[53]

The banning of factional activity was not regarded as an absolute measure. When Riazanov proposed an amendment to rule out elections to the central committee on the basis of separate groups, each standing on its separate platform, Lenin objected:

> We cannot deprive the party and the members of the central committee of the right to appeal to the party in the event of disagreement on fundamental issues... Supposing we are faced with a question like, say, the conclusion of the Brest

peace? Can you guarantee that no such question will arise? No, you cannot. In the circumstances, the elections may have to be based on platforms.[54]

That the banning of factions did not mean the banning of all inner-party opposition was clear not only from this exchange between Lenin and Riazanov, but also from the fact that the resolution 'On Party Unity' itself invited dissidents to state their views in the Bolshevik press as well as in special discussion sheets.

Lenin also went out of his way to emphasise that there was substance in the Workers' Opposition's criticisms of the situation in the party and state. He referred to 'the services of the Workers' Opposition'. In the resolution on party unity he included the following:

> the congress at the same time declares that every practical proposal concerning questions to which the so-called Workers' Opposition group, for example, has devoted special attention, such as purging the party of non-proletarian and unreliable elements, combatting bureaucratic practices, developing democracy and workers' initiative... must be examined with the greatest care and tested in practice.[55]

Even in the darkest days of the civil war, factions had not been banned in the Bolshevik Party. The Mensheviks and Social Revolutionaries were harassed, now outlawed, now allowed to come out into the open. Such policy changes were dictated by the circumstances of the war, and by the vacillations of these parties. But at the Tenth Party Congress in March 1921 not only were these parties outlawed, but so also were factions inside the ruling Bolshevik Party. There was a feeling among the Bolsheviks that there was no alternative. Perhaps the attitude of the party was best summed up in Radek's words to the congress:

> In voting for this resolution, I feel that it can well be turned against us, and nevertheless I support it... Let the central committee in a moment of danger take the severest of measures against the best party comrades, if it finds this necessary. Let the central committee even be mistaken! That is less dangerous than the wavering which is now observable.[56]

In general one can say that at this time Trotsky was an enthusiastic supporter of the claims of authority and centralisation in the party. He seems to have been less sensitive than Lenin to the dangers inherent in the situation— only later, in 1923, does he become aware of the bureaucratic threat. But while Trotsky supported this accumulation of bureaucratic power, he was not himself centrally involved in it. The party and state apparatus was increasingly falling under the control of Stalin and his faction—a fact that was to become immensely important after the departure of Lenin.

Chapter thirteen

First steps of the Communist International

AT THE OUTBREAK of the First World War both Lenin and Trotsky argued the need to build a new international. After the October revolution the time came to honour that pledge.

Marxists, beginning with Marx himself in **The German Ideology** of 1845, had always conceived revolution as an international process. Trotsky, in his classic work **Results and Prospects** (1906), had stated specifically that the Russian working class would be unable to maintain itself in power without direct state aid from the victorious European proletariat. Trotsky, Lenin and all the other leading Bolsheviks constantly repeated the same idea throughout the revolution—at that time the notion of building socialism in one country never entered anyone's head.

However, the devastating effects of the civil war lent a special urgency to this general consideration. As we have seen in the preceding chapters the forced militarisation of the Soviet Republic, the destruction of the already fragile economy, the straining of relations with the peasantry and the decimation of the minority working class, all generated increasing bureaucratic tendencies. Ultimately the only escape from these pressures lay in the spreading of the revolution internationally. This required international organisation.

On 24 January 1919 an invitation was issued to the Founding Congress of the Third or Communist International (Comintern). This invitation was drafted by Trotsky. The 'objects and tactics' of the new international were summed up thus:

1) The present era is the era of the disintegration and collapse of the entire world capitalist system, which will drag the

whole of European civilisation down with it if capitalism with its insoluble contradictions is not destroyed.

2) The task of the proletariat now is to seize state power immediately. The seizure of state power means the destruction of the state apparatus of the bourgeoisie and the organisation of a new proletarian apparatus of power.

3) The new apparatus of power should embody the dictatorship of the proletariat (and in some places also of the rural semi-proletariat, the village poor), that is, it should be the instrument for the systematic suppression of the exploiting classes and their expropriation...

4) The dictatorship of the proletariat must be the lever for the immediate expropriation of capital and for the abolition of private property in the means of production and their transformation into national property...

5) In order to safeguard the socialist revolution, to defend it against internal and external enemies, to assist other national sections of the fighting proletariat and so on, it is essential to disarm the bourgeoisie and their agents completely, and to arm the proletariat.

6) The world situation today demands the closest possible contact between the different sections of the revolutionary proletariat and the complete union of the countries where the socialist revolution has already been victorious.

7) The fundamental methods of struggle are mass actions of the proletariat leading to open armed conflict with the political rule of capital.[1]*

On 2-6 March 1919 the Founding Congress of the Communist International met in Moscow. It was a puny affair. There were 51 delegates: 35 with voting rights, representing 19 parties and organisations, and 19 with consultative votes, representing 16 organisations. These figures are actually very misleading, as the delegates were far from representative. Of the 35 with voting rights, only four were not then residing in Russia: one each from

* The inclusion of the invitation in the Russian edition of Trotsky's **Collected Works**,[2] published in 1926, is sufficient evidence of Trotsky's authorship; an editorial note in Lenin's **Collected Works**,[3] published in 1935, attributes the authorship to Lenin and Bukharin—the editorial process was by then under Stalin's control.

Norway and Sweden, neither of which had a Communist Party, and two others specially delegated to the congress from countries where a Communist Party did exist: Max Albert (the pseudonym of Hugo Eberlein) from Germany, and Gruber (the pseudonym of Karl Steinhardt) from Austria, representing a tiny communist group. The majority of the delegates represented national communist groups affiliated to the Bolshevik Federation of Foreign Communist Groups. Their membership was very small, ranging from about ten in the French group to 90 (in December 1918) in the Hungarian and 112 in the Yugoslav.[4]

In the history of the international labour movement there had never previously been a meeting so small and so unrepresentative that actually started such a massive and powerful international movement. Nothing was further from the Bolshevik leaders' minds, however, than the intention of giving an assortment of small sects the label of an International. When they founded the Communist International they were relying on what they foresaw was going to happen in Europe: mass communist parties would emerge in the revolutionary struggles ahead. They assumed correctly that in the revolutionary situation existing after the war and with the example of victorious Bolshevism, the communist sects would rise to achieve mass influence.

At the congress itself Trotsky made only a brief appearance, since at the time Kolchak started his spring offensive on the eastern front. Trotsky gave the congress a short explanation of the main lines of his military policy. Then he presented it with a manifesto he had written to introduce the new International to the world:

> Seventy-two years ago the Communist Party proclaimed its programme to the world in the form of a Manifesto written by the greatest heralds of the proletarian revolution, Karl Marx and Frederick Engels... The development of Communism during this three-quarters of a century proceeded along complex paths: side by side with periods of stormy upsurge it knew periods of decline; side by side with successes—cruel defeats. But essentially the movement proceeded along the path indicated in advance by the **Communist Manifesto**. The epoch of final, decisive struggle has come later than the apostles of the socialist

revolution had expected and hoped. But it has come. We Communists, the representatives of the revolutionary proletariat of the various countries of Europe, America and Asia who have gathered in Soviet Moscow, feel and consider ourselves to be the heirs and consummators of the cause whose programme was affirmed 72 years ago. Our task is to generalise the revolutionary experience of the working class, to purge the movement of the corroding admixture of opportunism and social patriotism, to unify the efforts of all genuinely revolutionary parties of the world proletariat and thereby facilitate and hasten the victory of the Communist revolution throughout the world.[5]

Trotsky's manifesto gave a sharp and incisive survey of the changes in the world economy during the First World War, the transformation of free-market capitalism into state-monopoly capitalism:

During the decades preceding the war, free competition, as the regulator of production and distribution, had already been thrust aside in the main fields of economic life by the system of trusts and monopolies; during the course of the war the regulating-directing role was torn from the hands of these economic groups and transferred directly into the hands of military-state power.[6]

Which class should dominate the state-controlled economy? This was the question facing humanity:

The state-isation of economic life, against which capitalist liberalism used to protest so much, has become an accomplished fact. There is no turning back from this fact—it is impossible to return not only to free competition but even to the domination of trusts, syndicates and other economic octopuses. Today the one and only issue is: who shall henceforth be the bearer of state-ised production—the imperialist state or the state of the victorious proletariat?[7]

The reformists, said the manifesto, evaded the issues facing the proletariat and preached conciliation:

The opportunists, who before the world war summoned the workers to practise moderation for the sake of gradual transition to socialism, and who during the war demanded class docility in the name of civil peace and national defence, are again demanding self-renunciation of the proletariat —this time for the purpose of overcoming the terrible consequences of the war. If these preachments were to find acceptance among the working masses, capitalist development in new, much more concentrated and monstrous forms would be restored on the bones of several generations—with the perspective of a new and inevitable world war. Fortunately for mankind this is not possible.[8]

The development of capitalism and imperialism put on the order of the day the need for an alliance of the proletariat of Europe and America with the national liberation movements of the colonies:

The last war, which was by and large a war for colonies, was at the same time a war conducted with the help of colonies. The colonial populations were drawn into the European war on an unprecedented scale. Indians, Negroes, Arabs and Madagascans fought on the territories of Europe—for the sake of what? For the sake of their right to continue to remain the slaves of England and France? Never before has the infamy of capitalist rule in the colonies been delineated so clearly; never before has the problem of colonial slavery been posed so sharply as it is today.[9]

The workers and peasants not only of Annam, Algiers and Bengal, but also of Persia and Armenia, will gain their opportunity of independent existence only in that hour when the workers of England and France, having overthrown Lloyd George and Clemenceau, will have taken state power into their own hands. Even now the struggle in the more developed colonies, while taking place only under the banner of national liberation, immediately assumes a more or less clearly defined social character. If capitalist Europe has violently dragged the most backward sections of the world into the whirlpool of capitalist relations, then socialist Europe will come to the aid of liberated colonies with her technology, her organisation and her ideological influence in order to facilitate their transition to a planned and organised socialist economy.

Colonial slaves of Africa and Asia! The hour of proletarian dictatorship in Europe will strike for you as the hour of your own emancipation![10]

The manifesto, however, was addressed primarily to the proletariat of Europe. It argued the case for the dictatorship of the proletariat very strongly:

> The entire bourgeois world accuses the Communists of destroying freedom and political democracy. These are lies. Upon assuming power the proletariat merely lays bare the complete impossibility of employing the methods of bourgeois democracy and creates the conditions and forms of a new and much higher workers' democracy.[11]

> The wails of the bourgeois world against civil war and against Red Terror represent the most monstrous hypocrisy yet known in the history of political struggles. There would be no civil war if the clique of exploiters who have brought mankind to the very brink of ruin did not resist every forward step of the toiling masses, if they did not organise conspiracies and assassinations, and did not summon armed assistance from without in order to maintain or restore their thievish privileges.
>
> Civil war is imposed upon the working class by its mortal enemies. Without renouncing itself and its own future, which is the future of all mankind, the working class cannot fail to answer blow for blow.
>
> While never provoking civil war artificially, the Communist parties seek to shorten as much as possible the duration of civil war whenever the latter does arrive with iron necessity; they seek to reduce to a minimum the number of victims and, above all, to assure victory to the proletariat.[12]

The new Communist International, it said, was the heir of all socialist traditions the world over:

> we Communists, united in the Third International, consider ourselves the direct continuators of the heroic endeavours and martyrdom of a long line of revolutionary generations from Babeuf—to Karl Liebknecht and Rosa Luxemburg.

If the First International presaged the future course of development and indicated its paths, if the Second International gathered and organised millions of workers, then the Third International is the International of open mass action, the International of revolutionary realisation, the International of the deed.[13]

Zinoviev, at the Eighth Congress of the Russian party, described this document by Trotsky as 'a second Communist Manifesto'.[14]

Trotsky was emphatic on the international significance of the Russian revolution. However, he was conscious of the radical differences in the conditions of the revolution in Russia compared with those facing the revolution in western and central Europe: it would be far more difficult to achieve victory in the advanced capitalist countries of Europe than in backward Russia.

A couple of weeks after the first congress of the Comintern, Trotsky compared the German revolution with the Russian revolution, showing why it would be much more difficult for the German proletariat to win power than the Russian:

History once again exhibited to the world one of its dialectic contradictions: precisely because the German working class had expended most of its energy in the previous epoch upon self-sufficient organisation construction, occupying the first place in the Second International both in party as well as trade union apparatus—precisely because of this, in a new epoch, at the moment of its transition to open revolutionary struggle for power the German working class proved to be extremely defenceless organisationally.[15]

The Russian proletariat was fortunate in having a revolutionary party; not so the proletariat of Germany:

In the absence of a centralised revolutionary party with a combat leadership whose authority is universally accepted by the working masses; in the absence of leading combat *nuclei* and leaders, tried in action and tested in experience throughout the various centres and regions of the proletarian movement; this movement upon breaking out into the streets became of necessity intermittent, chaotic, creeping in character.[16]

However in the coming struggles the German proletariat should be able to forge the needed instrument for victory:

> The difficulties, the partial defeats and the great sacrifices of the German proletariat should not for a moment dishearten us. History does not offer the proletariat a choice of ways. The stubborn, unabated, erupting and re-erupting, creeping revolution is clearly approaching the critical moment when, having mobilised and trained all its forces in advance for combat, the revolution will deal the class enemy the final mortal blow.[7]

A few days later Trotsky wrote a prophetic article pointing out the danger that the pioneering position of Russia in the world revolution would lead to national messianism. He delivers a clear antidote to this:

> In our analysis there is not an atom of 'messianism'. The revolutionary 'primogeniture' of the Russian proletariat is only temporary. The mightier the opportunist conservatism among the summits of the German, French or English proletariat, all the more grandiose will be the power generated for their revolutionary onslaught by the proletariat of these countries, a power which the proletariat is already generating today in Germany. The dictatorship of the Russian working class will be able to finally entrench itself and to develop into a genuine, all-sided socialist construction only from the hour when the European working class frees us from the economic yoke and especially the military yoke of the European bourgeoisie, and, having overthrown the latter, comes to our assistance with its organisation and its technology. Concurrently, the leading revolutionary role will pass over to the working class with the greater economic and organisational power. If today the centre of the Third International lies in Moscow—and of this we are profoundly convinced—then on the morrow this centre will shift westward: to Berlin, to Paris, to London. However joyously the Russian proletariat has greeted the representatives of the world working class within the Kremlin walls, it will with an even greater joy send its representives to the Second Congress of the Communist International in one of the

Western European capitals. For a world Communist Congress in Berlin or Paris would signify the complete triumph of the proletarian revolution in Europe and consequently throughout the world.[18]

This hope for a speedy victory of the revolution in the West was shared by Lenin and other Bolshevik leaders at the time.

A few months later Trotsky had second thoughts about the imminence of the revolution in the West. On 5 August 1919 he sent a secret memorandum from the front to the central committee urging a radical reorientation in international affairs. This memorandum, a product of Trotsky's fantastically creative imagination, in a way pioneered the 'Theses on the National and Colonial Question' that Lenin introduced at the Second Congress of the Comintern in July-August 1920. Trotsky wrote:

> the failure of the general strike demonstration [in Germany], the strangulation of the Hungarian Republic and the continuance of open support for the campaign against Russia are all symptoms of the sort that indicate that the incubatory preparatory period of the revolution in the West may last for indeed a considerable time yet...
>
> We have up to now devoted too little attention to agitation in Asia. However, the international situation is evidently shaping in such a way that the road to Paris and London lies via the towns of Afghanistan, the Punjab and Bengal.*
>
> Our military successes in the Urals and in Siberia should raise the prestige of the Soviet revolution throughout the whole of oppressed Asia to an exceptionally high level. It is essential to exploit this factor and concentrate somewhere in the Urals or in Turkestan a revolutionary academy, the political and military headquarters of the Asian revolution, which in the period immediately ahead may turn out to be far more effectual than the executive committee of the Third International. A start should already now be made with organising matters in this direction on a more serious basis, with assembling the necessary personnel, linguists and translators of books, and with recruiting indigenous

---

* It should be noted that the famous quotation attributed to Lenin, according to which the most direct road for the revolution in France or Britain ought to run by way of India, is not to be found in his **Works**.

revolutionaries—using all resources and means available to us...

Preservation of present-day slaughterhouse capitalism for even a few years infers inevitable attempts at intensifying colonial exploitation, but also, on the other hand, equally inevitable attempts at uprisings. Asia may become the arena of the next uprisings. Our task lies in effecting the necessary switch of the centre of gravity of our international orientation at the opportune moment.[19]

The Second Congress of the Comintern

By the time of its Second Congress, from 19 July to 7 August 1920, the International had transformed itself from a collection of small sects (if one excludes the Russian party) into a *mass* organisation. The Italian Socialist Party had voted to affiliate to the Comintern at its conference in Bologna in September 1919, adding 300,000 members to the International. In June 1919 the Bulgarian Socialists, known as *Tesniaki*—'narrow', who had consistently held a revolutionary internationalist position very close to Bolshevism, also voted to affiliate. This was a mass party with 35,478 members in 1920. The Yugoslav Socialist Party, another mass party, also joined. The Czechoslovak Social-Democratic Party split in December 1920, the Communist Left taking more than half the membership and establishing a Communist Party of 350,000 members. A separate split in the Social-Democratic Party of the German-speaking minority added further forces and after their unification the Czechoslovak party claimed 400,000 members. The Norwegian Labour Party affiliated in spring 1919, and in Sweden the majority of the Socialist Party, after a split, also joined the Comintern, adding another 17,000 members.

In Germany the Independent Social-Democratic Party (USPD), with its 800,000 members, which had split from the German Social-Democratic Party (SPD) in April 1917 under pressure from the revolutionary mood among the masses, veered markedly to the left in 1919 and 1920. At its Leipzig Congress in December 1919 it decided by 227 votes to 54 to leave the Second International—but by 169 to 114 not to join the Third International. In France the Socialist Party joined the Comintern with its 140,000 members.

Trotsky made only a brief appearance at the Second Congress of the Comintern in order to endorse the '21 Conditions' for membership of parties in the International. He did not participate in the rest of the discussion at the congress on important issues of strategy and tactics: on the role of Communist parties in the proletarian revolution, on parliamentarism, the trade union question, the national and colonial question, and the agrarian question. This was because he was overburdened by military affairs, as the Polish-Russian war was raging. He came to the congress just towards its end—at the time when the Red Army stood at the gates of Warsaw—to present the manifesto he had written on behalf of the International. Again his brilliant pen produced a masterpiece that merits extensive quotation.

The manifesto starts by summarising the international scene after the Treaty of Versailles, which had formally concluded the First World War:

> The bourgeoisie throughout the world sorrowfully recalled its yesteryears. All of its mainstays in foreign and domestic relations have been either overthrown or shaken. 'Tomorrow' looms like a black threat over the exploiters' world...
>
> The Versailles Treaty has created no new balance of power in place of the old...
>
> The programme of 'organising Europe', advanced by German imperialism at the moment of its greatest military successes, has been inherited by the victorious Entente. When the rulers of the Entente place the defeated bandits of the German Empire in the defendant's dock, the latter will truly be judged by a 'court of peers'—their peers in crime.
>
> But the victors' camp likewise contains a number of those who have themselves been vanquished.
>
> Intoxicated by chauvinist fumes of a victory which she won for others, bourgeois France considers herself the commandress of Europe. In reality, never before has *France* and the very foundations of her existence been so slavishly dependent upon the more powerful states—England and North America—as she is today...
>
> The power of ruined and blood-drained France is illusory, almost burlesque in character; sooner or later this will penetrate even into the brains of French social-patriots.[20]

The president of the United States, [Woodrow Wilson], the great prophet of platitudes, has descended from Mount Sinai in order to conquer Europe, '14 Points' in hand. Stockbrokers, cabinet members and businessmen never deceive themselves for a moment about the meaning of this new revelation. But by way of compensation the European 'Socialists', with doses of Kautskyan brew, have attained a condition of religious ecstasy and accompanied Wilson's sacred ark, dancing like King David.[21]

The Versailles Treaty, said the manifesto, had created 'Babylon on the eve of its destruction':[22]

The programme of liberation of small nations, advanced during the war, has led to the complete ruination and enslavement of the Balkan peoples, victors and vanquished alike, and to the Balkanisation of a large part of Europe.

Virtually each one of the newly created 'national' states has an *irridenta* of its own, [in other words] its own internal national ulcer...

Official, governmental, national, civilised, bourgeois Europe —as it has issued from the war and the Versailles peace— resembles an insane asylum. Artificially split-up little states, whose economy is choking to death within their borders, snarl at one another, and wage wars over harbours, provinces and insignificant towns.[23]

The world bourgeoisie was becoming ever more cruel and barbaric:

The war has inured [the bourgeoisie] to subjecting a whole number of countries to a hunger-blockade, to bombarding from the air and setting fire to cities and villages, expediently spreading the *bacilli* of cholera, carrying dynamite in diplomatic pouches, counterfeiting his opponents' currency; he has become accustomed to bribery, espionage and smuggling on a hitherto unequalled scale. The usages of war have been taken over, after the conclusion of peace, as the usages of commerce. The chief commercial operations are fused nowadays with the functions of the state, which steps to the fore as a world robber gang equipped with all the instruments of violence.[24]

The manifesto describes the counter-revolutionary bourgeois political regimes:

> Since the war, during which the federal electoral bodies played the part of impotent but noisy patriotic stooges for their respective ruling imperialist cliques, the parliaments have fallen into a state of complete prostration. All the important issues are now decided outside the parliament...
>
> The real masters of the situation and the rulers of state destiny are—Lord Rothschild and Lord Weir, Morgan and Rockefeller, Schneider and Loucheur, Hugo Stinnes and Felix Deutsch, Rizello and Agnelli—these gold, coal, oil, and metal-kings—who operate behind the scenes and who send their second-rank lieutenants into parliaments—to carry out their instructions.

In the sharp class conflict of today sheer force decided everything:

> There is not a single serious issue today which is decided by ballot. Of democracy nothing remains save memories in the skulls of reformists. The entire state organisation is reverting more and more to its primordial form, [that is] detachments of armed men. Instead of counting ballots, the bourgeoisie is busy counting up bayonets, machine guns and cannons which will be at its disposal at the moment when the question of power and property forms is posed point blank for decision.[25]

The decisive rampart of world capitalism was the bureaucracy of social democracy and the trade unions:

> the proletariat is being thwarted in its international revolutionary actions not so much by the half-destroyed barbed wire entanglements that remain set up between the countries since the war, as it is by the egotism, conservatism, stupidity and treachery of the old party and trade union organisations which have climbed upon its back during the preceding epoch.[26]

The manifesto also deals with two key issues discussed by the Second Congress: the fight against ultra-leftism and the colonial question. For the debate on ultra-leftism, Lenin produced his famous booklet **Left-wing Communism—an infantile disorder**, and on the colonial question he produced theses.

On the ultra-left policy of boycotting parliament and the reformist trade unions, Trotsky declared:

> Waging a merciless struggle against reformism in the trade unions and against parliamentary cretinism and careerism, the Communist International at the same time condemns all sectarian summonses to leave the ranks of the multimillioned trade union organisations or to turn one's back upon parliamentary and municipal institutions. The Communists do not separate themselves from the masses who are being deceived and betrayed by the reformists and the patriots, but engage the latter in an irreconcilable struggle within the mass organisations and institutions established by bourgeois society, in order to overthrow them the more surely and the more quickly...
>
> The *soviet* system is not an abstract principle opposed by Communists to the principle of parliamentarism. The *soviet* system is a class apparatus which is destined to do away with parliamentarism and to take its place during the struggle and as a result of the struggle.[27]

On the colonial question the manifesto emphasises the significance of the anti-imperialist struggle for the international proletarian revolution:

> The toilers of the colonial and semi-colonial countries have awakened. In the boundless areas of India, Egypt, Persia, over which the gigantic octopus of English imperialism sprawls— in this uncharted human ocean vast internal forces are constantly at work, upheaving huge waves that cause tremors in the City's stocks and hearts.
>
> In the movements of colonial peoples, the social element blends in diverse forms with the national element, but both of them are directed against imperialism. The road from the first stumbling baby-steps to the mature forms of struggle is being traversed by the colonies and backward countries in general through a forced march, under the pressure of modern imperialism and under the leadership of the revolutionary proletariat.[28]

The manifesto also offers a devastating indictment of socialists who fail to defend the rights of oppressed nationalities:

The socialist who aids directly or indirectly in perpetuating the privileged position of one nation at the expense of another, who accommodates himself to colonial slavery, who draws a line of distinction between races and colours in the matter of human rights, who helps the bourgeoisie of the metropolis to maintain its rule over the colonies instead of aiding the armed uprising of the colonies; the British socialist who fails to support by all possible means the uprisings in Ireland, Egypt and India against the London plutocracy —such a socialist deserves to be branded with infamy, if not with a bullet, but in no case merits either a mandate or the confidence of the proletariat.[29]

Chapter fourteen

The Comintern: Trotsky teaches strategy and tactics

The Third Congress

THE CONGRESSES of the Comintern were schools of strategy and tactics, and at them Lenin and Trotsky played the part of teachers, while the leaders of the young Communist Parties were the pupils. Especially significant were the Third and Fourth Congresses.

The revolutionary high tide of 1918-19 failed to produce victory for the proletariat. The revolutionary wave ebbed before the Communist parties grew up and reached the maturity they needed to lead the struggle for workers' power. This gave the bourgeoisie the opportunity to achieve the stabilisation of capitalism. When the Third Congress of the Communist International met (22 June–12 July 1921) the immediately revolutionary situation had passed. The crucial issue facing the congress was what revolutionary parties should do in a non-revolutionary situation.

Trotsky delivered the report on the world economic crisis and on the new tasks of the Communist International. This surveyed the various defeats suffered by the revolutionary movement since 1919 and proceeded to analyse the economic position of the leading powers, world trade, the prospects for economic recovery and its impact on the class struggle. Trotsky concluded that capitalism had managed to restore a temporary, uncertain and uneven equilibrium, while the situation at bottom remained revolutionary.

> In 1919 the European bourgeoisie was in a state of extreme confusion. Those were the days of panic, the days of a truly insane fear of Bolshevism...

The year 1919 was, without doubt, the most critical year for the bourgeoisie. In 1920 and 1921 we observe a gradual influx of self-assurance among the bourgeoisie and along with this an undeniable consolidation of its state apparatus, which immediately following the war was actually on the verge of disintegration in various countries...[1]

Why was the revolution not victorious?

In the most critical year for the bourgeoisie, the year 1919, the proletariat of Europe could undoubtedly have captured state power with minimum sacrifices, had there been at its head a genuine revolutionary organisation, setting forth clear aims and capably pursuing them, [in other words] a strong Communist Party. But there was none. On the contrary, in seeking after the war to conquer new living conditions for itself, and in assuming an offensive against bourgeois society, the working class had to drag on its back the parties and trade unions of the Second International, all of whose efforts, both conscious and instinctive, were essentially directed towards the preservation of capitalist society.[2]

By and large the Communist leaders in Europe had the illusion that as the Russian proletariat had managed to make a revolution it would not be difficult for the European proletariat to do the same. Trotsky had to reiterate what he had said at the First and Second Congresses of the Comintern: that the Western European bourgeoisie was far more formidable an enemy than the Russian bourgeoisie had been.

The economic recovery of capitalism after the war was intermittent and uneven. In 1921 there was a short-lived economic crisis. After analysing the economic situation of world capitalism at the Third Congress, Trotsky posed the question: what would be the impact of an economic recovery on the class struggle of the proletariat? He argued against a mechanical approach that identified economic crisis with a revolutionary situation and economic improvement with a decline of revolutionary prospects.

Many comrades say that if an improvement takes place in this epoch it would be fatal for our revolution. No, under no circumstances. In general, there is no automatic dependence of the proletarian revolutionary movement upon a crisis. There is only a dialectical interaction.

Let us look at the relations in Russia. The 1905 revolution was defeated. The workers bore great sacrifices. In 1906 and 1907 the last revolutionary flare-ups occurred and by the autumn of 1907 a great world crisis broke out... Throughout 1907 and 1908 and 1909 the most terrible crisis reigned in Russia too. It killed the movement completely, because the workers had suffered so greatly during the struggle that this depression could act only to dishearten them. There were many disputes among us over what would lead to the revolution: a crisis or a favourable conjuncture?

At the time many of us defended the viewpoint that the Russian revolutionary movement could be regenerated only by a favourable economic conjuncture. And that is what took place. In 1910, 1911 and 1912, there was an improvement in our economic situation and a favourable conjuncture which acted to reassemble the demoralised and devitalised workers who had lost their courage. They realised again how important they were in production; and they passed over to an offensive, first in the economic field and later in the political field as well. On the eve of the war the working class had become so consolidated, thanks to this period of prosperity, that it was able to pass to a direct assault.

This provided a lesson for 1921:

should we today, in the period of the greatest exhaustion of the working class resulting from the crisis and the continual struggle, fail to gain victory, which is possible, then a change in the conjuncture and a rise in living standards would not have a harmful effect upon the revolution, but would be on the contrary highly propitious.[3]

The question, which is raised by many comrades abstractly, of just what would lead to revolution, impoverishment or prosperity, is completely false when so formulated... Neither impoverishment nor prosperity as such can lead to revolution, but the alternation of prosperity and impoverishment, the crises, the uncertainty, the absence of stability—these are the motor factors of revolution.[4]

The 'Theses on the International Situation and the Tasks of the Comintern' written by Trotsky (aided by Varga) and adopted unanimously by the Third Congress summed up the world situation and the tactics needed by Communist parties. In a nutshell, the proletariat now faced defensive struggles:

The fundamental task of the Communist Party in the current crisis is to lead the present defensive struggles of the proletariat, to extend their scope, to deepen them, to unify them, and in harmony with the march of events, *to transform them into decisive political struggles for the ultimate goal...*

Whatever the shifts in the course of the struggle, the Communist Party always strives to consolidate organisationally new bases of support, trains the masses in active manoeuvring, arms them with new methods and practices, designed for direct and open clashes with the enemy forces. Utilising every breathing spell in order to assimilate the experience of the preceding phase of the struggle, the Communist Party seeks to deepen and extend the class conflicts, to co-ordinate them nationally and internationally by unity of goal and unity of practical action, and in this way, at the head of the proletariat, shatter all resistance on the road to its dictatorship and the socialist revolution.

After stating that there was no permanent reformist solution to the problems facing the working class and reaffirming that the destruction of capitalism remained the 'guiding and immediate mission', the 'Theses on Tactics' adopted by the Third Congress argued the need for Communists to fight for reforms:

the Communist parties must put forward demands whose fulfilment is an immediate and urgent working-class need, and they must fight for these demands in mass struggle, regardless of whether they are compatible with the profit economy of the capitalist class or not.

The task of the Communist parties is to extend, to deepen, and to unify this struggle for concrete demands...

Every objection to the putting forward of such partial demands, every charge of reformism on this account, is an emanation of the same inability to grasp the essential conditions of revolutionary action as was expressed in the hostility of some Communist groups to participation in the trade unions, or to making use of parliament. It is not a question of proclaiming the final goal to the proletariat, but of intensifying the practical struggle which is the only way of leading the proletariat to the struggle for the final goal.[5]

In one of the most important programmatic documents of revolutionary Marxism, Trotsky developed the theme of the united front. 'On the United Front', theses drafted for the enlarged plenum of the executive committee of the Comintern, states:

> The task of the Communist Party is to lead the proletarian revolution. In order to summon the proletariat for the direct conquest of power and to achieve it the Communist Party must base itself on the overwhelming majority of the working class.

So long as it does not hold this majority, the party must fight to win it. If the theme of the First and Second Congresses of the Comintern was the struggle for workers' power, then the theme of the Third Congress was 'To the Masses', that is, the conquest of power through a previous conquest of the masses achieved on the basis of their daily life and struggle.

The Communist Party can win the majority of the proletariat, said the theses, by leading it in clashes with the capitalists:

> In these clashes—insofar as they involve the vital interests of the entire working class, or of its majority, or of this or that section—the working masses sense the need of unity in action, of unity in resisting the onslaught of capitalism or unity in taking the offensive against it. Any party which mechanically counterposes itself to this need of the working class for unity in action will unfailingly be condemned in the minds of the workers.

Hence the need for a united front between Communists and Social Democrats:

> The problem of the united front—despite the fact *that a split is inevitable in this epoch between the various political organisations basing themselves on the working class*—grows out of the urgent need to secure for the working class the

possibility of a united front in the struggle against capitalism.

...wherever the Communist Party already constitutes a big, organised, political force, but not the decisive magnitude; wherever the party embraces organisationally, let us say, one-fourth, one-third, or even a larger proportion of the organised proletarian vanguard, it is confronted with the question of the united front in all its acuteness...

...the [Communist] party must assume the initiative in securing unity in these current struggles. Only in this way will the party draw closer to those two-thirds who do not as yet follow its leadership, who do not as yet trust the party because they do not understand it. Only in this way can the party win them over.

Should the reformist leaders be included in the united front?

Does the united front extend only to the working masses or does it also include the opportunist leaders?

The very posing of this question is a product of misunderstanding.

If we were able simply to unite the working masses around our own banner or around our practical immediate slogans, and skip over reformist organisations, whether party or trade union, that would of course be the best thing in the world. But then the very question of the united front would not exist in its present form.

The question arises from this, that certain very important sections of the working class belong to reformist organisations or support them. Their present experience is still insufficient to enable them to break with the reformist organisations and join us. It may be precisely after engaging in those mass activities, which are on the order of the day, that a major change will take place in this connection. That is just what we are striving for.

The policy of the united front does not assume that the reformist leaders will accept this policy wholeheartedly:

A policy aimed to secure the united front does not of course contain automatic guarantees that unity in action will actually be attained in all instances. On the contrary, in many cases, and perhaps even in the majority of cases, orgnisational agreements will be only half-attained or perhaps not at all. But it is necessary that the struggling masses should always be given the opportunity of convincing themselves that the non-achievement of unity in action was not due to our formalistic irreconcilability but to the lack of real will to struggle on the part of the reformists.

The involvement of the Communist Party in the united front in no way suspends its political independence from reformism and reformist parties:

We broke with the reformists and centrists in order to obtain complete freedom in criticising perfidy, betrayal, indecision and the half-way spirit in the labour movement. For this reason any sort of organisational agreement which restricts our freedom of criticism and agitation is absolutely unacceptable to us. We participate in a united front but do not for a single moment become dissolved in it. We function in the united front as an indepedent detachment. It is precisely in the course of struggle that broad masses must learn from experience that we fight better than the others, that we see more clearly than the others, that we are more audacious and resolute. In this way, we shall bring closer the hour of the united revolutionary front under the undisputed Communist leadership.[6]

The Communists had to carry out a two-edged policy: first, to secure success in achieving the immediate aims of the united front, secondly to win workers away from social democracy. To achieve both, the Communist Party had to know how to fight alongside social democracy and against it at one and the same time. Without sharp demarcation lines to divide it from social democracy, the Communist Party would slide into opportunism. The Communists should march separately from social democrats but strike together.

Powerful trends in a number of important Communist parties rejected the struggle for 'partial and immediate demands'. They thought this policy to be reformist. A set of ultra-left amendments to the 'Theses on Tactics' was submitted by the German, Austrian, Dutch and Italian parties. At one time these tendencies appeared to have a majority at the congress. Lenin wrote later: 'At that congress I was on the extreme right flank. I am convinced that it was the only correct stand to take...'[7] The same stand was taken by Trotsky. After a long, hard battle the line taken by Lenin and Trotsky finally carried the day.

The specific case around which the battle took place at the congress was that of the *Marzaktion*—the March Action in Germany.

Since the defeat of the Red Army at the gates of Warsaw the revolutionary fever in Europe had subsided. Against this background the leadership of the Communist Party of Germany (KPD), encourged by Zinoviev, president of the Comintern, by Bukharin and by Zinoviev's emissary Bela Kun, the leader of the failed Hungarian revolution, decided to 'spur on' the revolution in Germany by an act of insurrection—the *Marzaktion*.

Rioting in the coalfields of Mansfeld in Central Germany led on 16 March 1921 to the intervention of the Reichswehr, the German army. On the following day the central committee of the KPD (known as the Zentrale) called for a nationwide general strike on 24 March, urging the workers to seize arms, to organise themselves and to join the struggle against the counter-revolution. It was a desperate step, because all factories closed down in any case from Good Friday (25 March) through to Easter Monday. But the response to the Communist appeal was negligible.

In Berlin, the seat of the Zentrale, the strike movement failed completely. Most workers reported to their jobs on 24 March, and only a few factories were idle, despite attempts by the KPD to enforce shutdowns by attempted invasions by the unemployed. These methods aroused sharp criticism even within the party. Ernst Däumig, for instance, sent a furious letter to the Zentrale, in which he protested against the practice of pitting proletarians against proletarians. Equally indignant were the party officials in charge of trade union activities, who complained that the tactics employed by the Zentrale were wrecking their influence within the unions. The Zentrale obtained slightly more support in the Ruhr region and the Rhineland.[8]

But all in all, the general strike was a fiasco: the number of workers participating in it was estimated at only 200,000.[9] In his report to the Third Congress of the Comintern, Zinoviev spoke of the involvement of 500,000 workers.

The KPD-organised demonstrations were also pathetic. In Berlin they attracted fewer than 4000, while just a few weeks earlier the party had won 200,000 votes in elections.[10] By 1 April even the most stubborn diehards amongst the Communist leaders had to recognise the futility of the exercise. The Zentrale resolved to end the insurrection by calling off the 'nationwide' general strike. The collapse of the adventure was followed by a massive decline of the KPD: from some 400,000 members to 150,000 or less. Thousands of militants were thrown into prison and tens of thousands lost their jobs.

The German Communist Party leaders had tried to force the pace of struggle, to substitute the party militants for the mass movement. At the Third Congress these leaders and other ultra-lefts sought to justify their practice by means of a special 'Theory of the Offensive'. Trotsky launched a powerful attack on them:

> this famous philosophy of the offensive, absolutely non-Marxist, has arisen from the following propositions: 'A wall of passivity is gradually rising; this is a misfortune. The movement is stagnating. Therefore, forward march! Let us break through this wall!' It seems to me that a whole layer of leading and semi-leading comrades in the German party have been for quite some time educated in this spirit and they are waiting to hear what the congress has to say on this score...
>
> It is our duty to say clearly and precisely to the German workers that we consider this philosophy of the offensive to be the greatest danger. And in its practical implication to be the greatest political crime.[11]

In an article entitled 'The Main Lesson of the Third Congress', published in **Pravda** on 12 June 1921, Trotsky wrote:

> That trouble with revolutionary subjectivism, as Herzen put it, is this, that it mistakes the second or fifth month of pregnancy for the ninth. No one has yet done so with impunity.[12]

Trotsky returned to the theme in a speech a month later:

> through an impatient application of the most drastic form of revolutionary struggle, at a time when conditions have not

yet matured for a decisive collision, one can obtain only negative results, and even bring about a revolutionary abortion instead of a mighty revolutionary birth.[13]

In a speech on the balance sheet of the Third Congress delivered at the Second Congress of the Communist Youth International (14 July 1921), Trotsky returned again to this theme:

> The idea of replacing the will of the masses by the resoluteness of the so-called vanguard is absolutely impermissible and non-Marxist. Through the consciousness and will of the vanguard it is possible to exert influence over the masses, it is possible to gain their confidence, but it is impossible to replace the masses by this vanguard. And for this reason the Third Congress has placed before all the parties, as the most important and unpostponable task, the demand that the majority of the toiling people be attracted to our side.[14]

Again on the same theme Trotsky said:

> *Only a traitor* could deny the need for a revolutionary offensive; but only a simpleton would reduce all revolutionary strategy to an offensive.[15]

The ultra-left impatience of the German leadership was but the other side of the coin of opportunism, Trotsky argued:

> opportunism expresses itself not only in moods of gradualism but also in political impatience: it frequently seeks to reap where it has not sown, to realise successes which do not correspond to its influence.[16]

A few weeks after the Third Congress Trotsky summed up its role:

> The Third Congress of the Comintern, if one were to express its significance in a succinct formula, will in all likelihood be inscribed in the annals of the labour movement as the highest school of revolutionary strategy. The First Congress of our Communist International issued the summons to rally the forces of the world proletarian revolution. The Second Congress elaborated the programmatic basis for mobilising

the forces. The Third International in its sessions already came in contact with these forces, consolidated them and was thus confronted with the most important practical questions of the revolutionary movement. That is why the Third Congress became... the highest school of revolutionary strategy.[17]

Trotsky had to teach the leaders of the young Communist parties that what characterised Bolshevism was not only its revolutionary scope but also its revolutionary realism—two aspects that are inseparable.

Trotsky's struggle, alongside Lenin, against the theory of the offensive and his brilliant advocacy of the united front gives the lie to the persistent allegation that Trotsky was an ultra-left. This notion, originating within the Stalinist apparatus, has received much wider circulation and acceptance. Thus, for example, Gramsci, the supposed *guru* of Euro-Communism and academic Marxism, could write that 'Bronstein [Trotsky] ...can be considered the political theorist of frontal attack in a period in which it only leads to defeats.'[18] The facts, however, demonstrate clearly that such a judgment is a one-sided caricature and falsification of Trotsky's position.

The Comintern may have been a superb school but Trotsky and the other Bolshevik leaders faced great difficulties in the attempt to achieve a rapid dissemination of the principles of Bolshevism. Not only was there the youthful ultra-leftism of many of the newly radicalised elements to contend with, but also the sly and stubborn resistance of many of the older pre-war opportunist leaders who had come over to the Comintern under mass pressure but had not changed their underlying outlook or political practice.

An interesting case study of these problems is provided by Trotsky's relations with the French Communist Party.

Trotsky and the French Communist Party

Of the Bolshevik leaders Trotsky, having spent nearly two years of the war in Paris, had most personal knowledge of the principal members of the leadership of the French Communist Party (PCF). Hence the executive committee of the Comintern elected Trotsky to chair its French commission. This took up a lot of Trotsky's time. His writings and speeches on the state of the French Communist Party fill 139 pages of his **First Five Years of the Communist International**.

The PCF was in poor shape. It claimed a membership of 120,000 in 1920, but during its first year of existence it was torn by factionalism and its membership halved. The PCF leadership disagreed with the executive committee of the Comintern on a series of major issues, including its attitude towards the reformists, the weakness of its parliamentary work, its failure to infiltrate the trade unions, the lack of discipline shown by its press, the 'Theory of the Offensive', the question of the united front and the colonial revolution. Trotsky's efforts to overcome opposition in the PCF were a labour of Sisyphus; the results were minimal.

The Comintern leadership failed completely to overcome the national traditions out of which the PCF developed—persistent right opportunism.

Before the Russian Revolution, very few people in France opposed the war, refused to accept the principle of national defence, or called on socialist deputies to vote against war credits —no more than a hundred militants, without any influence on the masses. 'Excepting a few groups of the extreme left,' says Robert Wohl, historian of French Communism, 'the names of Lenin and Trotsky had been unknown until the February revolution.'[19]

After the war, as a result of the clear bankruptcy of French reformism, the victory of the October revolution, and the survival of Bolshevik power, hundreds of thousands of people in France, as elsewhere, moved towards Communism. At the Congress of the French Socialist Party in Tours in December 1920, the overwhelming majority decided to join the Communist International. The result was that of the 179,800 members of the French Socialist Party (SFIO), 110,000 joined the Communist Party, while the dissidents were scarcely able to rally 30,000.[20] But the Socialist-turned-Communist Party was far from being really revolutionary. It was 'a coalition of left-wing and centrist groups... an unwieldy and hybrid political formation... an unstable compound of conflicting elements'.[21] Its most prominent leaders were out-and-out opportunists.

Take the case of Marcel Cachin, who remained a leader of the party until his death in 1958. When the 1914 war broke out he was:

a social-patriot of the deepest conviction; in 1915, as an agent of the French government, he had tried to persuade the Italian socialists to enter the war on the side of the Entente. Legend has it that it was Cachin who handed Mussolini the French subsidies that enabled him to start his own newspaper and shift from anti-patriotism to violent nationalism.[22]

In March 1917 Cachin went to Russia as a member of a delegation with the blessing of the French government, in order 'to revive the interest of the Russian socialists in the pursuit of the war'.[23] He went so far as to accuse Lenin of being a German agent.[24]

The general secretary of the new French Communist Party, L O Frossard, had similar political characteristics. He joined the Comintern simply hoping 'to drape traditional French socialism, which was now in disgrace because of its participation in the sacred union, with the prestige of the Russian Revolution and the Bolshevik regime.'[25]

At the Strasbourg conference of the SFIO in February 1920 Frossard declared:

No one has the right to say that adopting an attitude [in favour of national defence] is a sufficient ground for expulsion... Those who consider it necessary to defend their fatherland even under capitalism will not let themselves be treated as *pariahs*.[26]

At the Tours congress Frossard told the right wing, who opposed communism and hence split from the party: 'For my part, tomorrow I will speak of you without bitterness. Tomorrow I will not utter a single wounding word about you. I consider you socialists and I will say so.'[27]

(In 1923 Frossard resigned from the French Communist Party. He rejoined the Socialist Party in 1936, held ministerial posts in several Third Republic governments, and was a member of Petain's first government in 1940).

On 5 December 1921 the executive committee of the Comintern sent a letter drafted by Trotsky to the Marseilles congress of the PCF. In it Trotsky stated that:

Unlike the Second International, the Comintern does not rest content with offering congratulations and greetings to its sections. Being guided solely by the interests of world revolution, it has the duty to fraternally point out to them their respective weaknesses and to try, in the process of intimate joint and harmonious collaboration, to eliminate these weaknesses...

The [PCF] has suffered from a weak leadership. The central committee immersed itself in a whole number of current administrative duties and failed to give firm political leadership to the party, failed to give day-to-day direction to the party's thought and diversified activities, failed to create a collective consciousness. The party has suffered from a lack of policy; it has lacked an agrarian policy, a trade union policy, an electoral policy...

Beginning with the Marseilles Convention, the central committee must steer a much firmer course and become a genuine leading political body, controlling and inspiring the press, guiding the parliamentary work, taking a definite position, day by day, on all the political questions, domestic and foreign...

...the party must sketch out its line of conduct on questions pertaining to the trade unions. It must loudly proclaim to the working class its right and its duty to concern itself with these questions. It must demand of its members that they remain Communists inside the trade unions as well as in the party. A Communist Party cannot tolerate the fact that its members support the policy of Jouhaux and of the Amsterdam International...

Similarly the party must wage an energetic struggle against the ideas of anarchists and ordinary trade unionists who deny the role of the party in the revolution.

The tradition of the French Socialist Party was that the party, being a parliamentary organisation, kept out of industrial disputes. This tradition had been carried over into the PCF.

Those who maintain that the economic struggle is of no concern to the party are either complete ignoramuses or individuals seeking to make a mockery of Communism. The party must draw into its ranks all the best elements of the working class; and as touches the ideological aspect, it must become the inspirer of all forms of proletarian struggle, including of course the economic struggle as well. The trade union as such is not subordinate to the party as such. In this sense the trade unions remain independent. But the Communists who work in the trade unions must invariably function as disciplined Communists.

Many of the leaders of the PCF showed no discipline at all, involving themselves in issuing proclamations that opposed the basic policies of the Comintern.

During the French delegation's stay in Moscow, on the occasion of the Third World Congress, the [executive committee of the Comintern] called the attention of the delegates to the need of placing the unofficial party press under the control of the central committee. The [executive committee] had primarily in mind the newspaper *La Vague* published by Brizon, and *Journal du Peuple* by Fabre. Both Brizon and Fabre were advocating a policy incompatible with the policy of the party and the Communist International. The Second World Congress adopted the principled position that no party member could use the freedom of the press as a flimsy pretext for publishing periodicals not subject to the party's absolute political control...

Any delay in solving this problem would be all the more unfortunate in view of the fact that since the adoption of this resolution, an opportunist tendency had crystallised round *Journal du Peuple*, a tendency which bemoans the split that occurred at Tours and which to this day sheds tears over the departure of the dissidents [the SFIO breakaway] and which even advocates open collaboration with bourgeois parties...[28]

In January 1922 the PCF central committee passed a resolution opposing the policy of the united front. A special delegate conference of the party endorsed the committee's resolution by a vote of 46 to 12.[29]

On 2 March 1922 the executive committee of the Comintern unanimously passed a long set of theses in which Trotsky elaborated the tasks of the PCF and advocated the expulsion of all who supported a government of the 'Left Bloc', an alliance between the workers' parties and the bourgeois Radicals:

The split of Tours drew a basic line of demarcation between reformism and Communism. But it was absolutely unavoidable for the Communist Party issuing from this split to retain in some of its segments certain survivals of its reformist and parliamentary past... The survivals of the past... are expressed in: (1) an urge to restore unity with the reformists; (2) an urge towards a bloc with the radical wing of the bourgeoisie; (3) a substitution of petty-bourgeois humanitarian pacifism for revolutionary anti-militarism; (4) a false interpretation of the party's relations with the trade unions; (5) a struggle against genuine centralist leadership in the party; (6) efforts to replace international discipline in action by a platonic federation of national parties.[30]

In June the executive committee of the Comintern again sharply criticised the leadership of the PCF in a resolution drafted by Trotsky:

The International categorically warns against the application of the principles of federalism and autonomy inside the revolutionary party, which must be the mighty leader of revolutionary action.

On the trade union question the resolution states:

The International affirms that the greatest danger to the French working class and especially to the trade union movement is represented by individualistic, petty-bourgeois elements, hostile to the spirit of proletarian discipline and artful in dodging all organisational control over their activities.[31]

Regarding the attitude to the united front of workers' parties on the one hand and the 'Left Bloc' with bourgeois parties on the other, the resolution states:

The International affirms that the press and the leading bodies of the French Communist Party have given completely incorrect information to the party concerning the meaning and the importance of the tactic of the united front. The International simply sweeps aside the superficial judgments of journalists, who strive to see a revival of reformism where there is an enhancement in the methods of struggle against reformism.

...The idea of the 'Left Bloc' under the present conditions can corrupt a great many workers who have little or no political experience. The French Communist Party must bear in mind this perspective, which represents a very serious danger. To the idea of the 'Left Bloc' in its entire day-to-day propaganda it must systematically counterpose the idea of a bloc of all workers against the bourgeoisie.[32]

A general strike in Le Havre on 29 August 1922 exposed the complete bankruptcy of the PCF. The metal workers and the shipyard workers of Le Havre had come out on strike on 19 June 1922, when the management announced that their wages would be cut by 10 per cent. During July and August tension between the employers and the strikers mounted. In mid-August the port workers and sailors joined the movement, bringing the number of strikers to 40,000. On 25 August, after the arrest of some workers, the local unions called a one-day general strike. The next day there were bloody encounters between the police and the strikers. Three workers were killed, fifteen more wounded. The CGTU—the left-wing General Confederation of Trade Unions —responded by calling a general strike for 29 August.

The night the general strike was declared there was no one at the offices of *L'Humanité*, the Communist Party daily, or at the party headquarters. The leaders were all on vacation. The next day's edition of *L'Humanité* did not even carry the strike order.[33]

Another clear expression of the deeply entrenched reformism of the PCF was its attitude to the colonial question, which should have been central for a party in the metropolis of a great empire. Thus, for instance, the Algerian branch of the PCF had 'come out clearly against nationalist movements and nationalist revolts, unanimously and without a single voice being raised to sustain a contrary point of view, without a single native comrade having made the slightest comment.'

When the Comintern drafted an appeal for the liberation of Algeria and Tunisia in May 1922, the Algerian section of Sidi Bel Abbès replied with a memorandum requesting that the publication of the Comintern appeal in Algeria be countermanded.

The Communists of the Sidi Bel Abbès section, despite their long tradition of leftism, could not accept the International's colonial policy, said the memorandum. The liberation of Algeria would be reactionary, not progressive, if it preceded a victorious revolution on the mainland. The native population of North Africa, it said, was composed mostly of elements hostile to the economic, social and intellectual development necessary to enable an autonomous state to build communism. The job of the PCF in North Africa, therefore, was to establish a favourable attitude towards communism.

These propositions were accepted unanimously by the Second Communist Interfederal Congress of North Africa, on 7 December 1922. The attitude of the North African Communists was that appeals to revolt and communist propaganda among the native population would be not only premature, but dangerous.[34]

At the Fourth Congress of the Comintern, Trotsky again moved a resolution critical of the PCF. The behaviour of the party during the Le Havre general strike, this said, was the result of its separation of politics from the industrial struggle:

> By severing, in a manner false in principle, the class struggle of the proletariat into two allegedly independent spheres —economic and political—the party failed to evince, on this occasion too, any independent initiative, confining its activity to backing up the CGTU, as if the murder of four proletarians by the capitalist government were actually an economic act and not a political event of first-rate importance.[35]

A further plague afflicting the PCF was Freemasonry. Many of its leaders were Freemasons, including the general secretary, Frossard. At the Fourth Congress Trotsky described Freemasonry as a petty-bourgeois body imbued with Catholicism, with bankers, lawyers, parliamentary deputies and journalists in place of the cardinals and abbots. Supposedly non-political, as was the church, the function of Freemasonry was to attract labour leaders into the bourgeois camp:

> The fact... that a considerable number of French Communists belong to the Masonic lodges, constitutes... the most striking evidence that our French party has preserved not only the psychologic heritage of French reformism, parliamentarism

and patriotism, but also its connections, purely material and highly compromising to the party leadership, with the secret institutions of the radical bourgeoisie... a whole slew of prominent party workers—deputies, journalists, right up to members of the central committee, retain intimate ties with the secret organisations of the class enemy...

The International considers it urgent to put an end once for all to these compromising and demoralising connections...

The congress instructs the central committee of the French Communist Party to liquidate prior to 1 January 1923 all the connections between the party, in the person of its individual members or groups, with the Freemasons. Every Communist belonging to a Masonic lodge who fails prior to 1 January to openly announce to his party and to make public through the party press his complete break with Freemasonry is thereby automatically expelled from the Communist Party and is forever barred from membership in it.[36]

Finally Trotsky sharply criticised the PCF's attitude to nations oppressed by French imperialism:

The Fourth Congress once again calls attention to the exceptional importance for the Communist Party to carry on correct and systematic work in the colonies. The congress categorically condemns the position of the Communist section in Sidi Bel Abbès, which employs pseudo-Marxist phraseology in order to cover up a purely slaveholder's point of view, essentially in support of the imperialist rule of French capitalism over its colonial slaves.[37]

In conclusion

Lenin and Trotsky aimed to build mass Communist parties welded together by a clear understanding of their historical tasks, parties founded on clear programmes, combined with a correct relationship with the masses, in other words parties of strict principle united by revolutionary realism. Instead, the Communist parties outside Russia exhibited opportunist vagueness on the one hand, and sectarian aloofness on the other. They oscillated violently between opportunism and adventurism—the two poles of left centrism.

Of course one could argue that Communist parties could not

be expected to come into existence fully fledged even in the most acute revolutionary situation, which is true; or that time would have welded the parties into real, consistent revolutionary organisations. That is possibly also true. But time was the one thing history did not grant. In fact the national traditions of the Communist parties of Europe were very resistant to the pressure of Bolshevism. The grafting of Bolshevism was largely unsuccessful, a fact which contributed powerfully to the failure of the international revolution and thus to the eventual triumph of Stalinism in Russia.

One thing, however, the Communist International did achieve, and Trotsky played a role in this second only to Lenin. In its debates, theses and manifestoes it laid down a record of undiluted, uncorrupted revolutionary Marxism which remains relevant to this day. As Trotsky himself put it in 1933:

> The first congresses of the Communist International left us an invaluable programmatic heritage: the character of the modern epoch as an epoch of imperialism, that is, of capitalist decline; the nature of modern reformism and the methods of struggle with it; the relation between democracy and proletarian dictatorship; the role of the party in the proletarian revolution; the relationship between the proletariat and the petty bourgeoisie, especially the peasantry (agrarian question); the problem of nationalities and the liberation struggle of colonial peoples; work in the trade unions; the policy of the united front; the relation to parliamentarism... all these questions have been subjected by the first four congresses to a principled analysis that has remained unsurpassed until now.[38]

Chapter fifteen

Lenin and Trotsky join forces to fight bureaucracy

'Stop the retreat'

LENIN, in his report to the Tenth Congress of the party, made it clear that the New Economic Policy would strengthen capitalism in the countryside: '...the switch from the appropriation of surpluses to the tax will mean more *kulaks* [rich peasants] under the new system. They will appear where they could not appear before.'[1] In his summing-up of the debate on his report, Lenin said: 'Speakers here have asked, and I have received written questions to the same effect: "How will you retain the workers' state, if capitalism develops in the rural areas?" This peril... is an extremely serious one.'[2]

Trotsky too never avoided looking dangers in the face. He was brutally clear about the nature of War Communism and the retreat to NEP. In 'Theses on the Economic Situation in Soviet Russia from the Standpoint of the Socialist Revolution'—a summing up of his report to the Fourth Congress of the Comintern—Trotsky wrote the following:

> The methods of War Communism, that is, the methods of an extremely crude centralised registration and distribution, are superceded under the new policy by market methods: by buying and selling, by commercial calculation and competition. But in this market the workers' state plays the leading part as the most powerful property owner, and buyer and seller. Directly concentrated in the hands of the workers' state are the overwhelming majority of the productive forces of industry as well as all means of railway traffic. The activity of the state organs is thus controlled by the market and to a

considerable extent also directed by it. The profitability of each separate enterprise is ascertained through competition and commercial calculation. The market serves as the connecting link between agriculture and industry, between city and country.[3]

The NEP was a struggle between socialism and capitalism:

insofar as a free market exists, it inevitably gives rise to private capital which enters into competition with state capital—at first in the sphere of trade only, but attempting later to penetrate into industry as well. In place of the recent civil war between the proletariat and the bourgeoisie there has come the competition between proletarian and bourgeois industry. And just as the contest in the civil war involved in the main which side would succeed in attracting the peasantry politically, so today the struggle revolves chiefly around the peasant market. In this struggle the proletariat has mighty advantages on its side: the country's most highly developed productive forces and the state power. On the side of the bourgeoisie lies the advantage of greater proficiency and to a certain extent connections with foreign capital, particularly that of the White Guard emigrés.[4]

The struggle between state industry and private enterprise would decide the future of Russia:

Whither is the NEP leading us: toward capitalism or toward socialism? This is, of course, the central question. The market, the free trade in grain, competition, leases, concessions—what will be the upshot of all this? If you give the devil a finger, mightn't it be necessary to give him next an arm and then a shoulder, and, in the end, the whole body, too? We are already witnessing a revival of private capital in the field of trade, especially along the channels between the city and the village. For the second time in our country private merchants' capital is passing through the stage of primitive capitalist accumulation, while the workers' state is passing through the period of primitive socialist accumulation. No sooner does private merchants' capital arise than it seeks ineluctably to worm its way into industry as well. The state is leasing factories and plants to private businessmen. The accumulation of private capital now goes on, in consequence, not merely in trade but also in industry. Isn't it then likely that *Messrs* Exploiters—the speculators, the merchants, the lessees and the concessionaires—will wax more powerful under the protection of the workers' state, gaining control of an ever larger sector of the national economy, draining off the elements of socialism through the medium of the market, and later at the propitious moment, gaining control of state power too?[5]

At the end of 1921 and the beginning of 1922 both Lenin and Trotsky called for a stop to the retreat in the face of capitalist pressure. Thus in an article entitled 'The Importance of Gold', written on 5 November 1921, Lenin stated: 'There are visible signs that the retreat is coming to an end; there are signs that we shall be able to stop this retreat in the not too distant future.'[6] On 27 March 1922 Lenin told the Eleventh Party Congress:

> The central committee approved my plan... strong emphasis should be laid on calling a halt to this retreat and the congress should give binding instructions on behalf of the whole party accordingly. For a year we have been retreating. On behalf of the party we must now call a halt.[7]

In notes for his speech at the congress, Lenin summed up his position thus: 'Halting the retreat. Preparation for the offensive *against private capital*—the watchword.'[8]

What about economic planning? Quite early Trotsky came to the conclusion that planning was imperative. It was not the first time that Trotsky had thought ahead of his party colleagues, including Lenin. As Trotsky had preceded Lenin in suggesting the need to give up grain requisitions and replace them with a tax in kind, allowing the peasants to trade, so now he argued for the planning of industry as a way to overcome the spontaneous capitalist tendencies of the NEP. Already before the NEP was announced, in his speech of March 1920 to the Ninth Party Congress, Trotsky argued the need for an overall economic plan. He elaborated this further in a memorandum to the central committee on 7 August 1921. He complained of the confusion in prevailing economic policy because of lack of planning:

> In the field of the economy a policy of major switches, and

all the more so where they lack intercoordination, is totally inadmissible. The lack of a real economic centre to watch over economic activity, conduct experiments in that field, record and disseminate results and coordinate in practice all sides of economic activity and thus actually work at a coordinated economic plan—the absence of a real centre of this sort not only inflicts the severest shocks on the economy, such as fuel and food crises, but also excludes the possibility of *the planned and coordinated elaboration of new premises of economic policy. Hence the system of push and pull which has severe repercussions downwards among the grass roots of our economy.*

What was required was both planning from the centre and initiative in the localities and in the specific industrial plants:

it is essential, on the one hand, to transfer the initiative and the responsibility to the institution on the spot and, on the other hand, to ensure that *the central economic apparatus does function in such a way as to ensure the genuine and uninterrupted regulation of economic life by actively eliminating bureaucratic hindrances and assisting in the establishment of straightforward relationships between interdependent organs and establishments...*

The economic plan must essentially be put together around large-scale nationalised industry, as a pivot... as a general rule coordination of the economic plan is to be worked out and ensured by Gosplan [the State Planning Commission] in the course of its daily work from the angle of large-scale nationalised industry being the governing economic factor.[9]

The urgent need for economic planning, Trotsky argued, was dictated by the economic situation under the NEP. The NEP established a mixed economy: large-scale industry and transport remained state-owned while small and medium-sized industry and trade were in the hands of private owners. The requisitioning of food was replaced by ordinary agricultural taxes. The first purpose of the NEP was to renew the exchange of manufactured products for food and raw materials. In this scheme the socialist and private sectors of the economy were to compete with each other on a commercial basis. It was hoped that in that competition the socialist sector would gradually expand *vis-à-vis* the private sector.

In fact things did not go as smoothly as this. Already in 1922 the peasantry harvested about three-quarters of the normal pre-war crop, while industry produced only a quarter of its pre-war output. But even the slow recovery of industry encompassed only light industry, especially textiles. Heavy industry remained paralysed. The country was without steel, coal and machinery. This threatened to bring light industry itself to a standstill, as it needed new machinery for repair and replacement of the old, as well as fuel. Prices of industrial goods soared. Stagnation in industry threatened to break again the link between town and country. The peasant was reluctant to sell food when he was unable to buy industrial goods.

Trotsky pointed out these developments and came to the conclusion that the situation demanded the speeding up of state industry. The state had to overcome the stagnation in heavy industry. Planning was necessary to invade the NEP. Trotsky did not pose the question of the market and planning as two hermetically separate alternatives. He argued for a combination of both.

For Trotsky the transition period between capitalism and socialism meant both a period in which socialist elements intertwined with capitalist elements and one in which a struggle to the death between them takes place.

> The industry of the workers' state is a socialist industry in its tendencies of development, but in order to develop, it utilises methods which were invented by capitalist economy and which we have far from outlived as yet...
>
> We observe, more than once in history, the development of economic phenomena, new in principle, within the old integuments, and moreover this occurs by means of the most diverse combinations.[10]

The introduction of a plan did not mean getting rid of the market at a stroke. Nor did it mean the end of the NEP. As Trotsky wrote in his theses for the Fourth Congress of the Comintern:

> The workers' state, while shifting its economy to the foundations of the market, does not, however, renounce the

beginnings of planned economy, not even for the period immediately ahead...

Under the conditions of the present period the state economic plan does not set itself the utopian task of substituting omniscient prescience for the elemental interplay of supply and demand. On the contrary, taking its starting point from the market, as the basic form of distribution of goods and of regulation of production, our present economic plan aims at securing the greatest possible preponderance of state enterprises in the market by means of combining all the factors of credit, tax, industry and trade; and this plan aims at introducing in the reciprocal relations between the state enterprises the maximum of foresight and uniformity so that by basing itself on the market, the state may aid in eliminating the market as quickly as possible, above all in the sphere of the reciprocal relations between the state-owned enterprises themselves.[11]

The plan, he said, should not be produced in a vacuum, as if the laws of the market did not affect it. The industrial plan should be disciplined by the market:

Before each enterprise can function planfully as a component cell of the socialist organism, we shall have to engage in large-scale transitional activities of operating the economy through the market over a period of many years. And in the course of this transitional epoch each enterprise and each set of enterprises must to a greater or lesser degree orientate itself independently in the market and test itself through the market...

...the state-owned enterprises are competing with one another on the market, and in part they have to compete with private enterprises... Only in this way will nationalised industry learn to function properly. There is no other way of our reaching this goal. Neither a priori economic plans hatched within hermetically sealed four office walls, nor abstract Communist sermons will secure it for us. It is necessary for each state-owned factory to be subjected not only to control from the top—by the state organs—but also from below, by the market, which will remain the regulator of the state economy for a long time to come.[12]

How radically different is Trotsky's concept of planning from Stalin's future command economy, which went under the misnomer of the Plan!

Planned state industry, said Trotsky, should pay special attention to aid peasant agriculture:

> The inclusion of the peasantry in planned state economy, that is, socialist economy, is a task... complicated and tedious. Organisationally the way is being paved for this by the state-controlled and state-directed cooperatives which satisfy the most pressing needs of the peasant and his individual enterprise. Economically this process will be speeded up all the more the greater is the volume of products which the state industry will be able to supply to the village through the medium of cooperative societies. But the socialist principle can gain complete victory in agriculture only through the electrification of agriculture, which will put a salutary end to the barbaric disjunction of peasant production.[13]

Again, how radically different this is from Stalin's future forced collectivisation!

Trotsky does not overlook the final aim of the long struggle between planning and the market: the total victory of the former and the withering of the latter:

> The organisation of economy consists in a correct and expedient allocation of forces and means among the various branches and enterprises; and in a rational [way], that is, the most efficient utilisation of these forces and means within each enterprise. Capitalism attains this goal through supply and demand, through competition, through booms and crises.
>
> Socialism will attain the same goal through the conscious upbuilding first of the national and later of the world economy, as a uniform whole. This upbuilding will proceed on a general plan, which takes as its starting point the existing means of production and the existing needs, and which will be at one and the same time completely comprehensive and extraordinarily flexible. Such a plan cannot be made *a priori*. It has to be worked out by departing from the economic heritage bequeathed to the proletariat by

the past; it has to be worked out by means of systematic alterations and recastings, with increasing boldness and resoluteness in proportion to the increase of economic 'know-how' and technical powers of the proletariat.

It is perfectly clear that a lengthy epoch must necessarily elapse between the capitalist regime and complete socialism; and that during this epoch the proletariat must, by making use of the methods and organisational forms of capitalist circulation (money, exchanges, banks, commercial calculation), gain an ever-increasing control of the market, centralising and unifying it and thereby, in the final analysis, abolishing the market in order to replace it by a centralised plan which stems from the whole previous economic development and which supplies the premise for the administration of economic life in the future. The Soviet Republic is now following this path. But it still is far nearer to its point of departure than to its ultimate goal.[14]

What a magnificent grasp of the dialectics of the transition period from capitalism and socialism, when elements of the past and the future intertwine, when the former are subordinated to the latter without immediately being obliterated by them. Again and again it is clear that Trotsky's concept of planned economy had nothing in common with the 'planned'—bureaucratic command—economy imposed by Stalin from 1928 onwards.

Trotsky's memorandum to the central committee in August 1921 called for the strengthening of Gosplan and the establishment of an economic plan on the basis of large-scale industry. It did not get Lenin's support. Lenin was less than enthusiastic about the idea. He was worried that the plan would remain on paper, that it would be make-believe encouraged by 'Communist conceit.' He wrote to G M Krzhizhanovsky, the head of Gosplan, on 19 February 1921: 'We are beggars. Hungry, ruined beggars. A complete, integrated real plan for us at present —"a bureaucratic utopia".'[15] So he did not support Trotsky's stand, either before his first stroke in May 1922 or after he returned to work in the autumn. Trotsky was therefore isolated in the politburo on this issue.

On 23 August 1922 Trotsky reproached Lenin with the fact that because of the lack of economic planning the government was not tackling economic matters with the necessary urgency:

> The most vital and urgent administrative-organisational economic measures are adopted by us with, what I estimate to be on an average, a delay of a year and a half to two years... With the change-over to the new economic policy state funds are a vital lever in the economic plan. Their allocation is predetermined by the economic plan. Outside of fixing the volume of monetary issues and allocating financial resources between departments there is not and cannot be any economic plan at the moment. Yet, as far as I can judge, Gosplan has no concern with these fundamental questions... How can one require efficiency and proper accountability from individual departments and organs if they do not have the slightest certainty as to what tomorrow will look like? How can one ensure even minimum stability of operation without at the least some rough and approximate, albeit short-term plan? How can one institute even a rough, short-term plan without a planning organ, one which does not have its head in the academic clouds but is directly engaged on controlling, knitting together, regulating and directing our industry?[16]

He stressed the need for planning as a means for rapid industrialisation, creating a firm base for the dictatorship of the proletariat.

Trotsky, amid the clouds gathering in the NEP sky, finally persuaded Lenin to change his mind. Both Lenin and Trotsky noticed that the successes of the NEP, achieved by resort to capitalist methods, brought about two evils characteristic of capitalism: large-scale unemployment and violent price fluctuations. The latter opened a new rift between industry and agriculture. In the winter of 1922-3 the terms of trade between agricultural and industrial goods, hitherto favourable to agriculture, began to move slowly but steadily the other way. This imbalance between industry and agriculture was bound to undermine the worker and peasant alliance (*smychka*) —the main purpose of the NEP. Above all no signs of stimulation for heavy industry, the key to industrial progress, were to be noticed.

On 27 December Lenin dictated from his sickbed a memorandum to the politburo in which he declared himself converted to Trotsky's view on planning. He wrote:

> *Granting legislative functions to the State Planning Commission.* This idea was suggested by Comrade Trotsky, it seems quite a long time ago. I was against it at the time, because I thought that there would then be a fundamental lack of co-ordination in the system of our legislative institutions. But after closer consideration of the matter I find that in substance there is a sound idea in it... I think that we must now take a step towards extending the competence of the State Planning Commission.[17]

This is another example of Trotsky's having better forethought than Lenin. The Stalinist story of the omniscient Lenin was very much a religious myth.

Lenin, in the last few months of his active political life, became a strong advocate of economic planning as an urgent need. It became more and more clear to him that the weakness of the proletariat was due to the weakness of industry. The balance of power between the proletariat and the peasantry, and the strength of the 'NEPmen', the growing capitalist sector, depended above all on the relative strength of industry and agriculture.

At the Fourth Congress of the Comintern on 13 November 1922, in the penultimate speech of his life, Lenin argued that 'all commanding heights' of the economy were in the hands of the state. But how 'commanding' was industry? While, as we have noted, agricultural output in 1922 was at about 75 per cent of its pre-war level, industry had achieved only a little more than 25 per cent of pre-war production; small industry—rural and artisan —was at 54 per cent of its pre-war level, while large-scale industry was at only 20 per cent. The 1922 output of the metal industry, the largest of Russia's pre-war industries and the basis of all large-scale industry, was only 7 per cent of its 1912 level.[18]

Lenin therefore sounded a note of alarm in his speech to the Fourth Congress of the Comintern:

> The salvation of Russia lies not only in a good harvest on the peasant farms—that is not enough; and not only in the good condition of light industry, which provides the peasantry with consumer goods—this, too, is not enough; we also need *heavy* industry. And to put it in good condition will require

several years of work.

Heavy industry needs state subsidies. If we are not able to provide them, we shall be doomed as a civilised state, let alone as a socialist state.[19]

Towards the end of his last published article, Lenin wrote of the need 'to change from the peasant, *muzhik* horse of poverty, from the horse of an economy designed for ruined peasant country, to the horse which the proletariat is seeking and must seek—the horse of large-scale machine industry, of electrification, of the Volkhov power station...' He called this 'the general plan of our work, of our policy, of our tactics, of our strategy.'[20] Building heavy industry was directly related to economic planning.

Trotsky's stand on the question of planning and industry was the theme of his economic policy in later years, the theme of the Left Opposition from 1923 onwards.

Defending the monopoly of foreign trade

Another issue intimately connected with that of economic planning was the monopoly of foreign trade. This became a live issue at the end of 1921 and beginning of 1922.

The monopoly of foreign trade had been established on 22 April 1918. During the civil war the question of its abolition never arose (not that there was any foreign trade to speak of). With the development of the NEP, however, the monopoly of foreign trade came under pressure due to the growing influence of private trade. Towards the end of 1921 Miliutin, the Soviet delegate to the Baltic Economic Conference in Riga, promised this monopoly would be abolished. A number of other Bolshevik leaders supported Miliutin in this. Sokolnikov, Bukharin and Piatakov opposed the retention of the foreign trade monopoly; Zinoviev, Kamenev and Stalin wanted it relaxed. On 3 March 1922 Lenin wrote to Kamenev:

The foreigners are already buying our officials with bribes, and carting out what is left of Russia. They may well succeed. [We must] publish right away... a firm, cold, fierce statement that we do not intend to retreat in the economy any further, and that those who attempt to cheat us (or circumvent the monopoly etc) will face terrorism.[21]

On 15 May Lenin wrote a draft decision for the politburo on

the subject, stating: 'The central committee reaffirms the monopoly of foreign trade.'[22] He also wrote in a letter to Stalin that *'a formal ban should be put on* all talk and negotiations and commissions... concerning the relaxation of the foreign trade monopoly.' Stalin wrote on Lenin's letter: 'I have no objection to a "formal ban" on measures to *mitigate* the foreign trade monopoly at the *present* stage. All the same, I think that *mitigation* is becoming indispensible.'[23]

The discussion continued. On 22 May Lenin's theses were adopted by the politburo. But later, during his absence after the stroke that paralysed him on 25 May, the opponents of the monopoly won the day. On 6 October a plenum of the central committee ratified Sokolnikov's proposal that the monopoly should be considerably relaxed. Lenin reacted sharply, and on 16 October the central committee agreed to put the question on the agenda again at the next plenum, to be held on 25 December.

On 11 October Lenin asked Trotsky to confer with him on this problem in particular. Two days earlier he had sent an urgent letter to all politburo members demanding the reversal of the decision. Once again Stalin appended a note to Lenin's letter: 'Comrade Lenin's letter has not made me change my mind as to the correctness of the decision of the plenum of the central committee of 6 October concerning foreign trade.'[24] The lion was mortally wounded, and the jackal raised his head.

On 12 December Lenin suggested to Trotsky that they should join forces in defence of the foreign trade monopoly: 'Comrade Trotsky: I am sending you Krestinsky's letter. Write me as soon as possible whether you agree: at the plenum, I am going to fight for the monopoly. What about you? Yours, Lenin.'[25]

Three days later, in a letter to Stalin, Lenin wrote: 'I have... come to an agreement with Trotsky on the defence of my views on the monopoly of foreign trade.' He added: '...any further vacillation over this extremely important question is absolutely impermissible and will wreck all our work.'[26]

The Lenin-Trotsky partnership on the question of the monopoly led the central committee to reverse its decision of 6 October. On 21 December, therefore, Lenin could write to Trotsky: 'It looks as though it has been possible to take the position without a single shot, by a simple manoeuvre. I suggest that we should not stop and should continue the offensive.'[27]

Lenin's bloc with Trotsky against Great Russian chauvinism

Lenin came politically closer to Trotsky, especially when the issue of fighting Great Russian chauvinism raised its ugly head. When Lenin, on his deathbed, was fighting for his life's work it was to Trotsky that he turned as an ally.

For a number of years there had been covert symptoms of Great Russian chauvinism in state and party. With the increasing centralisation of administration, and the appointment of more and more state and party officials by Moscow, the workers of other nationalities within the Soviet Union were bound to appear as second-class. Thus administrative convenience played into the hands of Moscow centralism and Great Russian chauvinism. The NEP, which gave economic and social power back to the Russian merchants and officials who had been identified with national oppression under the Tsarist regime, further strengthened the development of Great Russian chauvinism.

Lenin was alarmed. As early as the Ninth Party Congress in March 1920 he said: 'Scratch some communists, and you will find Great Russian chauvinists.'[28] At the Tenth Party Congress in March 1921, Sakharov, a delegate from Turkestan, analysed the composition of the local party and demanded a more active struggle against both Great Russian chauvinism and Moslem nationalism.[29] The Tenth Congress was first to recognise Great Russian chauvinism in the Communist apparatus by including in its resolutions a strongly worded condemnation of it.[30]

On 2 November 1920 Trotsky, in a message to Lenin and the politburo, bluntly stated that the Soviet administration in the Ukraine had from the outset been based on people sent from Moscow and not on local elections:

> The Soviet regime in the Ukraine has maintained itself in being up to now (but feebly at that) largely by virtue of the authority of Moscow, the Great-Russian Communists and the Russian Red Army... Economically the Ukraine still is the embodiment of anarchy, sheltering under the bureaucratic centralism of Moscow.[31]

He demanded a radical break with this method of government.

At the Eleventh Party Congress (March-April 1922) the

veteran Ukrainian Bolshevik, N Skrypnik, argued that the Communist Party apparatus had been infiltrated by adherents of **Smena Vekh*** ready to violate the party's solemn pledge to defend Ukrainian independence. 'The one and indivisible Russia is not our slogan', he exclaimed—at which point a voice from the audience shouted back ominously: 'The one and indivisible Communist Party!'[32]

The right of nations to self-determination was inevitably threatened in a situation where there was only *one* party —particularly as it was highly centralised and dominated by officials from the dominant nation. Since the central committee in Moscow—or increasingly the secretariat—imposed its will on the central committees of the national republics, little in real terms remained of national independence.

In August 1922 two associated topics brought the question of Great Russian chauvinism to a head in the Moscow party leadership. One was the establishment of the USSR, the other the national question in Georgia.

On 10 August 1922 the politburo directed the orgburo to set up a commission to investigate relations between the Russian Socialist Federal Soviet Republic (RSFSR) and the formally independent Soviet Republics of the Ukraine, Belorussia, Georgia, Armenia and Azerbaidzhan. Stalin drafted the commission's resolution: 'On the Relations Between the RSFSR and the Independent Republics'. He treated the government of the RSFSR as the *de facto* government of all six republics, not even formally recognising the legal fiction of independence. The government organs of the RSFSR, VTsIK, Sovnarkom and the Council of Labour and Defence (STO) were to take over the functions of the leading bodies of the six republics. Key commissariats (foreign affairs and foreign trade, military affairs, transport and communications) were to be taken over by the Russian government, while others (finance, labour and national economy) had to operate under the control of the corresponding agencies of RSFSR; only an insignificant few were to be entrusted entirely to the autonomous republics. Nearly all the national commissariats

---

* **Smena Vekh**, which translates into English as 'A changing of landmarks', was a volume of essays published in Prague in July 1921 by a group of emigré Russians, who argued for reconciliation between the Soviet regime and the Russian White emigrés.

were to become mere extensions of the Moscow administration.

Point Six of the resolution proposed that the documents should be kept secret until the various VTsIKs agreed: there was to be no consultation of congresses of *soviets*, let alone of the masses of workers and peasants.[33]

On 15 September 1922 the central committee of the Georgian Communist Party rejected this resolution. The party secretariat —which in this case meant Stalin—then acted improperly, by sending the commission's resolution to all members and candidate members of the party central committee without the question having been considered by the politburo. To add insult to injury on 28 August, even before his plans had been discussed by the politburo, Stalin appears to have sent a telegram to Mdivani, a leader of the Georgian opposition to Stalin, informing him that the decisions of the highest governing bodies of the RSFSR (VTsIK, Sovnarkom and STO) were henceforth binding on all the republics.[34]

When Lenin received the commission's resolution he was furious. It violated any concept of national equality, and openly formalised the hegemony of the RSFSR over the other republics. On 26 September he wrote to Kamenev: '...we consider ourselves, the Ukrainian SSR and others, equal, and enter with them, on an equal basis, into a new union, a new federation, the Union of the Soviet Republics of Europe and Asia.' He demanded the creation of an All-Union Central Executive Committee, Sovnarkom and STO, to supercede those of the RSFSR.[35]

Stalin was truculent and opposed the sick old man. He and Kamenev, probably at a meeting of the politburo, exchanged two brief notes on the subject of Lenin's memorandum. Kamenev's note reads: 'Ilyich is going to war to defend independence.' Stalin replied: 'In my opinion we have to be firm against Lenin.'[36]

On 27 September Stalin replied to Lenin. Among other hurtful remarks he accused Lenin of 'national liberalism'.[37]

On 6 October Lenin wrote a memorandum to the politburo, 'On Combatting Dominant National Chauvinism':

> I declare war to the death on dominant national chauvinism...
> It must be *absolutely* insisted that the Union Central Executive Committee should be *presided over* in turn by a Russian, Ukrainian, Georgian, etc. *Absolutely!*[38]

Recognising that he would be in a minority on the central committee, Stalin accepted Lenin's amendment to the commission's resolution. But this was only a cosmetic victory for Lenin, as shown by the issue of Georgia, around which the national question next arose.

Stalin and Ordzhonikidze, political and military leader of the Caucasian front during the civil war, wanted to combine the republics of Georgia, Azerbaidzhan and Armenia into a Caucasian Federation, violating the autonomy of the national republics. The local Georgian leaders, headed by Budu Mdivani, one of the earliest Bolsheviks in the Caucasus, and Filipp Ieseevich Makharadze, a member of the central committee of the Russian Communist Party and a Marxist since 1891, opposed the suggested federation. The conflict turned into a political and personal clash between two groups of Georgians: on the one hand Ordzhonikidze and his mentor Stalin, on the other the Georgian Communist Party central committee.

On 22 October the Georgian central committee resorted to the unprecedented step of tendering its resignation to the central committee of the Russian party. The resignation was accepted and Ordzhonikize appointed a new central committee, made up of incompetent but docile young men who accepted the federation without protest. The secretariat in Moscow eagerly accepted the resignation of the old Georgian central commitee and the new appointments.

But the members of the old central committee did not give up the struggle. A small but significant incident took place that opened Lenin's eyes to the real meaning of the conflict around the Georgian question. In the course of the continual debates and confrontations, Ordzhonikidze, losing his temper, went so far as to use physical violence against another party member, a supporter of Mdivani. It happened at a private session held at Ordzhonikidze's house, while Rykov, Lenin's deputy and a member of the politburo, was present. When a new request to reopen the enquiry into the Georgian question reached Moscow, signed by Makharadze and others, it could not be ignored. At this point Lenin was beginning to be anxious about the situation. He was suddenly alarmed by a letter from Okudzhava, a prominent member of the old Georgian central committee, accusing Ordzhonikize of personally insulting and threatening the

Georgian comrades.

Lenin's incapacity gave Ordzhonikidze and Stalin the opportunity to take the offensive against their Georgian opponents. On 21 December the central committee of the Russian Communist Party ordered the opposition leaders, Mdivani, Makharadze, Tsintsadze and Kavtaradze, to leave Georgia.[39]

When Lenin recovered from his stroke towards the end of December, he decided to return to the Georgian question. On 30 December he dictated the following:

> I suppose I have been very remiss with respect to the workers of Russia for not having intervened energetically and decisively enough in the notorious question of autonomisation, which, it appears, is officially called the question of the union of Soviet Socialist Republics...
>
> It is said that a united apparatus was needed. Where did that assurance come from? Did it not come from that same Russian apparatus which... we took over from Tsarism and slightly anointed with Soviet oil?
>
> ...It is quite natural that in such circumstances the 'freedom to secede from the union' by which we justify ourselves will be a mere scrap of paper, unable to defend the non-Russians from the onslaught of that really Russian man, the Great Russian chauvinist, in substance a rascal and a tyrant, such as the typical Russian bureaucrat is. There is no doubt that the infinitesimal percentage of Soviet and Sovietised will drown in that tide of chauvinistic Great Russian riff-raff like a fly in milk... were we careful enough to take measures to provide the non-Russians with a real safeguard against the truly Russian bully? I do not think we took such measures although we could and should have done so.

Lenin went on to refer to Stalin:

> I think that Stalin's haste and his infatuation with pure administration, together with his spite against the notorious 'nationalist-socialism' played a fatal role here. In politics spite generally plays the basest of roles.[40]

In another note dictated on 31 December Lenin went on to deal with the misdeeds of Ordzhonikidze: 'exemplary punishment must be inflicted on Comrade Ordzhonikidze.' He continued:

The political responsibility for all this truly Great Russian nationalist campaign must, of course, be laid on Stalin and Dzerzhinsky [the head of the Cheka].

Unless Great Russian chauvinism was fought to the death, the party's support for anti-imperialist national liberation movements would be completely hypocritical:

> we ourselves lapse... into imperialist attitudes towards oppressed nationalities, thus undermining all our principled sincerity, all our principled defence of the struggle against imperialism![41]

The Georgian question was uppermost in Lenin's mind throughout his last few weeks of political activity. His secretary, Fotieva, in the **Journal** entry of 14 February 1923, wrote: 'Called me in again. Impediment in speech, obviously tired. Spoke again on the three points of his instruction. In special detail on the subject that agitated him most of all, namely the Georgian question. Asked to hurry things up.'[42] On 5 March Lenin dictated the following letter to be telephoned to Trotsky:

> *Top secret*
> Personal
> Dear Comrade Trotsky: It is my earnest request that you should undertake the defence of the Georgian case in the party CC. This case is now under 'persecution' by Stalin and Dzerzhinsky, and I cannot rely on their impartiality. Quite to the contrary. I would feel at ease if you agreed to undertake its defence. If you should refuse to do so for any reason, return the whole case to me. I shall consider it a sign that you do not accept.
> With best comradely greetings,
> Lenin.[43]*

With this letter Lenin forwarded to Trotsky his memorandum on the national question.

Lenin was worried that Trotsky would not be decisive enough. Trotsky recounts in 1927:

---

* The closing words of the letter were so warm that Stalin, when forced to read it out before the central committee in July 1926—by which time his position was unassailable—changed them to 'With communist greetings'.

When Fotieva... brought me the so-called 'national' letter of Lenin, I suggested that since Kamenev was leaving that day for Georgia to the party congress, it might be advisable to show him the letter so that he might undertake the necessary measures. Fotieva replied: 'I don't know. Vladimir Ilyich didn't instruct me to transmit the letter to Comrade Kamenev, but I can ask him.' A few minutes later she returned with the following message: 'It is entirely out of the question. Vladimir Ilyich says that Kamenev would show the letter to Stalin and Stalin would make a rotten compromise in order then to deceive.'[44]

On 6 March Lenin sent a brief but very significant message to the leaders of the Georgian opposition:

To P G Mdivani, F Y Makharadze and others
Top Secret
Copy to Comrades Trotsky and Kamenev
Dear Comrades:
I am following your case with all my heart. I am indignant over Ordzhonikidze's rudeness and the connivance of Stalin and Dzerzhinsky. I am preparing for you notes and a speech.
Respectfully yours,
Lenin[45]

This was the last document Lenin dictated. On 7 March he suffered his third serious stroke. By 10 March half his body was paralysed. He never recovered the power of speech. His political life was over. Stalin and Ordzhonikidze were saved by this stroke.

Rabkrin

While dealing with the Georgian question Lenin became increasingly aware that it was only a symptom of a much deeper and more general sickness—the rule of the bureaucracy.

If the Georgian affair brought him into conflict with Stalin, his examination of the Workers' and Peasants' Inspectorate (Rabkrin) deepened that conflict. Stalin headed Rabkrin from 1919 until the spring of 1922, when he was appointed party general secretary. But he continued to exercise a strong influence on it for some time. The inspectorate's functions were wide: it was entitled to inspect the work of the commissariats and the civil servants, to oversee the efficiency and morale of the whole administration.

Lenin intended Rabkrin as a super-commissariat fighting bureaucracy and imposing democratic control. It acted through teams of workers and peasants who were free at any time to enter any government office. Unfortunately working in offices turned the workers themselves into bureaucrats. As Deutscher put it, Stalin transformed Rabkrin 'into his private police within the government'.[46] As its chief he came to control the whole state machinery, its working and personnel, far more closely than any other commissar.

Trotsky attacked Rabkrin as inefficient as early as 1920. He was not supported by Lenin, who continued to defend Rabkrin as late as 5 May 1922.[47] However Lenin's conflict with Stalin on the Georgian issue opened his eyes. In his last article, 'Better fewer, but better', he declared war on Rabkrin:

> Let us say frankly that the People's Commissariat of the Workers' and Peasants' Inspection does not at present enjoy the slightest authority. Everybody knows that no other institutions are worse organised than those of our Workers' and Peasants' Inspection, and that under present conditions nothing can be expected from this People's Commissariat.[48]

As Lenin's health did not permit him to carry out a struggle for reform himself he turned to Trotsky for help. Trotsky remembers his last conversation with Lenin not long before his third stroke:

> Lenin summoned me to his room in the Kremlin, spoke of the terrible growth of bureaucratism in our Soviet apparatus and of the necessity of finding a lever with which to get at that problem. He proposed to create a special commission of the central committee and asked me to take an active part in the work. I answered him: 'Vladimir Ilyich, it is my conviction that in the present struggle with bureaucratism in the Soviet apparatus, we must not forget that there is taking place, both in the provinces and in the centre, a special selection of functionaries and specialists, party and non-party, around certain ruling party personalities and groups—in the provinces, in the districts, in the party locals and in the

centre—that is, the central committee. Attacking a functionary you run into the party leader. The specialist is a member of his retinue. Under present circumstances I could not undertake this work.' Vladimir Ilyich reflected a moment and—here I quote him verbatim—said: 'That is, I propose a struggle with Soviet bureaucratism and you are proposing to include the bureaucratism of the Organisational Bureau of the party?'

I laughed at the unexpectedness of this, because no such finished formulation of the idea was in my mind.

I answered: 'I suppose that's it.'

Then Vladimir Ilyich said: 'Very well, then, I propose a bloc.' I said: 'It is a pleasure to form a bloc with a good man.'[49]

A dying man, making desperate efforts to save the revolution, Lenin turned to Trotsky as an ally. Again, as in 1917 and during the civil war, an intimate alliance was being forged between them.

Lenin's criticism of Rabkrin did not meet with unanimous support among the party leadership. Trotsky recalled:

How did the Political Bureau react to Lenin's project for the reorganisation of Rabkrin? Comrade Bukharin hesitated to print Lenin's article ['Better fewer, but better'], while Lenin, on his side, insisted upon its immediate appearance. N K Krupskaya told me by telephone and asked me to take steps to get it printed as soon as possible. At the meeting of the Political Bureau, called immediately upon my demand, all those present—comrades Stalin, Molotov, Kuibyshev, Rykov, Kalinin, Bukharin—were not only against comrade Lenin's plan but against the very printing of the article. The members of the secretariat were particularly harsh and categorical in their opposition. In view of the insistent demand of comrade Lenin that the article should be shown to him in print, comrade Kuibyshev, afterwards the head of Rabkrin, proposed at the above-mentioned session of the Political Bureau that one special number of *Pravda* should be printed with Lenin's article and shown to him in order to placate him, while the article itself should be concealed from the party... I was supported only by comrade Kamenev, who appeared at the meeting of the Political Bureau almost an hour late.

The chief argument that induced them to print the article was that an article by Lenin could not be concealed from the party in any case.[50]

On 4 March 1923 **Pravda** published Lenin's article. Unfortunately its impact within the party was insignificant.

Lenin's Testament

In the last few days of his political life Lenin was haunted by the question of his successor. Who would take his place at the head of the party and the state? He wrote about the subject. He undertook an analysis of the personnel of the top leadership of the party, which seemed to him to be of serious importance because of the perilous situation of the Soviet regime.

This question constituted a crucial element of Lenin's 'Testament'. This consisted of notes dictated between 23 and 31 December 1922, with a supplement dictated on 4 January. In the edition of Lenin's **Works** published after Khrushchev's revelations about Stalin 30 years later, these notes are called 'Letter to the Congress'.

The notes proposed changes in the central committee, the central control commission and Rabkrin—and then presented an analysis of the top leadership of the party. Lenin argued that a threat to the stability of the Soviet regime could exist first of all at its base—in the danger of a split between the proletariat and the peasantry:

> Our party relies on two classes and therefore its instability would be possible and its downfall inevitable if there were no agreement between these two classes... No measures of any kind could prevent a split in such a case.

This was a threat in the long run. In the short run Lenin foresaw the greater danger of a split resulting from *personal* relationships within the party leadership:

> I think that from this standpoint the prime factors in the question of stability are such members of the CC as Stalin and Trotsky. I think relations between them make up the greater part of the danger of a split.

After this prophetic judgment Lenin proceeded to sketch portraits of six leaders of the party: Stalin and Trotsky, Zinoviev and Kamenev, Bukharin and Piatakov:

> Comrade Stalin, having become secretary-general, has unlimited authority concentrated in his hands, and I am not sure whether he will always be capable of using that authority with sufficient caution. Comrade Trotsky, on the other hand, as his struggle against the CC on the question of the People's Commissariat for Communications has already proved, is distinguished not only by outstanding ability. He is personally perhaps the most capable man in the present CC, but he has displayed excessive self-assurance and shown excessive pre-occupation with the purely administrative side of the work.
>
> These two qualities of the two outstanding leaders of the present CC can inadvertently lead to a split, and if our party does not take steps to avert this, the split may come unexpectedly.

Only a single remark is made about Zinoviev and Kamenev: 'I shall just recall that the October episode with Zinoviev and Kamenev was, of course, no accident.' Of the two youngest men, Bukharin and Piatakov, Lenin writes:

> They are, in my opinion, the most outstanding figures (among the youngest ones), and the following must be borne in mind about them: Bukharin is not only a most valuable and major theorist of the party; he is also rightly considered the favourite of the whole party, but his theoretical views can be classified as fully Marxist only with great reserve, for there is something scholastic about him (he has never made a study of dialectics, and I think, never fully understood it).
>
> As for Piatakov, he is unquestionably a man of outstanding will and outstanding ability, but shows too much zeal for administrating and the administrative side of the work to be relied upon in a serious political matter.[51]

At this stage—on 23 and 25 December—Lenin suggested that a collective leadership should be preserved, based largely on the pre-eminence of Trotsky and Stalin, and with the safeguards of a larger central committee, among other measures. However, ten days later Lenin wrote an addendum that completely shifted the balance: a sharp, bitter attack on Stalin. This change of mind was a result of the Georgian affair, for Lenin now accused Stalin and Ordzhonikize of acting like Great Russian bullies, and of an incident on 22 December when Stalin used offensive language against Krupskaya. On 4 January 1923 Lenin added the following to his Testament:

> Stalin is too rude and this defect, although quite tolerable in our midst and in dealings among us communists, becomes intolerable in a secretary-general. That is why I suggest that the comrades think about a way of removing Stalin from that post and appointing another man in his stead who in all other respects differs from Comrade Stalin in having only one advantage, namely, that of being more tolerant, more loyal, more polite and more considerate to the comrades, less capricious, etc.[52]

Lenin's Testament looks, on the face of it, like a non-Marxist document—a personal fight against Stalin rather than a general political-social statement. However, Lenin well knew that politics develops by and through people. Personal traits in the party and state leadership may well become the expression of alien social forces.

The tragedy of Lenin's position pervades the whole of his Testament—that he had now to rely on changes at the personal level as *the main weapon of politics,* when throughout his revolutionary activity he had relied on the rank and file to put the necessary pressure on the conservative party machine.

Lenin and Trotsky could not turn to the proletarian element in the party because this was now only a small minority. They could not rely on inner-party democracy—even if by a miracle it had been restored—because the party was made up largely of factory managers, government officials, army officers and party officials; such a democracy would have reflected the aspirations of the bureaucracy. Lenin and Trotsky could not call on the 'Old Guard', first because these were a tiny minority of the party—a mere 2 per cent—and secondly because many of them made up an important part of the bureaucratic caste.

Lenin knew that the bureaucracy had arisen in the Soviet state to fill a political and administrative vacuum created by the exhaustion and dispersal of the revolutionary proletariat that had resulted from the cumulative suffering of the First World War, the revolution, the civil war and the accompanying devastation, famine, epidemics and physical annihilation. The measures that Lenin proposed to fight bureaucracy were all substitutes for an active proletariat—which now no longer existed.

One is 'incapable of making correct calculations... when one is heading for destruction', Lenin had written in a different context. Unfortunately, this remark now applied to Lenin himself.

Chapter sixteen
Trotsky and the triumvirate

IN DECEMBER 1922 or January 1923, when Lenin finally ceased to take part in politburo work, Stalin, together with Zinoviev and Kamenev, created a secret faction in the politburo. They pledged themselves to co-ordinate their moves and act in unison. (Stalin made the first public admission of the existence of this triumvirate, or *troika*, at the Twelfth Party Congress).[1]

Why did the three join forces? They wanted to oppose any move to give Trotsky the leadership of the party if Lenin died.

Stalin hated Trotsky, as we have seen, throughout the civil war. He was always full of envy of him. Trotsky was an intellectual giant, brilliant writer, orator, the organiser of the October insurrection and the supreme war leader. Stalin was inarticulate, his writing as dull as dishwater, almost unknown outside party circles, and had played no prominent role in the 1905 and 1917 revolutions. It is no accident that his name hardly appears in John Reed's **Ten days that shook the world**, and that Lunacharsky, in his **Revolutionary silhouettes**, published in 1923, did not find it necessary to include a silhouette of Stalin. Again, Khruschev, in his secret speech to the Twentieth Congress in 1956, said: 'I will probably not sin against the truth when I say that 99 per cent of the persons present here heard and knew very little about Stalin before the year 1924.'[2]

Zinoviev could not forgive Trotsky for his glorious success in October 1917 when Zinoviev himself, to his shame, had opposed the insurrection and was called a 'strikebreaker' by Lenin. Zinoviev opposed Trotsky's military policy throughout the civil war. He was also one of the most vocal opponents of Trotsky over the issue of the militarisation of labour and the trade unions.

Kamenev was Zinoviev's *alter ego*. He had sided with him on all these issues.

The administrative strength of the members of the *troika* was impressive. Stalin was the only person who was on all four leading bodies of the party—the central committee, the politburo, the orgburo and the secretariat. Zinoviev and Kamenev were the virtual bosses of Petrograd and Moscow respectively and enjoyed a good deal of local power. As against this, Trotsky had no party apparatus at his command.

In Lenin's absence the politburo consisted of six members: the *troika*, Trotsky, Tomsky and Bukharin. Tomsky, as the right-wing Bolshevik leader of the trade unions, came into sharp conflict with Trotsky's policy over the militarisation of labour and statification of the trade unions.

Uniting all of them, excluding Trotsky, was the *esprit de corps* of old Bolshevism, and both Zinoviev and Stalin had written sharp attacks on Trotsky in the years when he was outside the Bolshevik Party.

Trotsky procrastinates

Lenin and Trotsky had agreed to unite against Stalin and against the bureaucracy, concentrating their attack on two main issues: Georgia and Rabkrin. Trotsky reported a remark by Fotieva: 'Vladimir Ilyich is preparing a bomb for Stalin at the congress'. The word 'bomb' was Lenin's, not hers. 'Vladimir Ilyich asks you to take the Georgian case in your hands. He will then feel confident.'[3]

What would Trotsky do? On 6 March 1923 Kamenev came to see him. He was crestfallen and anxious to mollify him. Trotsky showed magnanimity and forgiveness. He told Kamenev that he had decided not to take any action against Stalin despite Lenin's clear stand. In his autobiography he described his meeting with Kamenev:

'I am against removing Stalin and expelling Ordzhonikidze... But I do agree with Lenin in substance. I want a radical change in the policy on the national question, a discontinuance of persecutions of the Georgian opponents of Stalin, a discontinuance of the administrative oppression of the party, a firmer policy in matters of industrialisation, and an honest co-operation in the higher centres... it is necessary that Stalin should write to Krupskaya at once to apologise for his rudeness, and that he revise his behaviour. Let him not overreach himself. There should be no more intrigues, but honest co-operation...' Kamenev gave a sigh of relief. He accepted all my proposals. His only fear was that Stalin would be obstinate. 'He's rude and capricious.'

'I don't think', I answered, 'that Stalin has any alternative now.' Late that night Kamenev informed me that he had been to see Stalin in the country, and that Stalin had accepted all the terms.[4]

Thus Trotsky made a 'rotten compromise', the very thing Lenin had warned against.

While Kamenev was acting as go-between, Lenin succumbed to another stroke. He was to survive it by ten months, but paralysed, speechless most of the time, and suffering from spells of unconsciousness. When it became clear that Lenin had finally left the political scene, Stalin took his own path with a vengeance.

The first and by far the most important opportunity for Trotsky to make use of the 'bomb' against Stalin was the Twelfth Party Congress (17-25 April 1923)—but he made no attempt to do so.

Stalin himself presented the report on the national question to the congress, while Lenin's attack on Stalin and Ordzhonikidze over the national question was kept from the delegates. Stalin viciously attacked the Georgian Communists, accusing them of 'Georgian chauvinism':

It is on this dangerous path that our comrades, the Georgian deviators, are pushing us by opposing federation in violation of all the laws of the party, by wanting to withdraw from the federation in order to retain an advantageous position. They are pushing us on to the path of granting them certain privileges at the expense of the Armenian and Azerbaidzhanian republics. But this is a path we cannot take, for it means certain death to our entire policy and to Soviet power in the Caucasus.

...under present conditions it is impossible to maintain peace in the Caucasus, impossible to establish equality, without the Transcaucasian Federation. One nation must not be allowed more privileges than another. This our comrades have sensed. That is why, after two years of contention, the Mdivani group is a small handful, repeatedly ejected by the party in Georgia itself.

To add insult to injury Stalin cited Lenin in support of his policy:

It was also no accident that Comrade Lenin was in such a hurry and was so insistent that the federation should be established immediately. Nor was it an accident that our central committee on three occasions affirmed the need for a federation in Transcaucasia.[5]

In vain did the Georgian delegates demand that Lenin's notes on the subject should be read out. The only member of the politburo to take up their case was Bukharin. Criticising Stalin and Zinoviev by name, and alluding to Lenin's supposed notes, he exposed Stalin's campaign against 'local deviations' as a fraud. Why, he asked, did Lenin 'sound the alarm' only against Great Russian chauvinism?

Why did Comrade Lenin begin to sound the alarm with such furious energy on the Georgian question? And why did Comrade Lenin say not a word in his letter about the mistakes of the deviators, but on the contrary, direct all his strong words against the policy which was being carried out against the deviators? If Comrade Lenin were here he would give it to the Russian chauvinists in a way that they would remember for ten years.[6]

Similar to Bukharin's attack on Great Russian chauvinism was Rakovsky's. He said:

The national question is one of those questions which is pregnant with very serious complications for Soviet Russia and the party. This is one of those questions which—this must be said openly and honestly at the party congress —threaten civil war, if we fail to show the necessary sensibility, the necessary understanding with regard to it. It is the question of the bond of the revolutionary Russian proletariat with the sixty million non-Russian peasants, who under the national banner raised their demands for a share in the economic and political life of the Soviet Union.[7]

Rakovsky referred to 'a multitude of comrades who regard the national question with a smile, with a sneer, [and say] "but we are a country that has gone beyond the stage of nationalities... where material and economic culture opposes national culture. National culture is for backward countries on the other side of the barricades, for capitalist countries; and we are a communist country".'[8]

The bureaucratic mentality, against whose spread Lenin had inveighed, was producing a Great Russian mentality, argued Rakovsky:

> Our central authorities begin to view the administration of the whole country from the viewpoint of the comfort of their office armchairs. Naturally, it is inconvenient to administer twelve republics, but if there were only one, if by pressing a single button one could administer the whole country, that would be very convenient.[9]

Rakovsky quoted the conduct of a high Ukrainian official who, as he was leaving a congress at which he had voted for a resolution asserting the equal rights of the Ukrainian language, replied curtly to a question addressed to him in Ukrainian: 'Speak to me in an intelligible language.'[10]

Rakovsky also cited a number of instances when the organs of the RSFSR had issued decrees and laws for the other Soviet republics, even before the union had been formally ratified and the authority of the federal government constitutionally ascertained. He charged that since December 1922 the union commissariats had actually governed the entire country, leaving the republics no self-rule whatsoever. To combat the mounting wave of Russian nationalism, Rakovsky concluded, it was necessary to strip the government of the USSR of nine-tenths of its commissariats.[11]

But the impact of Bukharin's and Rakovsky's speeches was minimal. Stalin in reply dared to say:

> Many speakers referred to notes and articles by Vladimir Ilyich. I do not want to quote my teacher, Comrade Lenin, since he is not here, and I am afraid that I might, perhaps, quote him wrongly and inappropriately.[12]

And what was Trotsky doing? He absented himself

completely from the debate on the national question, explaining that he had been occupied with amendments to his resolution on industry![13]

Stalin's resolution on the nationalities question was adopted unanimously.

Again, who presented to the Twelfth Congress the organisational report of the central committee, including the report on Rabkrin? Stalin!

Lenin's denunciation of Rabkrin, although known to delegates, because it had been published in **Pravda** and referred to by one delegate as 'something like a bombshell',[14] was easily defused by Stalin. In his report on party organisation Stalin expounded and defended Lenin's proposal for the organisation of Rabkrin. He repeated and endorsed Lenin's condemnation of bureaucracy:

> [Lenin] said that our policy was correct, but the apparatus was not working properly and, therefore, the car was not running in the right direction, it swerved. I remember that Shliapnikov, commenting on this, said that the drivers were no good. That is wrong, of course, absolutely wrong. The policy is correct, the driver is excellent, and the type of car is good, it is a Soviet car, but some of the parts of the state car, [for example] some of the officials in the state apparatus, are bad, they are not our men. That is why the car does not run properly and, on the whole, we get a distortion of the correct poliltical line... That is why the apparatus as a whole is not working properly. If we fail to repair it, the correct political line by itself will not carry us very far. These are the ideas Comrade Lenin elaborated as far back as a year ago, and which only this year he formulated in a harmonious system in the proposal to reorganise the central control commission and the Workers' and Peasants' Inspection.[15]

His main conclusion was the need to strengthen the 'registration and distribution department... the organ of the central committee whose function is to register our principal workers'.[16] In other words strengthen Usprad, Stalin's own organisational base!

The time had come, said Stalin, to train a generation of 'young leaders to take the place of the old... to draw new, fresh forces into the work of the central committee... to promote the most capable and independent of them'.[17] While carrying out Lenin's wish to enlarge and combine the central control commission and Workers' and Peasants' Inspection, Stalin made this body, apart from the secretariat itself, the most solidly reliable instrument at his command.

In his reply to the discussion of the central committee organisational report, after another vicious attack on the Georgian Communists, Stalin ended with the following words:

> In conclusion, a few words about the present congress. Comrades, I must say that I have not for a long time seen a congress so united and inspired by a single idea as this one is. I regret that Comrade Lenin is not here. If he were here he would be able to say: 'I tended the party for twenty-five years and made it great and strong'. *(Prolonged applause)*[18]

The congress passed a resolution 'On the Central Committee Report' which was very complacent regarding the state of organisation of the party, Rabkrin and the central control commission:

> While supporting the plan for the radical reorganisation of Rabkrin and the central control commission, the congress is convinced that an appropriate improvement in the central state and party control apparatuses, given the necessary organisational connection between them and the systematic combination of their efforts, will make it possible to attain both goals: (1) to undertake a decisive improvement of the state apparatus, and (2) to secure the party against the distortion of its line and against an actual breakaway of some groups of party workers from the party as a whole.
>
> The congress notes with satisfaction the improvement of the central committee's organisational apparatus and of all the organisational work of the party centre generally, and instructs the new central committee to give high priority to the work of the accounts and assignment section, which is now to play an especially important role in the correct assignment of personnel to ensure that the party exerts real leadership in all areas of the administration without exception.[19]

Trotsky again did not intervene in the discussion of the

central committee report. He spoke at the congress only on his industrial report. He did not give even a hint of any disagreement with Stalin. Trotsky went so far to avoid controversy that he actually reprimanded people who spoke up to defend him against the *troika*.[20]*

What about the publication of Lenin's 'Testament'? Members of the Politburo and the presidium of the central control commission were asked for their views at the beginning of June 1923.

Zinoviev was against publication. Stalin said: 'I submit that there is no necessity to publish, the more so since there is no sanction for its publication from Ilyich.' Kamenev's comment was: 'It must not be printed. It is an undelivered speech meant for the politburo. No more. Personal description is the basis and content of the article.' Tomsky affirmed: 'I am for Comrade Zinoviev's proposal—that only the members of the CC be informed. It should not be published for no one among the public at large will understand anything of this.' A Solts, of the presidium of the central control commission, said: 'This note by V I had in view not the public at large but the CC and that is why so much space is allotted to the description of persons... It should not be printed.' The same position was taken by Bukharin, Rudzutak, Molotov and Kuibyshev. The only one in favour of publication was Trotsky.[21]

But Trotsky was too late. Having remained silent at the Twelfth Congress, he was in no position to insist on publishing Lenin's Testament two months later.

Trotsky's report on industry

Trotsky gave the report to the congress on industry. It was analytically brilliant, but to avoid polemics with the majority of the politburo it avoided bringing the differences out into the open.

Trotsky argued that 'only the development of industry creates an unshakeable foundation for the proletarian dictatorship'. He urged a policy of the 'correct relating of market and plan' whereby the government should avoid either inept administrative

---

* That Trotsky was later very embarrassed by his behaviour at the Twelfth Congress is clear from the fact that no reference at all to the congress can be found in his autobiography, while four pages are devoted to describing duck hunting in precisely the place where a description of the congress would be expected.

interference with the market or insufficient regulation of the market. 'State activity as a whole must place its primary concern on the planned development of state industry.' Trotsky showed how the exchange of goods between agriculture and industry, which the NEP had been designed to promote, strengthened the production of consumer goods while having no impact on the production of heavy industry, which remained on a very low level. It was the task of the coming period to revive heavy industry, by 'draining off into the mill of socialism as large a part as possible of what we previously called the surplus value created by the whole labouring population of our union.'[22]

Trotsky then moved to expand a point that made his speech famous when the rest of it was forgotten. He exhibited a diagram showing the relation between the prices of agricultural products and prices of industrial products since the previous summer: and he showed how the prices diverged more and more widely, giving the diagram the aspect of an open pair of scissors. Unfortunately he was still fudging, hence he did not describe the appearance of the 'scissors' as a major crisis, though he explained that it revealed the lag of industry behind the recovery of private farming.

Trotsky now proceeded to his conclusions, which had been agreed in advance in the politburo. The first was the need to promote the export of grain. The second, which was accepted in principle by everyone but could appear as trite, was to increase the efficiency of industry by measures of concentration and by cutting down overhead costs.

Finally he wound up his speech with a long exposition of the principles of planning. What was needed, he said, was a 'single economic plan'. The development of planning would be in three stages: first, 'means of production to produce means of production'; then 'means of production to produce objects of consumption'; and finally, 'objects of consumption'. The aim of the plan was, in the final analysis, to overcome the market, to overcome the NEP:

The New Economic Policy is the arena which we ourselves have set up for the struggle between ourselves and private capital. We have set it up, we have legalised it, and within it we intend to wage the struggle seriously and for a long time.

Lenin had said that the NEP had been conceived 'seriously and for long'; and the opponents of planning often quoted this saying: 'Yes, seriously and for a long time', Trotsky retorted:

> But not forever. We have introduced NEP in order to defeat it on its own ground and largely by its own methods. In what way? By making effective use of the laws of the market economy... and also by intervening through our state-owned industry in the planning of these laws and by systematically broadening the scope of planning. Ultimately we shall extend this planning principle to the whole market, and in so doing swallow and eliminate it. In other words, our successes on the basis of the New Economic Policy automatically bring us nearer to its liquidation, to its replacement by the *newest* economic policy, which will be a socialist policy.[23]

The working class would have to shoulder the main burden of industrial reconstruction. Trotsky cited a remark from a report to the congress on the state industry of the Moscow region: 'The working class, being in power, has the possibility, when class interests require it, of giving industry a credit at the expense of the worker's wage.' 'In other words', paraphrased Trotsky, 'there may be moments when the government does not pay you a full wage or pays only a half, and you, the worker, give a credit to your state at the expense of your wages.'[24] Unless the worker was ready to produce surplus value for the workers' state there was no way forward for socialism. Trotsky concluded with a postscript on the inevitable hardships of a period of 'primitive socialist accumulation'. (The term 'primitive socialist accumulation' was first coined by Vladimir Smirnov.)[25]

The assumption behind the talk of 'giving up half the wages' to the state was the identification of the working class with the state—the same identifiction that had underlain Trotsky's position in the trade union debate. The question of the bureaucratisation of the state was thus overlooked, as was the weakness of the proletariat in a sea of peasantry. The term 'primitive socialist accumulation' would become a source of very sharp controversy in years to come.

The failure to recognise the conflict between management and workers was a thread running through Trotsky's resolution at the Twelfth Congress. The workers must be helped to understand that the 'director, who strives to earn profits, is serving the interests of the working class in the same degree as the trade-union worker who strives to raise the standard of living of the worker and to protect his health.' The director who 'proves himself by the positive result of his work' should be able to count on the unqualilfied 'protection and support' of party organs.[26]

The rationalisation of industry, Trotsky argued, would lead to unemployment: 'the necessity of dismissing men and women workers' was a 'hard, very hard nut', but it was less damaging than the 'concealed unemployment' of inefficient production.

Thus Trotsky stressed the dialectical relation between planning and the market. He saw the combination of the two as that of two antagonistic elements fighting for supremacy, in which one should end victorious. What was called for was not an abrupt ending of the NEP but the expansion of the state sector so that one day it would supercede the private sector and with it the NEP.

Trotsky's report to the congress passed without any overt dissent: an agreement between members of the politburo meant that no one would criticise Trotsky's report.* In exchange he kept quiet on the national question, Rabkrin and the rest.

Trotsky's report and the resolution accompanying it stopped short of any specific directive. Nine months after the congress Trotsky complained that 'at the Twelfth Congress questions concerning the planned direction of the economy were broached at bottom only formally. This is what explains in large measure why the ways and means set down in the resolution of this congress remained almost entirely unapplied up to recently...'[30]

The enigma: Why did Trotsky keep quiet?

When the Twelfth Congress opened, again and again there were massive displays of homage to Trotsky. As usual the chairman read greetings to the congress, which poured in from

---

* Zinoviev, however, hinted at disagreement with Trotsky: 'Our Vladimir Ilyich taught... that it is necessary to begin with the peasant economy';[27] the peasant question was 'the basic question of our revolution';[28] Lenin had 'scoffed at a number of comrades who were too excited about "paper" plans. We know from our daily work with Vladimir Ilyich that no one jeered as much as he at "new", "great", hypertrophic "plans".' A 'dictatorship of industry' would imperil the *smychka*, the alliance of workers and peasants. Talk of overcoming the NEP was adventurism. Kamenev repeated this same idea, that the 'dictatorship of industry' threatened the *smychka*[29]

party cells, trade unions, and groups of workers and students all over the country. In almost every message tributes were paid to Lenin and Trotsky. Only now and then did the greetings also refer to Zinoviev and Kamenev, while Stalin's name was hardly mentioned. The reading of the messages went on through several sessions.[31] Zinoviev, who delivered the political report of the central committee, was not received by the customary applause. He delivered it in virtual silence; the reaction of the delegates was clear. Stalin got a similar reception. The applause for Trotsky was tumultuous.

Why did Trotsky not use his popularity and the mandate he got from Lenin to launch a general offensive against Stalin, against the bureaucracy, against Great Russian chauvinism?

In later days Trotsky was convinced that had he spoken up at the Twelfth Congress, relying on the documents Lenin had supplied him with, he could probably have defeated Stalin quickly, even if in the long run this would not have prevented the victory of the bureaucracy. He wrote:

> Our joint action against the central committee at the beginning of 1923 would without the shadow of doubt have brought us victory. And what is more, I have no doubt that if I had come forward on the eve of the Twelfth Congress in the spirit of a 'bloc of Lenin and Trotsky' against the Stalin bureaucracy, I should have been victorious even if Lenin had taken no direct part in the struggle. How solid the victory would have been is, of course, another question. To decide that, one must take into account a number of objective processes in the country, in the working class, and in the party itself. That is a separate and large theme... In 1922-3... it was still possible to capture the commanding position by an open attack on the faction then rapidly being formed of national socialist officials, or usurpers of the apparatus, of the unlawful heirs of October, of the epigones of Bolshevism.[32]

'If... if...'. It is very difficult to speculate what would have happened if a certain action had been taken, how a change of one link in the historical chain of events would have shaped the rest of the chain. With this reservation in mind, one might say, accepting Trotsky's estimate that his intervention against Stalin in the spirit of a bloc with Lenin would have succeeded—at least temporarily, that this would have affected the policies carried out by the Comintern in Germany in the autumn of 1923 when the Communist Party was on the verge of taking power but was hindered by poor leadership, not least that in Moscow.

A few months after the congress, in September 1923, the leaders of the German Communist Party asked the politburo of the Russian party to send Trotsky to Germany to direct the coming insurrection. Stalin, Zinoviev and company blocked the assignment. Had Trotsky thrown the 'bomb' at Stalin during the Twelfth Congress, the *troika* might perhaps not have been able to prevent Trotsky going to Germany, which was then in the midst of a revolutionary situation. If Trotsky, the organiser of the Russian October insurrection, had taken hold of the German party, who knows whether the German October would not have ended in victory instead of defeat?

Of course, we can speculate only on probabilities. Every prognosis inevitably includes a conditional element. The shorter the period over which this prognosis extends, the greater this element. Time is an important element in politics, particularly in a revolutionary epoch.

Trotsky himself argued, in his book **The Lessons of October**, published in 1924, that correct leadership in Germany might radically have changed the situation of the proletarian revolution in Russia, with enormous consequences.

For lack of a ha'porth of tar a ship sank.

Small incidents can play a disproportionate role in history. If Rosa Luxemburg had hidden herself more effectively in January 1919 and not been murdered, the German Communist Party would not have been led for years afterwards by inexperienced and relatively weak people.

What was the reason for Trotsky's silence at the Twelfth Congress? There are a number of explanations. One is given by Trotsky himself, who said that he avoided coming out against Stalin as this could have been interpreted as fighting for personal power while Lenin was still alive. This is what Trotsky wrote in his autobiography:

The chief obstacle was Lenin's condition. He was expected to rise again as he had after his first stroke and to take part in the Twelfth Congress as he had in the Eleventh. He himself hoped for this. The doctors spoke encouragingly, though with dwindling assurance... Independent action on my part would have been interpreted, or, to be more exact, represented as my personal fight for Lenin's place in the party and the state. The very thought of this made me shudder. I considered that it would have brought such a demoralisation in our ranks that we would have had to pay too painful a price for it even in case of victory. In all plans and calculations, there remained the positive element of uncertainty—Lenin and his physical condition. Would he be able to state his own views? Would he still have time? Would the party understand that it was the case of a fight by Lenin and Trotsky for the future of the revolution, and not a fight by Trotsky for the place held by Lenin, who was ill?[33]

Hoping for Lenin's recovery and believing that their joint action would be much more effective than his own solitary effort, said Trotsky, he bided his time.

Another much less flattering explanation of Trotsky's astonishing behaviour was given by his close friend and admirer, Adolf Ioffe. In a letter written to Trotsky an hour before Ioffe committed suicide in 1927, he wrote:

I have never doubted the rightness of the road you pointed out, and as you know I have gone with you for more than twenty years, since the days of 'permanent revolution'. But I have always believed that you lacked Lenin's *unbending will*, his *unwillingness to yield*, his readiness even to remain alone on the path that he thought right in anticipation of a future majority, of a future recognition by everyone of the rightness of his path... you have often *abandoned your rightness* for the sake of an overvalued agreement or compromise. This is a mistake... the guarantee of the victory of your rightness lies in nothing but the extreme unwillingness to yield, the strictest straightforwardness, the absolute rejection of all compromise; in this very thing lay the secret of Lenin's victories.[34]

Ioffe's judgment was based on the experience of the period 1923-7, when Trotsky made many compromises and concessions.

This was due not to lack of character but to lack of theoretical and political clarity. (This will be dealt with in the next volume of this biography). Once Trotsky had clearly grasped the counter-revolutionary nature of Stalinism he was completely uncompromising despite *extraordinary* pressures. There is no doubt that Lenin, with his sense of urgency, his understanding of the need to concentrate on the decisive link in the chain of events at the time, even at the cost of secondary elements, would not have been influenced by such secondary considerations as how his fight against Stalin would look to bystanders.

Isaac Deutscher suggests a different explanation for Trotsky's behaviour:

> The truth is that Trotsky refrained from attacking Stalin because he felt secure. No contemporary, and he least of all, saw in the Stalin of 1923 the menacing and towering figure he was to become. It seemed to Trotsky almost a bad joke that Stalin, the wilful and sly but shabby and inarticulate man in the background, should be his rival. He was not going to be bothered about him. He was not going to stoop to him or even to Zinoviev; and, above all, he was not going to give the party the impression that he, too, participated in the undignified game played by Lenin's disciples over Lenin's still empty coffin.[35]

Trotsky's disdainful attitude towards Stalin was of long standing. He wrote later that he was hardly aware of Stalin's existence until after the October revolution.[36] Yet Stalin had been the editor of the party's paper, **Pravda**, and a member of the central committee. Trotsky's attitude reveals how far he was from Lenin in grasping the personal-administrative elements in the Bolshevik Party, which he had belatedly joined.

Another factor probably affected Trotsky's behaviour at the Twelfth Congress. He knew of his very high popularity among the masses, but he felt insecure among the party *cadres*. In the eyes of many Old Bolsheviks Trotsky was still an outsider. At the Eleventh Congress, the previous year, an incident occurred that demonstrated this. In the course of the debate Lenin, Zinoviev and Trotsky expressed the same view on the merger of party and state and argued for the need to separate them. Mikoyan, a young Armenian delegate, remarked that he was not surprised to hear this view from Trotsky who was 'a man of the state but not of the party', but he could not understand how Lenin and Zinoviev took the same stand.[37] From the time Trotsky joined the Bolsheviks he depended very much on Lenin's support to bridge the gulf with the Old Bolsheviks; now Lenin was not there to support him. This undermined his confidence *vis-à-vis* the party *cadres*.

Above all, Trotsky's hesitation in carrying Lenin's struggle against Stalin into the open was due to his fear of splitting the party and encouraging the counter-revolution. His vast knowledge of the French Revolution of 1789 must have made him aware of this danger. He must have recalled how the extreme left in the French revolution, in the days following *9 Thermidor* and the fall of Robespierre, motivated by sheer hatred of Robespierre, supported the right. Gracchus Babeuf, the first modern communist, went so far as to declare on 5 September 1794: '*10 Thermidor* was the end of our confinement; since then we have been in labour to be reborn into liberty.'[38] After a time Babeuf regretted having been one of the first to inveigh against the 'Robespierre system'.[39] But it was too late. Although there was no collusion between Babeuf and the neo-Hébertists on the one hand and the Monarchist reactionaries and the Thermidorians on the other, the campaign of Babeuf and his companions did help towards the success of reaction.

It was this fear of counter-revolution that dominated Trotsky's thinking. On 10 May 1922, more than a year after the Kronstadt rising, writing in **Pravda** on the signs of economic recovery and general improvement of conditions in the country, Trotsky posed the question whether the time had not come to put an end to the one-party system and to lift the ban at least on the Mensheviks. His answer was a categoric 'No'. Why? Because 'within the boundaries of capitalist encirclement they were and remain the semi-political, semi-military agencies of imperialism, armed to its teeth.'[40]

Trotsky had to ask himself whether he could take responsibility for possibly sparking off a new Kronstadt uprising. He clearly considered it the duty of revolutionaries, in the absence of any existing alternative, to remain loyal to the party of the revolution to the last possible moment. This was a weighty consideration, much easier to dismiss when the degeneration of the party had run its course than in the midst of the struggle.

The main influences on Trotsky's behaviour were the same circumstances that made Lenin's grasp so unsure, so vacillating, contradicting his whole character, his whole political past. Neither Lenin nor Trotsky could see a solution. There was a possibility that the siege of Russia might eventually be lifted by the international revolution. But what to do in the meantime? The proletariat was weakened and atomised, and the party no longer enjoyed the working-class support it had commanded when it entered the civil war; yet a revolutionary party and government that had fought a cruel and devastating civil war could neither abdicate the day after its victory, nor submit to its defeated enemies and their revenge, even when it discovered that it could not rule according to its own principles.

Lenin and Trotsky knew very well that the workers were exhausted. Trotsky's own supporters, as he put it later, were not stirred on by a hope of great and serious changes. On the other hand, the bureaucracy fought with extraordinary ferocity.[41] To fight with little hope is very difficult indeed. As Trotsky wrote many years later:

> The Left Opposition could not achieve power, and did not hope even to do so—certainly not its most thoughtful leaders. A struggle for power by the Left Opposition, by a revolutionary Marxist organisation, was conceivable only under the conditions of a revolutionary upsurge. Under such conditions the strategy is based on aggression, on direct appeal to the masses, on frontal attack against the government. Quite a few members of the Left Opposition had played no minor part in such a struggle and had first-hand knowledge of how to wage it. But during the early 1920s and later, there was no revolutionary upsurge in Russia, quite the contrary. Under such circumstances it was out of the question to launch a struggle for power.

Inability to foresee victory must engender paralysis of will power. The 'danger was that, having become convinced of the impossibility of open association with the masses, even with their vanguard, the opposition would give up the struggle and lie low until better times.'[42]

Gramsci refers to 'the optimism of the will and the pessimism of the intellect'. The tragedy was that at the time of the Twelfth

Congress Trotsky could not point to any mass support to which to attach that *will*. The Russian proletariat was exhausted and isolated.

At the end of the Twelfth Congress Stalin's position was strengthened: he was again re-elected to the post of general secretary; Ordzhonikidze was put in charge of Rabkrin; Dzerzhinsky became the chairman of VSNKh (the National Economic Council) and Kuibyshev, again Stalin's close associate, was appointed to preside over the central control commission! Among the 40 members elected by the Twelfth Congress to the central committee, Trotsky had no more than three political friends: Rakovsky, Radek and Piatakov.

After the congress Stalin strengthened his position in the politburo by the replacement of Radek with his ally Rykov. Of the four candidate members, of whom Bukharin now became one, three—Kalinin, Molotov and Rudzutak—were all good Stalinists.

The Twelfth Congress of the party was a watershed in the development of the Soviet regime. It was the first congress of the party in which Lenin did not participate and it was not yet clear whether he would ever return to political activity. Things were still in limbo. Only after the congress, when it became obvious that Lenin would never return, did the *troika*—Stalin, Zinoviev and Kamenev—dare to launch a massive campaign against 'Trotskyism'.

For a few months after the congress there was still a prospect of immediate victory for the proletarian revolution in Germany —an event that would radically have altered the situation in Soviet Russia. But after October-November 1923 it became clear that the revolutionary opportunity in Germany had been missed. The defeat of the German revolution opened the door to Stalin's newly formulated concept of 'Socialism in one country'. This became the whip used by Stalin and his theoretical aide Bukharin to fight Trotsky and his supporters.

During the years 1923-7 (the theme of my next volume) the rising bureaucracy became increasingly independent of the proletariat, and relied more and more on the rich peasants—the *kulaks*—and the rising merchants—the NEPmen. Trotsky challenged the three social forces that benefitted from the NEP— the bureaucracy, the *kulaks* and the NEPmen. He developed a policy of planned industrialisation of the country, aimed at increasing the social weight of the proletariat, enlarging its size, raising its living standards and expanding workers' democracy. Stalin (and Bukharin) opposed both the demand for planned industrialisation and the call for democratisation.

Objective circumstances in Russia helped Stalin to defeat Trotsky. The proletariat was still smaller in size than it had been in 1917, and its confidence was undermined by widespread unemployment and the harassment of the managers of industry. At the same time the *kulaks* and NEPmen—blessed by Bukharin, who called to them: 'Enrich yourselves'—went from strength to strength.

The right turn of the Stalin-Bukharin bloc in internal matters was accompanied by a massive shift to the right in Comintern affairs. Thus on the occasion of the Chinese Revolution (1925-7) the Communist Party of China was forced by Moscow to subordinate itself to the bourgeois party of the Kuomintang. The Kuomintang was accepted into the Comintern as a sympathetic section, while the Chinese Communist Party was forced to be in the Kuomintang and under its discipline. When Chiang Kai-shek's Kuomintang army entered Shanghai in March 1927 Stalin sent a cable congratulating him. When Chiang ordered the workers disarmed, the Chinese Communist Party was instructed by the Comintern leadership not to resist. A few days later Chiang's troops murdered tens of thousands of Shanghai workers and Communists.

Similarly right-wing policies were adopted by the Comintern for Britain. On the eve of the general strike of May 1926, and during the strike itself, the Comintern's policy was to collaborate with the Trades Union Congress and bolster trust in the left officials of the unions, while these acted as a figleaf for the right-wing officials. The sabotage of the general strike by the TUC led to the unmitigated defeat of the working class. This was a decisive turning point in British history: a long, though not uninterrupted period of working-class militancy came to an end, giving way to a prolonged period of dominance of the unions by openly class-collaborationist right-wing leaders, and a massive reinforcement of the Labour Party right.

Trotsky's writings on China and Britain are amongst the best Marxist essays on strategy and tactics ever produced.

Nonetheless, however correct his analysis, the defeats

inflicted on the working class by Stalin's policies did not strengthen Trotsky's position, but Stalin's. A weakened Communist movement was opened up to the blandishments of the bureaucracy and its appeal for 'socialism in one country', for defence of the *status quo* and against any revolutionary upheavals.

To add to Trotsky's difficulties, the implications of the degeneration of the state, party and Comintern were less clear at the time than with the benefit of hindsight. Lack of theoretical and political clarity led Trotsky to make a number of concessions and compromises, above all to Zinoviev and Kamenev, who were to become his new allies in the United Opposition of 1926-7. Nothing was more alien to Trotsky's character than hesitation and fudging. When by 1927 he grasped the enormity of Stalin's crimes, and called Stalin 'the gravedigger of the revolution', he became completely uncompromising.

Notes

PREFACE

1. Tony Cliff, **Trotsky: Towards October 1879-1917** (Bookmarks: London 1989).
2. Tony Cliff, **Lenin** (four volumes, Pluto Press: London 1975-9; reprinted in three volumes, Bookmarks: London 1985-7).

Chapter 1: THE CONSOLIDATION OF SOVIET POWER

1. Leon Trotsky, **My Life** (New York 1960) page 337.
2. Trotsky, **My Life**, pages 337-8.
3. Trotsky, **My Life**, pages 340-1.
4. John Reed, **Ten days that shook the world** (London 1961) page 28.
5. N N Sukhanov, **The Russian Revolution 1917: A personal record** (London 1955) page 636.
6. Sukhanov, pages 639-40.
7. **Vtoroi Vserossiiskii Sezd Sovetovv RiSD**, pages 84-7; J Bunyan and H H Fisher, **The Bolshevik Revolution, 1917-1918: Documents and Materials** (Stanford 1924) pages 135-6.
8. L H Haimson, **The Mensheviks** (Chicago 1974) pages 59-60.
9. **The Bolsheviks and the October Revolution: Minutes of the Central Committee of the Russian Social-Democratic Labour Party (Bolsheviks) August 1917-February 1918** (London 1974) (hereafter referred to as **CC Minutes**), page 292.
10. **CC Minutes**, page 127.
11. **CC Minutes**, page 127 note.
12. **CC Minutes**, pages 291-5.
13. **CC Minutes**, pages 128-35.
14. Quoted in Trotsky, **The Stalin School of Falsification** (New York 1962) pages 107-123.
15. **Biulleten Oppozitsiu**, number 7 (1929) pages 30-2.
16. Trotsky, **Stalin School**, pages 107-23.
17. J L H Keep (editor) **The Debate on Soviet Power: Minutes of the All-Russian Central Executive Committee of Soviets** (Oxford

1979) page 68.

18. **Debate on Soviet Power**, page 71.

19. Trotsky, **Sochineniia** (Moscow) volume 3, book 2, pages 104-6 and 402.

20. Quoted in Haimson, page 75.

21. **CC Minutes**, page 143.

22. **CC Minutes**, page 150.

23. O H Radkey, **The Sickle under the Hammer** (New York 1963) pages 66- 7.

24. Bunyan and Fisher, page 190.

25. Haimson, pages 67-8.

26. Victor Serge, **Year One of the Russian Revolution** (London 1972) page 79.

27. Quoted in Trotsky, **On Lenin** (London 1971) page 115.

28. Trotsky, **Sochineniia**, volume 2, book 2, page 202.

29. Trotsky, **Sochineniia**, volume 3, book 2, page 133.

30. Trotsky, **Sochineniia**, volume 3, book 2, page 138.

31. M Latsis, **Chrezvychainaia Komissiia po borbe s kontr-revoliutsiei** (Moscow 1920).

32. Serge, **Year One**, page 307.

33. Latsis, page 9.

34. Serge, **Year One**, page 189.

35. V I Lenin, **Collected Works**, translated from the fourth Russian edition (Moscow) volume 30, page 223.

36. Serge, **Year One**, page 298.

37. Karl Marx and Friedrich Engels, **Historisch-Kritische Gesamtausgabe**, Ier Teil, volume 7, page 423.

38. Trotsky, **Terrorism and Communism** (Ann Arbor 1972) pages 54-5.

Chapter 2: THE PEACE OF BREST-LITOVSK

1. **Izvestiia**, 10 November 1917; Trotsky, **Sochineniia**, volume 3, book 2, pages 164-5.

2. **Izvestiia**, 19 November 1917; Trotsky, **Sochineniia**, page 178.

3. **Izvestiia**, 6 December 1917; Trotsky, **Sochineniia**, pages 206-7.

4. Trotsky's preface to A A Ioffe (editor) **Mirnye peregovorii v Brest-Litovsk** (Moscow 1920).

5. Ottokar Czernin, **In the World War** (London 1919) pages 232- 3

6. Trotsky, **My Life**, page 365.

7. Czernin, page 232.

8. Lenin, **Works**, volume 26, pages 444 and 447-8.

9. Trotsky, **On Lenin**, pages 93-5.

10. J W Wheeler-Bennett, **Brest-Litovsk: The Forgotten Peace, March 1918** (London 1938) page 196.

11. **CC Minutes**, pages 176-7.

12. **CC Minutes**, pages 177-8.

13. **CC Minutes**, page 174.

14. **CC Minutes**, page 179.
15. Ioffe, page 66.
16. Ioffe, page 102.
17. Trotsky, **My Life**, page 373.
18. Czernin, page 372.
19. Ioffe, pages 207-8; Wheeler-Bennett, pages 226-7.
20. Wheeler-Bennett, page 166.
21. **Pravda**, 12 February 1918, in Wheeler-Bennett, page 237.
22. Trotsky, **The History of the Russian Revolution to Brest-Litovsk** (London 1919) page 142.
23. General Max von Hoffmann, **War Diaries and other papers** (London 1929) volume 1, pages 206-7.
24. Trotsky, **My Life**, page 387.
25. **CC Minutes**, pages 204-5.
26. **CC Minutes**, pages 210-11.
27. **CC Minutes**, pages 218-9.
28. **CC Minutes**, pages 221-2.
29. **CC Minutes**, page 223.
30. **CC Minutes**, pages 223-4.
31. **CC Minutes**, page 233.
32. **CC Minutes**, page 235.
33. **Sedmoi sezd RKP(b)** (Moscow 1923) page 83.
34. Bunyan and Fisher, pages 523-4.
35. **Leninskii sbornik**, volume 11, pages 59-61
36. **Kommunisticheskaia partiia sovetskogo soiuza v rezoliutsiakh i resheniiakh sezdov, konferentsii i plenumov TsK**, seventh edition (Moscow 1953) (hereafter given as **KPSS v Rezoliutsiakh**), volume 1, pages 404-5.
37. **CC Minutes**, pages 212-5.
38. Lenin, **Works**, volume 27, page 37.
39. Lenin, **Works**, volume 27, page 39.
40. Wheeler-Bennett, page 81.
41. Czernin, page 215.
42. Czernin, page 223.
43. Czernin, page 228.
44. Czernin, page 233.
45. Czernin, pages 237-8.
46. Czernin, page 239.
47. Wheeler-Bennett, page 170.
48. Czernin, page 240.
49. Czernin, page 318.
50. Wheeler-Bennett, pages 229-30.
51. Wheeler-Bennett, page 231
52. See General Ludendorff, **My War Memoirs, 1914-1918** (London 1919) volume 2, pages 547-60.
53. K Liebknecht, **Politische Aufzeichnungen aus seinem Nachlass**

(Verlag Die Aktion 1921) quoted in Trotsky, **My Life**, page 378.

54. Quoted in Trotsky, **My Life**, pages 390-1.

55. N K Krupskaya, **Reminiscences of Lenin** (Moscow 1959) page 449.

56. Trotsky, **How the Revolution Armed** (five volumes, London 1979-1981) (hereafter referred to as **HRA**) volume 1, page 507.

Chapter 3: BUILDING THE RED ARMY

1. See Cliff, **Trotsky**, volume 1, pages 168-72.

2. H W Nelson, **Leon Trotsky and the Art of Insurrection, 1905-1917** (London 1988) pages 53 and 58.

3. Nelson, pages 58-9.

4. Nelson, pages 63-4. Nelson refers to a number of examples from Trotsky's writings, especially his **Sochineniia**, volume 6, pages 145-7, 151-2 and 172.

5. Trotsky, **Sochineniia**, volume 9, page 190.

6. Trotsky, **Sochineniia**, volume 9, page 190.

7. Nelson, pages 86-7.

8. Trotsky, **Sochineniia**, volume 9, page 195; Nelson, pages 91-2.

9. Lissagaray, **History of the Paris Commune of 1871** (London 1976) page 135.

10. Lissagaray, page 173.

11. Lissagaray, page 258.

12. Trotsky, **HRA**, volume 5, page 337.

13. **Pravda**, 14 March 1923, quoted in **The Case of Leon Trotsky** (London 1937) pages 102-3.

Chapter 4: THE STRUCTURE OF THE RED ARMY

1. K Muratov, **Revoliutsionnoe dvizhenie v russkoi armii v 1917** (Moscow 1958) page 313.

2. Trotsky, **HRA**, volume 1, page 413.

3. A S Bubnov, S S Kamenev and R P Eideman (editors) **Grazhdanskaia voina 1918-1921** (Moscow 1928) (hereafter referred to as Bubnov) volume 2, page 50.

4. E Eriaklov, **Krasnaia Gvardiia v borbe za vlast sovetov** (Moscow 1937) page 39.

5. Y Akhapkin (editor) **First Decrees of Soviet Power** (London 1970) page 86.

6. Trotsky, **HRA**, volume 1, page 245.

7. Lenin, **Works**, volume 24, pages 100-1.

8. Akhapkin, pages 67-8.

9. R Wade, **Red Guards and Workers' Militias in the Russian Revolution** (Stanford 1984) page 311.

10. **Direktivy komandovaniia frontov Krasnoi Armii (1917-1927)** volume 4 (Moscow 1978) page 20.

11. Trotsky, **HRA**, volume 1, pages 157-9.

12. Akhapkin, page 137.

13. Trotsky, **HRA**, volume 1, page 564.
14. Trotsky, **My Life**, page 437.
15. **Direktivy komandovaniia frontov Krasnoi Armii (1917- 1927)** volume 4, page 112.
16. Trotsky, **HRA**, volume 1, page 115.
17. Bubnov, volume 2, page 85.
18. Bubnov, volume 2, page 83
19. Bubnov, volume 2, page 87
20. M Bouloiseau, **The Jacobin Republic, 1792-1794** (Cambridge 1987) page 128.
21. Bouloiseau, page 136.
22. Trotsky, **HRA**, volume 1, page 476.
23. Trotsky, **HRA**, volume 2, page 39.
24. Trotsky, **My Life**, pages 411-12.
25. Trotsky, **HRA**, volume 3, page 6.
26. Quoted in D N Fedotoff-White, **Growth of the Red Army** (Princeton 1944) page 105.
27. Trotsky, **HRA**, volume 1, page 442.
28. Trotsky, **HRA**, volume 3, pages 173-4.
29. Trotsky, **HRA**, volume 2, pages 155-6.
30. Trotsky, **HRA**, volume 3, page 10
31. G S Pukhov, **Kak vooruzhalatsia Petrograd** (Moscow 1933) page 113.
32. Bubnov, volume 2, pages 67-8.
33. Trotsky, **HRA**, volume 1, page 242.
34. Trotsky, **HRA**, volume 2, page 368.
35. Bubnov, volume 2, page 126.
36. Trotsky, **HRA**, volume 1, page 8.
37. Trotsky, **HRA**, volume 1, pages 23 and 38.
38. Trotsky, **HRA**, volume 1, page 10.
39. Trotsky, **HRA**, volume 3, page 11.
40. Trotsky, **HRA**, volume 3, pages 12-13.
41. Bubnov, volume 2, page 95.
42. Bubnov, volume 2, page 97.
43. Bubnov, volume 2, page 96.
44. Bubnov, volume 2, page 96.
45. Trotsky, **HRA**, volume 4, page 390.
46. F Benvenuti, **The Bolsheviks and the Red Army, 1918-1922** (Cambridge 1988) page 209.
47. Trotsky, **HRA**, volume 1, page 196.
48. Trotsky, **HRA**, volume 1, page 183.
49. Trotsky, **HRA**, volume 2, page 113.
50. Trotsky, **HRA**, volume 4, pages 194-5.
51. Trotsky, **HRA**, volume 2, pages 116-8.
52. Trotsky, **HRA**, volume 1, pages 557-8.
53. Trotsky, **HRA**, volume 1, page 249.

54. Trotsky, **HRA**, volume 1, page 298.

Chapter 5: THE SPIRIT OF THE RED ARMY

1. Trotsky, **HRA**, volume 1, page 301.
2. Trotsky, **HRA**, volume 2, pages 18-19.
3. Trotsky, **HRA**, page 20.
4. E H Carr, **The Bolshevik Revolution, 1917-1923** (London 1953) volume 3, page 16.
5. J Erickson, **The Soviet High Command** (London 1962) page 25.
6. Erickson, page 675.
7. Trotsky, **HRA**, volume 1, page 21.
8. Trotsky, **HRA**, volume 1, page 160.
9. Trotsky, **HRA**, volume 2, pages 580-1.
10. Trotsky, **HRA**, volume 3, page 209.
11. Trotsky, **HRA**, volume 1, page 24.
12. Trotsky, **HRA**, volume 1, pages 419-20.
13. Trotsky, **HRA**, volume 4, page 95.
14. Trotsky, **HRA**, volume 1, pages 459-60.
15. Trotsky, **HRA**, volume 2, pages 289-90.
16. Trotsky, **HRA**, volume 4, pages 151-2.
17. Trotsky, **HRA**, volume 1, pages 356-8.
18. Bubnov, volume 1, page 168.
19. Trotsky, **HRA**, volume 1, page 322.

Chapter 6: THE RED ARMY BLOODED

1. Trotsky, **HRA**, volume 1, pages 309-10.
2. Trotsky, **My Life**, page 396.
3. Trotsky, **My Life**, page 397.
4. Trotsky, **My Life**, page 397.
5. **Proletarskaia Revoliutsiia**, number 2 (25) (1924), quoted in Trotsky, **My Life**, page 399.
6. Trotsky, **My Life**, page 407.
7. Trotsky, **My Life**, page 410.
8. Trotsky, **My Life**, pages 411 and 413-14.
9. Trotsky, **My Life**, page 415.
10. Trotsky, **My Life**, page 418.
11. Trotsky, **My Life**, page 417.
12. Trotsky, **My Life**, page 420.
13. Trotsky, **HRA**, volume 1, page xxix.

Chapter 7: OPPOSITION TO TROTSKY IN THE RED ARMY

1. Trotsky, **HRA**, volume 1, page 9.
2. Trotsky, **HRA**, volume 1, pages 427-8.
3. Trotsky, **HRA**, volume 1, page 8.
4. Trotsky, **HRA**, volume 4, pages 85-6.
5. Trotsky, **HRA**, volume 4, page 86.

6. Trotsky, **HRA**, volume 4, pages 86-7.
7. Trotsky, **HRA**, volume 1, pages 215-6.
8. Trotsky, **HRA**, volume 2, pages 259-60.
9. Trotsky, **HRA**, volume 2, pages 407-8.
10. Trotsky, **Stalin** (London 1947) page 277.
11. Trotsky, **Stalin** pages 297-8.
12. **Theses of the Left Communists, 1918** (Glasgow 1977) pages 16-17.
13. Trotsky, **My Life**, pages 439-40.
14. Trotsky, **Stalin**, pages 280-1.
15. Trotsky, **My Life**, page 440.
16. Trotsky, **My Life**, page 441.
17. J V Stalin, **Works** (Moscow 1953) volume 4, page 120.
18. Stalin, **Works**, volume 4, page 123.
19. Stalin, **Works**, volume 4, pages 124 and 126.
20. Stalin, **Works**, volume 4, page 133.
21. J Meijer (editor) **The Trotsky Papers (The Hague 1971)** (hereafter referred to as **Trotsky Papers**) volume 1, pages 135 and 137.
22. Trotsky, **HRA**, volume 1, page 474.
23. See Trotsky's message to Lenin of 14 December 1918, in **Trotsky Papers**, volume 1, page 197.
24. Trotsky, **HRA**, volume 1, page 465.
25. Trotsky, **Stalin**, page 291.
26. **Pravda**, 29 November 1918, quoted in Benvenuti, pages 79-80.
27. **Trotsky Papers**, volume 1, page 155.
28. **Trotsky Papers**, volume 1, page 155.
29. **Trotsky Papers**, volume 1, page 253.
30. **Trotsky Papers**, volume 1, pages 361-3 and 367.
31. Trotsky, **Stalin**, page 328.
32. **Pravda**, 25 December 1918; Benvenuti, pages 82-3.
33. **Trotsky Papers**, volume 1, pages 207-9.
34. **Pravda**, 26 December 1918; Benvenuti, page 85.
35. Trotsky, **Stalin School**, page 45.
36. Trotsky, **My Life**, page 446.
37. Trotsky, **My Life**, page 398.
38. **Petrogradskaia Pravda**, 3, 11 and 13 April 1918.
39. Quoted in A F Ilyin-Zhenevsky, **The Bolsheviks in Power** (London 1984) pages 63-4.
40. Quoted in Ilyin-Zhenevsky, page 71.
41. Quoted in Ilyin-Zhenevsky, pages 71-2.
42. Stalin, **Works**, volume 4, page 194.
43. Stalin, **Works**, volume 4, page 213.
44. Stalin, **Works**, volume 4, pages 216-7.
45. Stalin, **Works**, volume 4, page 214.
46. Trotsky, **HRA**, volume 1, page 172.
47. Trotsky, **HRA**, volume 1, page 223.
48. Trotsky, **HRA**, volume 1, page 221.

49. **Trotsky Papers**, volume 1, pages 107-9.
50. Lenin, **Works**, volume 28, page 195.
51. Trotsky, **My Life**, page 447.
52. Lenin, **Works**, volume 29, page 7.
53. R Medvedev, 'Hell Black Night', in **Inostranaia literatura**, March 1989, page 170.
54. Trotsky, **Stalin**, page 277.
55. Trotsky, **Stalin School**, page 98.
56. **Trotsky Papers**, volume 2, page 841.
57. Trotsky, **HRA**, volume 1, pages 243-56.
58. A V Danilevsky, **V I Lenin i voprosy voennogo stroitelstva na viii sezde RKP(b)** (Moscow 1964) pages 71 and 76.
59. Danilevsky, pages 75-6.
60. Lenin, **Works**, volume 29, pages 153-4.
61. **Leninskii sbornik**, volume 37, page 137.
62. **Leninskii sbornik**, volume 38, pages 135-40.
63. **Trotsky Papers**, volume 1, pages 319 and 322.
64. **Trotsky Papers**, volume 1, pages 325-35.

Chapter 8: DISPUTES ON MILITARY STRATEGY

1. **Trotsky Papers**, volume 1, page 521.
2. **Trotsky Papers**, volume 1, page 521.
3. **Trotsky Papers**, volume 1, page 523.
4. **Trotsky Papers**, volume 1, page 525.
5. Stalin, **Works**, volume 4, page 271.
6. **Trotsky Papers**, volume 1, page 523.
7. Stalin, **Works**, volume 4, page 273.
8. Lenin to Sokolnikov, 20 April 1919, quoted in **Trotsky Papers**, volume 1, page 369.
9. Lenin to Antonov-Ovsienko, 22 April 1919, quoted in **Trotsky Papers**, volume 1, page 373.
10. 24 April-1 May 1919, quoted in **Trotsky Papers**, volume 1, pages 377-87.
11. **Trotsky Papers**, volume 1, pages 566-7.
12. **Trotsky Papers**, volume 1, pages 581-2, note 4.
13. **Trotsky Papers**, volume 1, page 483.
14. Trotsky, **My Life**, page 452.
15. Minutes of the central committee, quoted in **Trotsky Papers**, volume 1, pages 578-81.
16. Trotsky, **Stalin**, page 313.
17. **Trotsky Papers**, volume 1, pages 591 and 593.
18. **Trotsky Papers**, volume 1, page 589.
19. Trotsky, **HRA**, volume 2, page 135.
20. Trotsky, **HRA**, volume 2, pages 70-78.
21. Trotsky, **HRA**, volume 2, pages 334-9
22. Meijer's comment in **Trotsky Papers**, volume 1, pages 587-8.

23. Trotsky, **Stalin School**, page 222.
24. **Trotsky Papers**, volume 1, page 597.
25. **Trotsky Papers**, volume 1, page 599.
26. **Trotsky Papers**, volume 1, page 611.
27. **Trotsky Papers**, volume 1, page 667.
28. Trotsky, **HRA**, volume 2, pages 429-30.
29. Trotsky, **HRA**, volume 2, pages 412-14.
30. Trotsky, **HRA**, volume 2, pages 540-1; Trotsky, **Sochineniia**, volume 17, book 2, pages 266-7.
31. Trotsky, **HRA**, volume 2, page 565; Trotsky, **Sochineniia**, volume 17, book 2, page 287.
32. Trotsky, **My Life**, page 429.
33. Klara Zetkin, **Reminiscences of Lenin** (London 1929) pages 19-21.
34. Stalin, **Works**, volume 4, pages 345-6.
35. Trotsky, **Stalin**, pages 329 and 322.
36. Lenin, **Works**, volume 32, page 173.
37. Zetkin, page 20.
38. Trotsky, **My Life**, pages 457-8.

Chapter 9: THE DEBATE ON MILITARY DOCTRINE

1. M Frunze, **Sobranie Sochinenii** (Moscow 1929) pages 207-227.
2. Trotsky, **HRA**, volume 2, pages 227-8.
3. Trotsky, **HRA**, volume 2, pages 85-6.
4. Trotsky, **HRA**, volume 5, pages 396-7.
5. Trotsky, **HRA**, pages 125-6.
6. Trotsky, **HRA**, page 317.
7. Trotsky, **HRA**, pages 317 and 319-20.
8. Trotsky, **HRA**, page 361.
9. Trotsky, **HRA**, pages 409-11.
10. Trotsky, **HRA**, page 397.
11. Trotsky, **HRA**, page 342.
12. Trotsky, **HRA**, pages 345-6.
13. Trotsky, **HRA**, pages 394-5.
14. Trotsky, **HRA**, pages 340-1
15. M N Tukhachevsky, **Voina klassov** (Moscow 1921) pages 138-40.
16. Trotsky, **HRA**, volume 4, pages 132 and 134.
17. Trotsky, **HRA**, volume 5, page 389.
18. Lenin, **Works**, volume 23, page 319.
19. Lenin, **Works**, volume 24, page 180.
20. Trotsky, **HRA**, volume 2, pages 190-2.
21. Trotsky, **HRA**, volume 2, pages 167-9.
22. Trotsky, **HRA**, volume 2, pages 16-18.
23. **Desiatii sezd RKP(b)** (Moscow 1933) pages 294, 614 and 674-84.

Chapter 10: THE RED ARMY AND THE RISE OF THE STALINIST BUREAUCRACY

1. Trotsky, **Stalin**, page 275.
2. T H Rigby, **Lenin's Government: Sovnarkom 1917-1922** (Cambridge 1979) page 89.
3. L N Kritzman, **Die heroische Periode der grossen russischen Revolution** (Frankfurt-am-Main 1971) page 265.
4. **Perepiska sekretariata TsK RSDRP(b) s mestnymi partiinymi organizatsiiakh** (Moscow 1957) volume 4, document 111.
5. **Pravda**, 3 January 1919, quoted in Benvenuti, page 63.
6. **Deviatii sezd RKP(b)** (Moscow 1920) pages 101-2.
7. Trotsky, **HRA**, volume 1, page xxv.
8. Rigby, page 182.
9. Rigby, page 181.
10. Trotsky, **Stalin**, page 295.
11. S I Gusev, **Uroki grazhdanskoi voiny** (Moscow 1921) page 8.
12. Trotsky, **The Revolution Betrayed** (New York 1987) pages 89-90.
13. Trotsky, **Stalin**, pages 384-5.

Chapter 11: WAR COMMUNISM AT AN IMPASSE

1. Kritzman, page 80.
2. Kritzman, page 293.
3. K Leites, **Recent Economic Development in Russia** (Oxford 1922 pages 152 and 199.
4. J Bunyan, **The Origin of Forced Labor in the Soviet State, 1917- 1921** (Baltimore 1967) pages 173-4.
5. V Brügmann, **Die russischen Gewerksschaften in Revolution und Bürgerkrieg 1917-1919** (Frankfurt-am-Main 1972) page 151.
6. Kritzman, page 252.
7. Kritzman, page 276.
8. Kritzman, page 287.
9. F Lorimer, **The Population of the Soviet Union** (Geneva 1948) page 41.
10. Kritzman, page 288.
11. Trotsky, **The New Course** (New York 1943) page 63; Trotsky, **Sochineniia**, volume 17, book 2, pages 543-4.
12. Trotsky, **My Life**, page 564.
13. **Desiatii sezd RKP(b)** (Moscow 1921) pages 191-2.
14. **Leninskii sbornik**, volume 7, page 363.
15. **Leninskii sbornik**, volume 35, page 175.
16. Lenin, **Works**, volume 31, page 505.
17. Lenin, **Works**, volume 32, page 133.
18. **Trotsky Papers**, volume 2, pages 3-7.
19. **Trotsky Papers**, volume 2, page 9.
20. Trotsky, **Sochineniia**, volume 15, pages 269-71.

21. Trotsky, **Sochineniia**, volume 15, pages 5-6.
22. Trotsky, **Sochineniia**, volume 15, pages 111-2.
23. Trotsky, **Sochineniia**, volume 15, page 133.
24. Trotsky, **Sochineniia**, volume 15, page 181.
25. **Desiatii sezd RKP(b)**, page 101.
26. Trotsky, **Sochineniia**, volume 15, page 287; Trotsky, **HRA**, volume 3, page 83.
27. Lenin, **Works**, volume 30, page 312.
28. Lenin, **Works**, volume 30, pages 332-4.
29. Trotsky, **HRA**, volume 3, page 107.
30. Trotsky, **HRA**, volume 3, page 109.
31. Trotsky, **HRA**, volume 3, page 113.
32. Trotsky, **Terrorism and Communism**, pages 140-2.
33. Marx, **Capital**, volume 1 (London 1954) page 191.
34. Kritzman, page 283.
35. **Sobranie uzakonenii** (1920) number 8, article 52, and number 10, article 64.
36. **Trotsky Papers**, volume 2, page 23.
37. **Trotsky Papers**, volume 2, page 115.
38. Trotsky, **Sochineniia**, volume 15, pages 345-7.
39. Trotsky, **Sochineniia**, volume 15, pages 347-8, 359, 399 and 445.
40. Trotsky, **Sochineniia**, volume 15, pages 385-6.
41. Trotsky, **Sochineniia**, volume 15, pages 452-85.
42. Quoted in Trotsky, **The New Course**, page 80.
43. **Desiatii sezd RKP(b)**, page 372.
44. Lenin, **Works**, volume 31, pages 374-5.
45. **Otchety o deiatelnosti tsentralnogo komiteta RKP(b)** (Moscow 1921) pages 47-8.
46. **Otchety o deiatelnosti tsentralnogo komiteta RKP(b)**, pages 47-9.
47. **KPSS v rezoliutsiiakh**, volume 1, pages 490-1.
48. **Desiatii sezd RKP(b)**, pages 350-1.
49. Lenin, **Works**, volume 32, pages 20-1.
50. Lenin, **Works**, volume 32, page 37.
51. Lenin, **Works**, volume 32, page 50.
52. Trotsky, Concluding Speech to the Second All-Russian Congress of Miners, 26 January 1921, in Trotsky, **Stalin School**, page 31.
53. Lenin, **Works**, volume 32, page 204.
54. Trotsky, **The New Course**, page 32.
55. **The Case of Leon Trotsky**, page 408.
56. See N Bukharin, **Dengi v spokhe proletarskoi diktatury** (Moscow 1920).
57. Lenin, **Works**, volume 36, page 595.
58. Trotsky, **Stalin School**, page 29.
59. **Desiatii sezd RKP(b)**, page 221.
60. **Desiatii sezd RKP(b)**, page 214.

61. Trotsky, **My Life**, pages 465-6.
62. S Singleton, 'The Tambov Revolt, 1920-1921', in **Slavic Review** (September 1966).
63. P Avrich, **Kronstadt 1921** (New York 1974) page 35.
64. Avrich, page 37
65. Avrich, page 39.
66. Serge, **Memoirs of a Revolutionary** (London 1963) page 123.
67. Avrich, page 42.
68. Avrich, page 45.
69. Avrich, page 42.
70. Avrich, pages 46-7.
71. Avrich, pages 89-90.
72. Avrich, page 93.
73. Avrich, page 69.
74. Avrich, pages 179-80.
75. **Desiatii sezd RKP(b)**, page 253.
76. Avrich, page 184.
77. Lenin, **Works**, volume 32, page 279.
78. Trotsky, **Revolution Betrayed**, page 96.
79. **Odinnadtsatii sezd RKP(b)** (Moscow 1936) page 468.

Chapter 12: THE DECLINE OF THE PROLETARIAT AND THE RISE OF THE BUREAUCRACY

1. I S Rosenfeld, **Promyshlennaia politika SSSR** (Moscow 1926) page 37.
2. Brügmann, pages 215-6.
3. Lenin, **Works**, volume 33, page 256.
4. Kritzman, page 217.
5. Kritzman, page 218.
6. **Trudy I vserossiiskogo sezda sovetov narodnogo khoziaistva** (Moscow 1918) page 434.
7. **Chetvertii vserossiiskii sezd professionalnykh soiuzov** (Moscow 1921) page 119.
8. Lenin, **Works**, volume 29, page 555.
9. Lenin, **Works**, volume 33, page 65.
10. Lenin, **Works**, volume 32, page 412.
11. **Odinnadtsatii sezd RKP(b)**, page 109.
12. G V Vernadsky, **A History of Russia** (New York 1944) page 319.
13. W Pietsch, **Revolution und Statt: Institutionen als Träger der Macht in der Sowjetrussland (1917-1922)** (Cologne 1969) page 137.
14. Lenin, **Works**, volume 31, page 178.
15. Lenin, **Works**, volume 29, page 183.
16. Lenin, **Works**, volume 33, page 77.
17. Lenin, **Works**, pages 428-9.
18. N Bukharin and P Preobrazhensky, **The ABC of Communism**

(London 1969) page 240.

19. Sukhanov, pages 528-9.
20. Carr, volume 1, page 183.
21. Bukharin and Preobrazhensky, page 436.
22. Serge, **Year One**, page 336.
23. T H Rigby, **Communist Party Membership in the USSR, 1917-1967** (Princeton 1968, pages 470-1.
24. Trotsky, **The New Course**, page 27.
25. Trotsky, **The Real Situation in Russia** (London 1928) page 94.
26. Serge, **Year One**, page 264.
27. Rigby, **Communist Party Membership**, pages 241-2.
28. **Izvestiia TsK RKP(b)**, 28 March 1920.
29. **Desiatii sezd RKP(b)**, pages 29-30 and 76.
30. **Odinnadtsatii sezd RKP(b)**, page 422.
31. **Izvestiia Tsk RKP(b)**, 24 March 1920.
32. **Odinnadtsatii sezd RKP(b)**, page 420.
33. Lenin, **Works**, volume 28, page 257.
34. **KPSS v rezoliutsiiakh**, volume 1, pages 442 and 463.
35. **KPSS v rezoliutsiiakh**, volume 1, page 525.
36. **CC Minutes**, pages 126-251.
37. Pietsch, page 153.
38. R H McNeal (editor) **Resolutions and Decisiions of the Communist Party of the Soviet Union** (Toronto 1974) volume 2, page 13.
39. **Vosmaia konferentsiia RKP(b)** (Moscow 1961) page 221.
40. **Desiatii sezd RKP(b)**, pages 56.
41. **Izvestiia TsK RKP(B)**, 5 March 1921.
42. **Dvenadtsatii sezd RKP(b)** (Moscow 1923) page 207.
43. **Izvestiia TsK RKP(b)**, March 1923.
44. **Desiatii sezd RKP(b)**, page 52.
45. **Desiatii sezd RKP(b)**, page 54.
46. **Desiatii sezd RKP(b)**, pages 62-3.
47. **Desiatii sezd RKP(b)**, pages 56-7.
48. Carr, volume 1, page 188.
49. A G Löwy, **Die Weltgeschichte ist das Weltgericht** (Vienna 1968) page 111.
50. R V Daniels, **The Conscience of the Revolution: Communist Opposition in Soviet Russia** (Cambridge, Massachusetts 1965) page 129.
51. Serge, **Year One**, page 366.
52. **KPSS v rezoliutsiiakh**, volume 1, page 529.
53. **KPSS v rezoliutsiiakh**, volume 1, pages 529-30.
54. Lenin, **Works**, volume 32, page 261.
55. Lenin, **Works**, volume 32, page 243.
56. **Desiatii sezd RKP(b)**, page 540.

Chapter 13: FIRST STEPS OF THE COMMUNIST INTERNATIONAL

1. Trotsky, **The First Five Years of the Communist International**, volume 1 (London 1973) pages 37-9.
2. Trotsky, **Sochineniia**, volume 13, pages 33-7.
3. Lenin, **Sochineniia**, volume 24, page 724.
4. Vosmoi sezd RKP(b) **(Moscow 1939) pages 501-4.**
5. Trotsky, **First Five Years**, volume 1, page 43.
6. Trotsky, **First Five Years**, volume 1, page 46.
7. Trotsky, **First Five Years**, volume 1, page 47.
8. Trotsky, **First Five Years**, volume 1, pages 46-7.
9. Trotsky, **First Five Years**, volume 1, page 48.
10. Trotsky, **First Five Years**, volume 1, page 49.
11. Trotsky, **First Five Years**, volume 1, page 49.
12. Trotsky, **First Five Years**, volume 1, page 52.
13. Trotsky, **First Five Years**, volume 1, pages 53-4.
14. **Sedmoi sezd RKP(b)**, page 138.
15. Trotsky, **First Five Years**, volume 1, page 69.
16. Trotsky, **First Five Years**, volume 1, page 70.
17. Trotsky, **First Five Years**, volume 1, page 71.
18. Trotsky, **First Five Years**, volume 1, pages 86-7.
19. **Trotsky Papers**, volume 1, pages 61-7.
20. Trotsky, **First Five Years**, volume 1, pages 130-1.
21. Trotsky, **First Five Years**, volume 1, page 132.
22. Trotsky, **First Five Years**, volume 1, page 145.
23. Trotsky, **First Five Years**, volume 1, pages 133-5.
24. Trotsky, **First Five Years**, volume 1, pages 137-8.
25. Trotsky, **First Five Years**, volume 1, pages 143-4 and 147.
26. Trotsky, **First Five Years**, volume 1, page 153.
27. Trotsky, **First Five Years**, volume 1, page 159.
28. Trotsky, **First Five Years**, volume 1, pages 152-3.
29. Trotsky, **First Five Years**, volume 1, page 153.

Chapter 14: THE COMINTERN: TROTSKY TEACHES STRATEGY AND TACTICS

1. Trotsky, **First Five Years**, volume 1, pages 228-9.
2. Trotsky, **First Five Years**, volume 1, page 346.
3. Trotsky, **First Five Years**, volume 1, pages 261-2.
4. Trotsky, **First Five Years**, volume 1, pages 285-6.
5. J Degras (editor) **The Communist International 1919-1943: Documents** volume 1 (London 1971) pages 248-50.
6. Trotsky, **First Five Years**, volume 2, pages 91-6.
7. Lenin, **Works**, volume 33, page 208.
8. Angress, **Stillborn Revolution: The Communist Bid for Power in Germany, 1921-1923** (Princeton 1963) pages 156-7.
9. H Malzahn, in **Protokoll des III Kongress der**

Kommunistischen Internationale (Hamburg 1921) page 259.

10. P Broué, **Révolution en Allemagne 1917-23** (Paris 1971) page 484

11. Trotsky, **First Five Years**, volume 1, pages 328-9.

12. Trotsky, **First Five Years**, volume 1, page 348.

13. Trotsky, **First Five Years**, volume 2, page 32.

14. Trotsky, **First Five Years**, volume 2, page 353.

15. Trotsky, **First Five Years**, volume 2, page 29.

16. Trotsky, **First Five Years**, volume 1, page 13.

17. Trotsky, **First Five Years**, volume 1, page 349.

18. Antonio Gramsci, **Selections from the Prison Notebooks** (London 1982) page 238.

19. R Wohl, **French Communism in the Making, 1919-1924** (Stanford 1966) page 91.

20. Wohl, pages 218-9.

21. Wohl, pages 438-9.

22. Wohl, page 174.

23. Wohl, pages 89-90.

24. Wohl, page 96.

25. Wohl, page 307.

26. J Braunthal, **History of the International** (London 1967) volume 2, page 193.

27. Wohl, page 218.

28. Trotsky, **First Five Years**, volume 2, pages 53-6.

29. Degras, volume 1, page 308.

30. Trotsky, **First Five Years**, volume 2, pages 110-11.

31. Trotsky, **First Five Years**, volume 2, page 145.

32. Trotsky, **First Five Years**, volume 2, pages 146-7.

33. Wohl, page 288.

34. Wohl, pages 407-8.

35. Trotsky, **First Five Years**, volume 2, pages 278-9.

36. Trotsky, **First Five Years**, volume 2, pages 281-2.

37. Trotsky, **First Five Years**, volume 2, page 284.

38. **Writings of Leon Trotsky (1933-34)** (New York 1972) page 40.

Chapter 15: LENIN AND TROTSKY JOIN FORCES TO FIGHT BUREAUCRACY

1. Lenin, **Works**, volume 32, page 225.

2. Lenin, **Works**, page 236.

3. Trotsky, **First Five Years**, volume 2, page 268.

4. Trotsky, **First Five Years**, volume 2, pages 268-9.

5. Trotsky, **First Five Years**, volume 2, page 238.

6. Lenin, **Works**, volume 33, page 116.

7. Lenin, **Works**, volume 33, page 280.

8. Lenin, **Works**, volume 36, page 571.

9. **Trotsky Papers**, volume 2, pages 579-83.

10. Trotsky, **First Five Years**, volume 2, page 245.

11. Trotsky, **First Five Years**, volume 2, pages 270-1.
12. Trotsky, **First Five Years**, volume 2, pages 236-7.
13. Trotsky, **First Five Years**, volume 2, page 271.
14. Trotsky, **First Five Years**, volume 2, pages 271-2.
15. Lenin, **Works**, volume 35, page 475.
16. **Trotsky Papers**, volume 2, pages 745-9.
17. Lenin, **Works**, volume 36, page 598.
18. Carr, volume 2, pages 310-11.
19. Lenin, **Works**, volume 33, page 426.
20. Lenin, **Works**, volume 33, page 501.
21. Lenin, **Works**, volume 45, page 497.
22. Lenin, **Works**, volume 42, page 418.
23. Lenin, **Works**, volume 42, page 600.
24. Quoted by L A Fotieva, **Iz vospominanii o Lenine** (Moscow 1964) pages 28-9.
25. Lenin, **Works**, volume 45, page 601.
26. Lenin, **Works**, volume 33, pages 460-1.
27. Lenin, **Works**, volume 45, page 606.
28. Lenin, **Works**, volume 29, page 194.
29. **Desiatii sezd RKP(b)**, pages 163-8.
30. **KPSS v rezoliutsiiakh**, volume 1, page 562.
31. **Trotsky Papers**, volume 2, pages 347-9.
32. **Odinnadtsatii sezd RKP(b)**, pages 72-5.
33. Lenin, **Works**, volume 42, pages 602-3.
34. R Pipes, **The Formation of the Soviet Union: Communism and Nationalism, 1917-1923** (Cambridge 1964) page 271.
35. Lenin, **Works**, volume 42, pages 421-3.
36. P N Pospelov and others, **Vladimir Ilyich Lenin: Biografiia** (Moscow 1963) page 611.
37. Trotsky, **Stalin School**, pages 66-7.
38. Lenin, **Works**, volume 33, page 372.
39. **Dvenadtsatii sezd RKP(b)**, page 150.
40. Lenin, **Works**, volume 36, pages 605-6.
41. Lenin, **Works**, volume 36, pages 610-11.
42. Lenin, **Works**, volume 42, page 493.
43. Lenin, **Works**, volume 45, page 607.
44. Trotsky to the Bureau of Party History, 21 October 1927, quoted in Trotsky, **Stalin School**, page 71.
45. Lenin, **Works**, volume 45, page 608.
46. I Deutscher, **The Prophet Unarmed** (London 1959) page 47.
47. Lenin, **Works**, volume 33, pages 353-4.
48. Lenin, **Works**, volume 33, page 490.
49. Trotsky, **Stalin School**, pages 73-4.
50. Trotsky, **Stalin School**, page 72.
51. Lenin, **Works**, volume 36, pages 594-5.
52. Lenin, **Works**, volume 36, page 596.

Chapter 16: TROTSKY AND THE TROIKA

1. See Stalin, **Works**, volume 5, page 231.
2. **The Anti-Stalin Campaign and International Communism** (New York 1956) page 76.
3. Trotsky, **My Life**, page 482.
4. Trotsky, **My Life**, page 486.
5. Stalin, **Works**, volume 5, pages 261-2.
6. **Denadtsatii sezd RKP(b)**, page 563.
7. **Denadtsatii sezd RKP(b)**, page 529.
8. **Denadtsatii sezd RKP(b)**, page 530.
9. **Denadtsatii sezd RKP(b)**, page 532.
10. **Denadtsatii sezd RKP(b)**, page 526.
11. **Denadtsatii sezd RKP(b)**, pages 531-2.
12. Stalin, **Works**, volume 5, page 271.
13. **Denadtsatii sezd RKP(b)**, page 577.
14. **Denadtsatii sezd RKP(b)**, page 96.
15. Stalin, **Works**, volume 5, pages 209-10.
16. Stalin, **Works**, volume 5, page 213.
17. Stalin, **Works**, volume 5, page 223.
18. Stalin, **Works**, volume 5, page 240.
19. **KPSS v rezoliutsiiakh**, volume 1, page 685.
20. **Dvenadtsatii sezd RKP(b)**, page 365.
21. **Trotsky Papers**, volume 2, pages 813-5.
22. **Dvenadtsatii sezd RKP(b)**, pages 321-2.
23. **Dvenadtsatii sezd RKP(b)**, page 331.
24. **Dvenadtsatii sezd RKP(b)**, page 315.
25. **Dvenadtsatii sezd RKP(b)**, page 321.
26. **KPSS v rezoliutsiiakh**, volume 1, page 702.
27. **Dvenadtsatii sezd RKP(b)**, page 25.
28. **Dvenadtsatii sezd RKP(b)**, page 36.
29. **Dvenadtsatii sezd RKP(b)**, page 394.
30. Trotsky, **The New Course**, page 8.
31. **Dvenadtsatii sezd RKP(b)**, pages 89, 48, 496 and 502-3.
32. Trotsky, **My Life**, page 481.
33. Trotsky, **My Life**, pages 481-2.
34. Trotsky, **My Life**, page 537.
35. Deutscher, page 93.
36. Trotsky, **Stalin**, pages 242-3.
37. **Odinnadtsatii sezd RKP(b)**, pages 453-7.
38. A Soboul, **The French Revolution, 1787-1799** (London 1974) volume 2, page 422.
39. Soboul, page 439.
40. Trotsky, **First Five Years**, volume 2, page 122.
41. Trotsky, **Stalin**, page 387.
42. Trotsky, **Stalin**, pages 403-4.

Index

Other publications from Bookmarks

Trotsky: Towards October 1879-1917 / *Tony Cliff*
The first volume of this biography shows how Trotsky learned from the revolution of 1905 and developed the theory of permanent revolution, giving him the grasp of the revolutionary process that he needed to organise the insurrection of October 1917. 320 pages. £6.95 / $11.95

State Capitalism in Russia / *Tony Cliff*
The classic analysis of Russia under Stalin, when a new state capitalist ruling class rose to power on the ashes of the revolution, now republished with a postscript covering the years between Stalin and Gorbachev. 377 pages. £5.95 / $9.00

Lenin: Building the Party 1893-1914 / *Tony Cliff*
The first volume of Tony Cliff's political biography of Lenin, showing his battle to turn Marxist ideas into practical daily action through the medium of the Bolshevik Party. 398 pages. £7.95 / $12.50

Lenin: All power to the Soviets 1914-1917 / *Tony Cliff*
This second volume shows the crucial interaction between the working class, the party and Lenin, which led to the climax of insurrection in October 1917. 424 pages. £7.95 / $12.50

Lenin: Revolution Besieged 1917-1923 / *Tony Cliff*
This final volume covers Lenin's struggle after 1917 to defend fragile workers' power against attack from without and bureaucracy from within. 496 pages. £8.95 / $16.50

Rosa Luxemburg / *Tony Cliff*
A political biography of the most original contributor to Marxism after Marx himself, who was murdered during the German revolution of 1919. 96 pages. £2.50 / $4.75

Russia: From workers' state to state capitalism
/ Peter Binns, Tony Cliff and Chris Harman

In 1917 the hopes of millions were placed on the revolution in Russia—but what went wrong? This book offers some hard answers to tough questions. 112 pages. £2.50 / $4.75

The Lost Revolution: Germany 1918-1923 */ Chris Harman*

Revolutions that are defeated are soon forgotten—yet the defeat of the great working-class upheavals that shook Germany after the First World War was a key link in the rise to power of both Hitler and Stalin. 336 pages. £5.95 / $11.00

The Comintern */ Duncan Hallas*

The Communist International, born of 1917, aimed to spread workers' power throughout the world. This book traces it from the vital contributions of the early years to its degeneration into a tool of Stalin's foreign policy. 184 pages. £4.95 / $7.95

Lenin's Moscow */ Alfred Rosmer*

An account of the 'centre of world revolution', when Moscow was capital city of the first workers' revolution and headquarters of the Communist International—of which Rosmer was a leading member. 288 pages. £4.95 / $9.95

The Quiet Revolutionary */ The autobiography of Margaret Dewar*

A schoolgirl in Moscow during 1917, forced to leave Russia during the famine years, then a revolutionary socialist in Germany during Hitler's rise to power—this is the story of one of the 'ordinary' people who are the real movers of history. 224 pages. £5.95 / $11.95

Bolsheviks in the Tsarist Duma */ A Y Badayev*

Six Bolsheviks were elected to the Duma, the Russian parliament, in 1912 at the height of the working-class upsurge which—though interrupted by the First World War—led on to the victory of 1917. Badayev was one of them. 208 pages. £5.95 / $11.00

The Western Soviets */ Donny Gluckstein*

In 1915-20 the workers' councils of Italy, Germany, Britain and Russia proposed an alternative mass democracy to the parliamentary channels that had failed in 1914 and have failed the workers since. This book shows what they offered. 280 pages. £6.95 / $11.00

Women and perestroika / *Chanie Rosenberg*

This study of the lives of women in Russia—under the Tsar, the 1917 revolution, Stalin and Gorbachev—uses their changing conditions as a touchstone by which to judge the effects of perestroika on the lives of workers, women and men alike. 128 pages. £3.95 / $7.50

Festival of the Oppressed / *Colin Barker*

The trade union Solidarity was the largest working-class movement for half a century—and shook the Eastern bloc to its foundations. This book tells the story of its rise and analyses the causes of its setback in 1981. 272 pages. £4.95 / $8.50

Class struggles in Eastern Europe 1945-83 / *Chris Harman*

Gorbachev and his reformers want to change Russia from above—but will he unleash change from below? This book looks at Hungary 1956, Czechoslovakia 1968 and Poland 1980, and reveals some of the potential for upheavals to come. 382 pages. £7.95 / $13.50

All available from good bookshops, or by post from Bookmarks (add 10 per cent to cover postage—minimum 35p or $1).

BOOKMARKS

265 Seven Sisters Road, London N4 2DE, England.
PO Box 16085, Chicago, IL 60616, USA.
GPO Box 1473N, Melbourne 3001, Australia.

Bookmarks bookshop
in London runs a large socialist mail order service. We have stocks of
books and pamphlets from many publishers in socialism, internationalism,
trade union struggle, women's issues, economics, the Marxist classics,
workine-class history and much, much more. We will send books anywhere
in the world.
Write for our latest booklists to:
BOOKMARKS
265 Seven Sisters Road, Finsbury Park, London N4 2DE, England.
Phone 081-802 6145.